Climate Change Denial

Heads in the Sand

Haydn Washington and John Cook

earthscan

publishing for a sustainable future

London • Washington, DC

First published in 2011 by Earthscan

Copyright © Haydn Washington and John Cook 2011

The moral right of the authors has been asserted.

Earthscan Ltd, Dunstan House, 14a St Cross Street, London EC1N 8XA, UK
Earthscan LLC, 1616 P Street, NW, Washington, DC 20036, USA

Earthscan publishes in association with the International Institute for Environment and Development

For more information on Earthscan publications, see www.earthscan.co.uk or write to earthinfo@earthscan.co.uk

ISBN   978-1-84971-335-1 hardback
       978-1-84971-336-8 paperback

Typeset by FiSH Books, Enfield
Cover design by Rogue Four Design, www.roguefour.com

A catalogue record for this book is available from the British Library

Library of Congress Cataloging-in-Publication Data

Washington, Haydn, 1955-
  Climate change denial : heads in the sand / Haydn Washington and John Cook.
    p. cm.
  Includes bibliographical references and index.
  ISBN 978-1-84971-335-1 (hardback) -- ISBN 978-1-84971-336-8 (pbk.) 1. Climatic changes.
2. Global warming. 3. Climatic changes--Psychological aspects. 4. Global warming--Psychological aspects. 5. Denial (Psychology) I. Cook, John. II. Title.

  QC903.W37 2010
  363.738'74--dc22

                          2010046147

At Earthscan we strive to minimize our environmental impacts and carbon footprint through reducing waste, recycling and offsetting our CO_2 emissions, including those created through publication of this book. For more details of our environmental policy, see www.earthscan.co.uk.

Printed and bound in the UK by CPI Antony Rowe.

For Stephen Schneider, who led in both climate science and climate action; and for Paul and Anne Ehrlich, who led the way in warning us about denial.

Contents

List of Figures

Acknowledgements

We would like to acknowledge the assistance of Earthscan and especially their editor Nick Bellorini. We would also like to thank the many people who contributed to the book and made comments. In particular we would like to thank Prof. Naomi Oreskes of the University of California (San Diego) for her foreword and Prof. Riley Dunlap of Oklahoma State University for his insights. We would like also to thank Dr Mark Diesendorf and Dr David Roser of the University of NSW, Prof. David Karoly of the University of Melbourne, and Dr Gavin Mudd from Monash University. We would also like to thank Mr Rodney Falconer for his drawing of an ostrich with its head in the sand. And as always our thanks go to our friends and family for their support.

Foreword

People who refuse to accept the scientific evidence of anthropogenic climate change like to call themselves skeptics. But as Haydn Washington and John Cook note in this straightforward and much-needed book, these men (and they *are* nearly all men) are not skeptics. A skeptic is a person who challenges his opponents to provide evidence for their beliefs. A skeptic rejects articles of faith and positions that defy refutation in the face of facts. In this sense, all scientists are skeptics. They insist that any claim be supported by evidence, and they insist on a substantial debate about the quantity and quality of that evidence before accepting it. The more radical the claim, the higher the bar to acceptance.

When Svante Arrhenius first suggested that increased atmospheric concentrations of carbon dioxide from burning fossil fuels could lead to global climate change, it was a radical claim. Who in the late 19th century believed that human activities could match the scale of natural forces? In any case there was no way to test the idea. Arrhenius was making a prediction about something that could happen in the future, not a claim about something that was already happening.[1]

The first scientist to claim that climate change was under way was British engineer Guy Stuart Callendar. In the early 1930s Callendar compiled available global data (mostly in Europe), which suggested that both atmospheric carbon dioxide and average global temperatures were starting to rise. Other scientists addressed the issue theoretically. American physicist E. O. Hulburt, a physicist at the US Naval Research Laboratory, calculated the effect of doubling CO_2 on global climate based on physical principles, and concluded that doubling CO_2 would increase average global temperature by 4°C, while tripling would increase it by 7°C. This, he noted, this was sufficient to change Earth's climate dramatically.[2]

A lot has happened since the 1930s, and climate change is no longer a radical claim. In fact, it's not a 'claim' at all. It's an established scientific fact. In over 10,000 peer-reviewed scientific papers, as well as thousands of pages of summary produced by the Intergovernmental Panel on Climate Change (IPCC), scientists have demonstrated that atmospheric CO_2 has increased, and global temperature has increased too.[3] As a result, spring is coming earlier than it used to. Rivers and lakes are warming. Glaciers are shrinking, while glacial lakes are expanding. Permafrost is becoming unstable. Plants and animals are shifting their ranges upwards in terms of both latitude and elevation.[4] And extreme weather events – droughts, floods, hurricanes – are becoming a little bit more common, and a little bit more extreme.

While scientists knew for a long time that such changes *could* happen, it was only in the 1980s that they began to think that they surely *would* happen. In 1979, the US National Academy of Sciences wrote, 'If carbon dioxide continues to increase, the study group finds no reason to doubt that climate changes will result and no reason to believe that these changes will be negligible.'[5]

And that's when the denial began to set in...

As Erik Conway and I wrote in our recent book, *Merchants of Doubt: How a Handful of Scientists Obscured the Truth on Issues from Tobacco to Global Warming*, almost as soon as the proverbial ink was dry on the National Academy report, some people began to challenge its conclusions. They did so for reasons that had very little to do with the science, and everything to do with politics and ideology.

In 1983, the Academy undertook a larger, more comprehensive report, chaired by conservative scientist William Nierenberg, who argued that the results of climate change *would* be negligible, because people were highly adaptable, and technological innovation, flourishing under free market conditions, would enable us to address any adverse impacts that arose. It was not an empirical argument – it was not based on evidence drawn from history, or sociology, or anthropology (indeed, there were no social scientists other than economists on the committee). It was an ideological argument, rooted in Nierenberg's anti-communism and commitment to free market principles.

Nierenberg was a Cold War scientist who had began his career working on the Manhattan Project – the crash programme to build an atomic bomb during World War II – and in the years that followed, he built a career close to the corridors of power. By the 1980s, he had ties to the administration of President Ronald Reagan, who favoured free market solutions to social problems. We know now, from historical research, that while Nierenberg was chairing the climate change committee, he was also appointed by the Reagan administration to review the scientific evidence of acid rain, and he *altered* the Executive Summary of that committee's report – under the guidance of White House science adviser George Keyworth – to make the problem of acid rain seem less urgent than the committee believed.

The very next year – 1984 – Nierenberg joined forces with two other politically conservative physicists – Robert Jastrow and Frederick Seitz – to create the George C. Marshall Institute, a think tank that would defend Reagan administration policies with respect to strategic defence and nuclear weaponry. Seitz was a former President of the Rockefeller University, with long-standing ties to the tobacco industry; Jastrow was an astrophysicist involved in the US space programme. By the end of the 1980s, Seitz, Jastrow and Nierenberg were challenging the evidence of global warming and the ozone hole. Their work laid the ground for a host of others – individuals, think tanks, private institutes and corporations – to launch a full-scale attack on climate science. Climate change denial began in the 1980s, and it continues to this day.

In the early 2000s, when I first begin to lecture about the history of climate science, I would be asked the same skeptical questions over and over again. 'What about the sun?' 'Isn't it true that warming has stopped?' 'Why should I believe a computer?' 'The climate has always been changing, so why should I worry?' And, less belligerently, 'Where can I go to get good clear answers to my questions?' I knew the answers to the first four questions, but there wasn't a good answer to the last one, and it was telling that the same questions came up over and over again. Clearly, scientists had not succeeded in communicating to the general public what they had long known, whereas skeptical claims *had* percolated into public consciousness.

As a university professor who competes daily with the internet for my students' attention, I understood the power of the web, and it frustrated me that scientists hadn't done more to use it. So I was happy indeed when I discovered John Cook's wonderful website, www.skepticalscience.com, which calmly and systematically debunks the most common 'denialist' arguments. When I discovered that Cook even had an iPhone app, I knew these were people I wanted to know.

For too long, scientists have debated climate science in the halls of science, thinking it was someone else's job to communicate the science to the rest of us. Meanwhile, vocal groups with an ideological or economic interest in challenging the scientific evidence did exactly that, in well-organized, well-funded and persistent campaigns. Many of the same groups and individuals who now challenge the scientific evidence of anthropogenic climate change previously challenged the evidence of tobacco smoking, acid rain and the ozone hole. Some have even tried to reopen the debate over DDT, claiming that DDT was never dangerous, and that millions of people have died unnecessarily from malaria because of the US decision to ban DDT in the United States.

Most of these claims are just false. The attempt to rehabilitate DDT, for example, is based on claims that are demonstrably erroneous. DDT *does* cause cancer; it was never the miracle chemical that its supporters claimed (and continue to claim); and the World Health Organization moved away from it in malaria prevention not because of environmental hysteria but because mosquitoes were developing resistance.[6]

Other 'denialist' claims have been shown to be incorrect as well – or at least to be misleading half-truths. Washington and Cook note that there are common patterns in the denial of scientific evidence: the most common is to claim that observed changes are natural variability. And if they are natural, then there is no cause for concern and no reason for change from 'business as usual'.

This can be hard to refute, because the natural world *is* highly variable. It is the job of scientists to sort out the diverse causes of natural change, to determine their magnitude and rate, and to differentiate them from human effects. What we know, after half a century of scientific work, is that the human footprint on the planet is now so large that human drivers of change are in many cases overwhelming natural drivers. There *is* natural climate variability – including changes caused by natural fluctuations in solar irradiance and atmospheric CO_2 – but natural variability is being overridden by planetary warming dominated by human activity: the production of greenhouse gases and the destruction of forests, mangrove swamps, and other natural carbon sinks. Similarly, there is natural variability in stratospheric ozone, but the depletions observed in the 1980s were caused primarily by the synthetic chemicals known as chlorofluorocarbons. There is natural acidic rain, but it was vastly increased in the 20th century by pollution from coal-fired electrical utilities, smelters and automobiles.

How do denialists make such half-truths seem credible? By relying on scientists to make them. In the 1950s, tobacco industry executives realized that if they attacked the scientific evidence of the harms of their product, the conflict of interest would be obvious. But if *scientists* raised questions about the science, that would be a whole different matter. So they set out to find scientists who were willing to do just that.

We see the same pattern in the challenges to climate science. Washington and Cook directly address the recent claims of Ian Plimer, who has received enormous attention in Australia (where both authors of this book live) for his view that the observed increase in atmospheric carbon dioxide is caused by volcanoes, and that it doesn't matter anyway since 'you can double carbon dioxide and it has no effect'.[7]

These are very strange claims. Irish experimentalist John Tyndall first demonstrated in the 1850s that carbon dioxide was a powerful greenhouse gas, and that its presence in the atmosphere, even at extremely low concentrations, was crucial for Earth's benevolent climate. Since then numerous other studies have confirmed the high sensitivity of the planetary climate to atmospheric CO_2. We've increased atmospheric CO_2 by about one-third, and we've seen an increase in average global temperature already of just under 1°C. Climate sensitivity isn't just a theory, it's an *observation*.

As for the source of the recent increase in CO_2, that was worked out in 2003 – and it's not volcanoes.[8] Many of us know that there are two forms of carbon: ordinary C-12, and radioactive C-14, which is used to date archeological relics and other things. But there is a third kind of carbon, C-13, the concentration of which varies in natural reservoirs. Plants and materials derived from them, notably coal, have much lower concentrations of C-13 than other materials, including the CO_2 emitted from volcanoes. Isotope geochemists Prosenjit Ghosh and Willi A. Brand· measured the C-13 content of atmospheric CO_2 and showed that as total CO_2 rose, the C-13 content fell. This result is just what you'd expect if that CO_2 came from fossil fuels.

Plimer speculates that invisible, undetected, underwater volcanoes are responsible for the increased atmospheric CO_2. Besides the obvious point that he is asking us to believe in something that no one has seen, felt or observed in any form, he asks us to disbelieve what scientists *have* seen and measured. It's a bit like asking us to believe in Santa Claus after we have seen our parents putting the presents under the tree.

Plimer is a geologist, not a climate scientist, and as a former exploration geologist myself – who cut my teeth in the Australian mining industry – I would never assume that a mining geologist is not a fine human being. But when it comes to judging a person's claims, it is reasonable to ask: Is this person actually an expert? And if his claims go against the conclusions of genuine experts, then why is he insisting on them? Indeed, why is he even involved in the debate at all? And why are we listening?

The answer to the questions above might simply be that Plimer's strong links to the mining industry may be influencing his views on the matter. While many business leaders accept the scientific evidence of anthropogenic climate change and see business opportunities in addressing it, those in the traditional business of extracting resources from the ground have been having a harder time. People fear change because they fear loss, and in doing something about climate change, there will be winners and losers. Hard rock mining will not necessarily lose – particularly mining for uranium for nuclear power, or materials necessary for solar cells or wind turbines – but the fossil fuel industry *will* lose, unless it moves briskly into new areas. Here we see the tobacco problem all over again. The tobacco industry was hugely profitable and its primary product was deadly. That was a serious difficulty. The industry did not respond well to it. The fossil fuel industry is repeating the pattern.

But if this is an old pattern, why are we falling for it?

Why Do Denialist Claims Persist?

Given that virtually every denialist claim of the past 20 years has been shown to have been misleading, or just plain false, why do these claims persist? Why do so many of us listen to them?

Most scientists think the problem is scientific illiteracy, so the solution is to get more information to more people. Climate modeller James Hansen, one of the first scientists to speak out publicly on the threat of unmitigated climate change (and one of the most passionate voices now calling for immediate action), has concluded that if the public had a better understanding of the climate crisis they would 'do what needed to be done'.[9]

Sadly, the evidence is against this conclusion. Scientists *have* been communicating what they know for a long time. The raison d'être of the IPCC – much maligned by climate deniers – was to communicate relevant science to governments and other interested parties. This information is readily available. But availability of information does not guarantee that people will accept it.[10] In both the United States and Australia, many highly educated people have rejected the conclusions of climate science, including chairmen of the boards of leading corporations, members of US Congress, and even occupants of the American White House.

There are many reasons why people resist bad news, but it is clear that a major driver here is fear. Fear that our current way of life is unsustainable. Fear that addressing the issue will limit economic growth. Fear that if we accept government interventions in the market place – through a cap-and-trade system to control greenhouse gas emissions, a carbon tax, or some more severe approach – it will lead to a loss of personal freedom.

Or maybe just plain old fear of change. Psychologists have shown that most of us anticipate change as loss. Climate change is easy to interpret as loss: loss of prosperity, loss of freedom, loss of the good life as we have known it.

So What Can We Do?

Washington and Cook conclude by referring to the concept of 'implicatory denial'. Most of us are aware that scientists say climate change is under way, but even if we accept it as true we act as if it had no *implications*. We deny what it means, and continue business as usual. As I write these words, a large portion of Queensland is flooded, in what the global reinsurance company Munich Re estimates may be the most costly natural disaster in Australian history. An area larger than Germany and France combined has been inundated; over 200,000 people have been affected; 60,000 homes are without electricity; and three-quarters of the state has been declared a disaster area. Among other things, witnesses described an 'inland tsunami' – a wall of water 21 feet high and half a mile across – that swept over the Lockyer Valley. While the death toll is not yet known, at least 20 are known dead, many others missing.[11]

Some commentators were willing to describe the flooding as 'biblical', yet almost none were willing to make the connection to climate change.[12] Of course, as scientists have repeatedly emphasized, 'climate' is by definition a matter of patterns, and one event does not a pattern make. But the Queensland floods *are* part of a pattern – a pattern that in 2010–2011 included devastating floods in China and Pakistan, unprecedented heatwaves and fires in Russia, and catastrophic mudslides in Brazil. Moreover, this pattern is consistent with what scientists have long predicted: that climate change would lead to an increase in extreme weather events. The reason is simple: conservation of energy. If you trap more energy in the atmosphere, it has to go somewhere, and one of the places it goes into is weather.

Australian Premier of Queensland Anna Bligh has said that the devastation in Queensland 'may be breaking our hearts, but it will not break our will'.[13] Yet the will that is needed – which *has* been needed for the past two decades – is not the will to keep calm and carry on in the face of tragedy. It is the will to change the way we live in order to avoid an even greater tragedy; a tragedy that will affect not just Queensland, or even all Australia, but the whole world, including the plants and animals with whom we share this rock upon which we live. For, as Washington and Cook rightly note, climate change *is* about the way we live. It is about how we use energy without regard for the long-term consequences, and how we inflict environmental damage without concern for other people and species. It is about a way of life that does not reckon the true cost of living, an economics that does not take into account environmental damage and loss.

Climate change is the ultimate accounting: it is the bill for a century of unprecedented prosperity, generated by the energy stored in fossil fuels. By and large, this prosperity has been a good thing. More people live longer and healthier lives than before the industrial revolution. The problem, however, is that those people did not pay the full cost of that prosperity. And the remainder of the bill has now come due.

Anna Bligh is right. What we need now is will: the will to face the facts, the will to accept their implications and the will to do something about it. Let us hope this fine book helps us to move in that direction.

Naomi Oreskes
Professor of History and Science Studies
University of California (San Diego)
January 2011

Notes

1 Spencer Weart (2004) *The Discovery of Global Warming*, Harvard University Press, Cambridge, MA; James Roger Fleming (1998) *Historical Perspectives on Climate Change*, Oxford University Press, New York, NY.

2 James Roget Fleming (2009) *The Callendar Effect: The Life and Work of Guy Stewart Callendar (1898-1964), The Scientist Who Established the Carbon Dioxide Theory of Climate Change*, The American Meteorological Society, Boston, MA; E. O. Hulburt (1931) 'The temperature of the lower atmosphere of the Earth', *Physical Review*, vol 38, 15 November, pp1876–1890.

3 Naomi Oreskes (2004) 'The scientific consensus on climate change', *Science*, vol 306, p1686; see also Peter T. Doran and Maggie Kendall Zimmerman (2009) 'Examining the scientific consensus on climate change', *EOS, Transactions, American Geophysical Union*, vol 90, no 3, p22, doi:10.1029/2009EO030002.

4 IPCC (2007) 'Summary for policymakers', in *Climate Change 2007: Impacts, Adaptation and Vulnerability. Contribution of Working Group II to the Fourth Assessment Report of the Intergovernmental Panel on Climate Change*, M. L. Parry, O. F. Canziani, J. P. Palutikof, P. J. van der Linden and C.E. Hanson (eds), Cambridge University Press, Cambridge, UK, pp7–22.

5 Verner E. Suomi, in Jule Charney et al (1979) *Carbon Dioxide and Climate: A Scientific Assessment*, Report of an Ad-Hoc Study Group on Carbon Dioxide and Climate, Woods Hole, Massachusetts, 23–27 July, to the Climate Research Board, National Research Council, National Academies Press, Washington, DC, p2.

6 Naomi Oreskes and Erik M. Conway (2010) *Merchants of Doubt: How a Handful of Scientists Obscured the Truth on Issues from Tobacco Smoke to Global Warming*, Bloomsbury Press, New York, NY.

7 Quote: 'you can double [carbon dioxide] and quadruple it and it has no effect ... To demonize it shows that you don't understand schoolchild science' (Ian Plimer, interviewed on ABN Newswire, June 2009, cited at www.sourcewatch.org/index.php?title=Ian_Plimer).

8 Prosenjit Ghosh and Willi A. Brand (2003) 'Stable isotope ratio mass spectrometry in global climate change research', *International Journal of Mass Spectrometry*, vol 228, no 1, pp1–33.

9   James Hansen (2010) *Storms of My Grandchildren*, Bloomsbury Press, New York, NY, p238.

10 On public opinion about climate change, see Anthony Leiserowitz et al (2010) *Knowledge of Climate Change Across Global Warming's Six Americas*, Yale Project on Climate Change Communication, http://environment.yale.edu/climate/files/ Knowledge%20Across%20Six%20Americas.pdf.

11 See www.smh.com.au/business/insured-losses-from-deluge-could-reach-6bn-worldwide-20110114-19re8.html;
www.ft.com/cms/s/0/caeec346-1ffe-11e0-a6fb-00144feab49a.html#axzz1B3enDB27;
www.ecoworld.com/waters/inland-tsunami-kills-10-in-queensland-australia.html.

12 See http://news.nationalgeographic.com/news/2011/01/pictures/110106-australia-flood-drought-water-storms.

13 See www.heraldsun.com.au/news/special-reports/two-killed-in-raging-flash-flood-in-queensland/story-fn7kabp3-1225985264224.

1

Denial and the Nature of Science

What Is Denial?

Denial is as old as humanity, and possibly nobody is free from it (Zerubavel, 2006). But what is denial? Is it the same as skepticism, as some people seem to think? This is a crucial question for the whole climate change debate. The Oxford English Dictionary definition of a skeptic is:

> A seeker after truth; an inquirer who has not yet arrived at definite conclusions.

So we should *all* be skeptics in many ways, as we should all seek the truth. Skepticism is about seeking the truth and realizing the world is a complex place. Skepticism is about stepping away from superstition and dogma. Genuine skepticism in science is one of the ways that science progresses, examining assumptions and conclusions (Pittock, 2009). Denial is something very different, it is a refusal to believe something no matter what the evidence. Those in denial demonstrate a 'wilful ignorance' and invoke logical fallacies to buttress their unshakeable beliefs (Specter, 2009). In fact deniers commonly use 'Bulverism', a method of argument that avoids the need to prove that someone is wrong by first assuming they are wrong, then explaining why they hold such a fallacious view (Hamilton, 2010). For example, climate scientists are just wrong, and they are wrong because they are too 'liberal'. Denial isn't about searching for truth, it's about the denial of a truth one doesn't like. So skepticism and denial are in some ways opposites. An objective scientist *should* be skeptical: one should not jump to conclusions or believe something simply because it is fashionable and agrees with current dogma. When the sociologist Robert Merton (1973) wrote about the structure of science, he stated that scientists operated by four principles – organized skepticism, universalism, communalism and disinterestedness. More precisely, in the scientific method skeptics need to do three things – apply critical faculties to both sides of an argument, admit uncertainties on both sides of the argument and accept that risk management may require appropriate policy responses despite the uncertainty (Pittock, 2009). Deniers don't do these three things, while genuine 'skeptics' do.

It is thus important to understand the difference between skepticism and denial, especially in terms of the climate change debate. Many climate change deniers call themselves climate 'skeptics'; indeed there is a 'climate skeptics' political party in Australia (www.climatesceptics.com.au). However, refusing to accept the overwhelming 'preponderance of evidence' is not skepticism, it is *denial* and should be called by its true name. Accordingly, in this book we will refer to climate change deniers, not skeptics. Others use the term 'denialists', but 'deniers' is more succinct and also acknowledges that everybody denies something. In the US it is also common to use the term 'contrarians' for climate change deniers (Hansen, 2009). The use of the term 'climate skeptic' is a distortion of reality, of what is really going on, similar to the term 'junk science' that deniers apply to mainstream science. Skepticism is healthy in both science and society; denial is not.

So denial and skepticism are very different, but what of 'denial', how common is it? We all deny, and the ability to deny is an 'amazing human phenomenon, largely unexplained and often inexplicable' (Cohen, 2001). Stanley Cohen believes this is 'a product of the sheer complexity of our emotional, linguistic, moral and intellectual lives'. But what is it that we deny? The answer is many things – the things we don't want to admit exist. In our daily lives most of us tend to deny something, whether it's about our looks, age, finances or health. We deny some things as they force us to confront change. We deny other things because they are just too painful. For example, some of us cannot face the death of a loved one. We deny other things because they worry us and make us afraid. Sometimes we can't see a solution, so things appear unsolvable. Often we go around in a 'mind loop' considering the problem, worrying about it, not finding a solution and then returning to the problem. These 'knots' can be very stressful (Laing, 1970). Thus many of us deny the root cause of the problem. After all, it would be much easier for us if the world just went along in the same old comfortable way. Psychoanalysis sees denial as an 'unconscious defence mechanism for coping with guilt, anxiety or other disturbing emotions aroused by reality' (Cohen, 2001). Sociologist Eviatar Zerubavel (2006), in his book *The Elephant in the Room*, notes that the most public form of denial is silence, where some things are not spoken of. Silence about climate change has certainly been one aspect of its denial over the last few decades. But now the silence in general society has been broken. We now 'talk' about climate change, though the denial continues on in other ways, as we shall see.

Zerubavel (2006) cites the fable of the Emperor's new clothes as a classic example of a conspiracy of silence, a situation where everyone refuses to acknowledge an obvious truth. But the denial of social realities – whether incest, alcoholism, corruption or even genocide – is no fairytale. Nor is the denial of climate change. Zerubavel sheds light on the social and political underpinnings of silence and denial – the keeping of 'open secrets'. He shows that conspiracies of silence exist at every level of society, ranging from small groups to large corporations, from personal friendships to politics. Zerubavel shows how such conspiracies evolve, illuminating the social pressures that cause people to deny what is right before their eyes. Each conspirator's denial is complemented by the others', and the silence is usually more intense when more people conspire, and especially when there are significant power differences among them. Denial is thus common, and it is important we understand this. As a form of denial, silence helps us avoid pain. When facing a frightening situation we often resort to denial. The early reports of Nazi massacres of Jews were actually dismissed by many Jews in Europe as sheer lies (Zerubavel, 2006). The prospect of the 'final solution' was just too frightening to believe. Zerubavel also refers to the 'ominous silence surrounding the spectre of a nuclear war'. He points out that denial is inherently *delusional* and inevitably distorts one's sense of reality. People often get upset when confronted with information challenging their self-delusional view of the world around them. Many indeed prefer such illusions to painful realities and thus cherish their 'right to be an ostrich'. They seem to believe that 'ignorance is bliss' and that 'what you don't know won't hurt you'. The longer we ignore the 'elephants', the larger they loom in our minds, as each avoidance triggers an even greater spiral of denial (Zerubavel, 2006). Climate change has now got to the point where the elephant is all but filling the room. We may now talk about it, but we still deny it.

It can be seen from the above that denial is everywhere. Our society – and each of us who makes up society – is involved in denial at some level. It is thus a fundamental part of the human psyche that needs to be acknowledged. Denial is, however, a delusion, one that we will argue can become a *pathology* when it endangers the ecosystems humans rely on. However, while some people will accept that denial exists, like all things people will seek to coopt it, to define it for themselves, and define it for their particular purposes. For example, journalist Michael Specter (2009) defines 'denialism' as the replacement of 'the rigorous and open-minded skepticism of science with the inflexible certainty of ideological commitment'. He provides evidence of the denial that HIV causes AIDS, denial about the value of vaccines and denial about some practices in alternative medicine. For him 'denialism' is limited to the denial of science, particularly the denial of science he agrees with. His definition is thus narrow, ignoring all the other things we deny, and ignoring just how prevalent denial is within our society. Specter relies on 'facts' that he approves of, but denies others he does not support. He thus supports nuclear power and genetic engineering, conveniently ignoring any science that raises concerns about these. Similarly, he discounts the problems of pesticides, mercury and population. It seems that while he is not in denial about some things, he *is* in denial about others he disapproves of (and doesn't acknowledge there is a scientific debate about). Indeed he uses denial as a means of espousing human mastery of nature. Specter (2009) wishes to usher in the technological dream of humans 'being able to program life' and 'teach nature' how to solve problems. However, many others (for example Hamilton, 2010; Oreskes and Conway, 2010) point out that this dream of mastery is what got us into this mess in the first place. Nonetheless, the main problem with Specter's treatment of 'denialism' is its narrowness and the fact that it ignores how prevalent denial really is within our society.

So denial is an understandable and very human trait. However, that does not mean it isn't dangerous, for it sometimes is. Just as the parable from historian Pliny the Elder of the ostrich sticking its head in the sand doesn't work for the ostrich, neither does denial of something that could be life-threatening. Ignoring a serious disease can lead to one's death. Similarly, denial of serious environmental problems may lead to the collapse of ecosystems upon which humans rely. It is in this category – denial of something that worries you – where climate change denial fits in. The ramifications of climate change denial are serious, including a changed climate where many species could go extinct, sea levels rise (flooding cities), and a world where agriculture could be hit hard, increasing famine. These examples could just be the harbinger of things to come.

Global climate change is arguably the single most significant environmental problem of our time, with potentially drastic consequences for human society and global ecosystems (IPCC, 2007). It is also a highly significant global environmental justice issue (Agarwal and Narain, 1991; Baer et al, 2000; Athanasiou and Baer, 2002; Norgaard, 2003). Despite the seriousness of this global environmental problem, there has been (until recently) meagre public response in the way of social movement activity, behavioural changes or public pressure on governments (Norgaard, 2003, 2006a and 2006b). Public apathy with respect to global warming has been identified as a significant concern by environmental sociologists (Kempton et al, 1995; Dunlap, 1998; Bulkeley, 2000; Rosa, 2001) and social psychologists working in the area of risk perception (Stern, 1992; Slovic, 2000). The study of public response to global warming comes predominantly from the fields of environmental sociology, risk analysis and perception, and the concept of a 'risk society' (Beck, 1992). Paradoxically, as evidence for climate change pours in and scientific consensus has increased, interest in the issue in some industrialized countries (such as Norway) is on the decline (Norgaard, 2003 and 2006a). National survey research found a downward trend in Norwegian interest and concern about environmental issues over the past decade. The percentage of respondents who replied that they were 'very much worried' about climate change declined steadily from 40 per cent in 1989 to less than 10 per cent in 2001 (Hellevik, 2002). In Australia in 2009 the Lowy Institute reported that 56 per cent of those surveyed thought climate change was very important. However this is down 10 per cent from 2008 and 19 per cent from 2007 (ABC, 2009). How can this be?

Existing research in environmental sociology and social psychology has previously emphasized the notion that *information* is the limiting factor in public non-response to this issue, an approach that has been characterized as the 'information deficit model' (Bulkeley, 2000; Norgaard, 2003). There is the sense that 'if people only knew' they would act differently: drive less, 'rise up' and put pressure on their governments (Halford and Sheehan, 1991). However, other scholars (for example Hulme, 2009) have come to believe that the 'deficit model' explanation is no longer tenable. There are other barriers than lack of scientific knowledge to changing the status of climate change in the minds of the public – psychological, emotional and behavioural barriers. We need to understand the complex 'cultural circuits' of science communication in which framing, language, imagery, marketing devices, media norms and agendas all play their part.

People in Norway avoided thinking about climate change *because* doing so raised feelings of 'helplessness' and 'guilt' that threatened individual self-identity ('ontological security', Norgaard, 2003) and also a collective sense of identity (Giddens, 1991). Instead of integrating this information into daily life, community members used a number of strategies to hold information about climate change at arm's length, thereby minimizing 'cognitive dissonance' and maintaining a sense of normal reality (Norgaard, 2003 and 2006b). 'Cognitive dissonance' is the uncomfortable feeling caused by holding two contradictory ideas simultaneously (Norgaard, 2003) or when we realize that something we believe to be true is contradicted by evidence (Hamilton, 2010). We shall return to consider these issues later.

Biologist Jared Diamond (2005) has argued in his book *Collapse* that societies that deny or ignore their environmental problems tend to collapse. He notes that many of them tend to collapse at the height of their power, when presumably the idea of possible collapse would have seemed unthinkable. Thus, denial of some problems can be not only life-threatening, but even society-threatening. Climate change, even rapid climate change, is not going to send humans extinct, or turn the world into a burnt cinder. However, runaway climate change could stress societies to the point of collapse. There are already large numbers of environmental refugees around the world, with a prediction that there will be between 200 million and a billion refugees by 2050 (Assadourian, 2010). These will be victims of environmental degradation, often in the form of drought or overpopulation (Conisbee and Simms, 2003). Hundreds of millions of extra environmental refugees could well push societies over the edge. Water will become a critical issue, one that could even lead to war (Shiva, 2002). The cause of all this is not that the problems are impossible to solve, it's that *we deny them*.

Science, Uncertainty and the 'Preponderance of Evidence'

UN Secretary General Ban Ki-moon opened the 2007 Bali Climate Conference with the words (quoted in Hulme, 2009):

> We gather because the time for equivocation is over. Climate change is the defining challenge of our age. The science is clear; climate change is happening, the impact is real. The time to act is now.

However, despite this statement, climate change and climate change science *are* still being denied. Why is this? The word science derives from the Latin, *scientia*, for knowledge. Various definitions of science have been given, such as 'organized knowledge', 'a highly integrated form of knowledge which makes a worldview' and 'proven knowledge' (Chalmers, 1976; Bronowski, 1978; Medawar, 1984). Science is thus seen as an organized, proven, highly integrated form of knowledge that can answer questions and give explanations and predictions.

The scientific method is about *probability* rather than certainty. It can thus not be seen as the road to absolute truth. The Universe is not certain, nor is the world or our lives. We may fool ourselves into believing in 'certainty', but it is a delusion. We are all at the mercy of fate or, to put it another way, there is always uncertainty. That is the nature of reality, one that many people tend to *deny*. Indeed this uncertainty is scary unless one accepts it. Uncertainty is not tidy, it is not black and white, cut and dried. It is messy and pretty random. It has been pointed out by Mike Hulme (2009) that the 'assumption of certainty' is a recent thing in our society and that for most of human history 'we have accepted that lack of certainty is our natural lot'.

Science has been said to be 'proven knowledge' (Chalmers, 1976), but in fact science doesn't *prove* anything. It finds the most likely theory to fit the observations. Sometimes things are so likely – or probable – that we call them *facts*, as in 'the Sun will rise tomorrow'. This is actually a declarative statement based on high probability. We are pretty certain the Earth will turn so that the Sun will appear to rise (as it always has in recorded history), and we have a lot of evidence about orbital mechanics to believe this will continue for millions of years. So, very probable things we call facts or 'laws', and very improbable things we often say are impossible. Nevertheless, it's all about probability, as nothing is absolutely certain. It is common in the physical sciences to say that something is 'true' or 'well-established' if the evidence suggests that there is less than a 5 per cent chance of it being wrong (Pittock, 2009). Because of uncertainty, climate scientists often talk about *probability density functions* to assess how likely or uncertain things are (Schneider, 2009). Scientific knowledge about climate change will always be incomplete and it will always be uncertain (to some degree). Good science thus always speaks with a 'conditional' voice (Hulme, 2009).

This may seem obvious to some, but it's important that we accept the *uncertain nature of reality*, for much of the denial of climate change hinges around this. Many non-scientists think things are black and white, either fact or fiction. However, scientists observe the world and come up with the most probable explanation. They therefore deal in probabilities, not absolute and clear cut 'facts', and they tend to emphasize the uncertainties rather than the settled knowledge (Oreskes and Conway, 2010). Many concerned citizens in the public have looked to scientists in the past to make a clear statement, such as 'climate change is happening and is a serious problem'. Nonetheless, for scientists this is asking them to step away from discussing probability, asking them instead to make a definitive statement. This goes against the grain for most scientists. Many scientists are also quite conservative (Passmore, 1975) or reticent (Hansen, 2009) and do not wish to put themselves forward in a strong and definitive way – yet this is what the public is often looking for. This has delayed climate change action for decades. Those scientists who did understand the public's desire for a definitive answer, and who were brave enough to come forward to give one, have often been criticized by their peers. Professor Stephen Schneider of Stanford University and Dr James Hansen of NASA are eminent climate change scientists who have been concerned enough to step forward and make strong and definitive statements. As a result they have received criticism, not only from climate change deniers (not surprisingly) but also from other serious scientists.

The most commonly quoted conclusion of the IPCC is that there is a 90 per cent chance that recent climate trends are caused by humanity (IPCC, 2007). This is a statement of probability, and it took decades for the IPCC to agree through consensus that such a statement was acceptable, that the statement was necessary as the risk posed by climate change was sufficiently great. For scientists to make such a strong statement was a genuine expression of concern. So scientists can't 'prove' things, they can show what is most probable. Some things scientists have come to understand fairly well and have a high degree of probability, so statements about them are sometimes called 'laws'. For example, the role of natural selection in evolution, gravity or the laws of thermodynamics have never been conclusively 'proven' (Ehrlich and Ehrlich, 1998). But these concepts are supported by such massive evidence that scientists treat them as certain in their daily operations. Other things still puzzle scientists and they continue to look for explanations. This applies to any field of scientific endeavour, so one is never 100 per cent sure about everything in any field of science, whether it is physics, chemistry, biology or geology. Indeed physics has enshrined its own 'uncertainty principle' and mathematics has developed 'chaos theory' to deal with an uncertain world.

Over centuries some things have come to be well understood (i.e. they have a very good probability), while other aspects of a topic are still intriguing and poorly explained. Statements about these thus have a lower probability. This is as true of climate science as of any other science. As climatologist Stephen Schneider has pointed out, just because there are aspects of climate change that puzzle us does not mean that there is not a large body of climate change science that is very well understood (Schneider, 2009). In other words, climate scientists are very certain about some things, such as the basics of climate change, but less certain about other things (for example, how much cloud formation there will be in a warmer world; Houghton, 2008). The poorly understood aspects of climate change do *not* invalidate the very well understood parts – yet this is what climate change deniers often claim. We know a lot about our atmosphere and how it works, but that doesn't mean we know it all, and it is only a statement of humility to acknowledge this.

Science works over time by the slow piecing together of observations (data) and finding a theory that explains these observations best. It is always in a state of flux, as we always learn new things. In the end nothing is fully settled in science, as deniers commonly note (see, for example, Plimer, 2009). However, a consensus does emerge as to what is going on – just as it has with climate change. In fact that consensus has been developing since the 1960s (Oreskes, 2007a). The consensus, or *preponderance of evidence,* has become a dirty word to deniers precisely because it does not support their denial. Because scientists keep an open mind to new evidence does not mean they ignore the balance of existing evidence. Because some parts of climate change are poorly understood does not negate the truth that a great deal *is* very well understood. All scientific work is incomplete, but that does not confer on us a freedom to ignore the knowledge we already have, or postpone action based on that (Oreskes and Conway, 2010). One cannot advance the debate about climate change denial without understanding this. Otherwise one will always face fatuous arguments about the 5 per cent that is poorly understood disproving the 95 per cent that is well understood.

Science is also 'adversarial' in that scientists test each other's data, ideas and theories (Ehrlich and Ehrlich, 1998). When dealing with the complex world, scientists may well evaluate the same evidence differently and differing conclusions are legitimate (Hansen, 2009). Science thus thrives on disagreement (Hulme, 2009). In this way science does not often progress by consensus. Scientists will often test each other's work and can be highly critical. So the *process* does not work by consensus, but over time a consensus develops on the science about the topic being researched. Consensus is a way of distilling evidence. Indeed, as Hulme (2009) notes, while there may be problems with a consensus approach, if it is:

> open, transparent and well governed, if it seeks to be true to the many
> uncertainties which persist, then consensus may well offer policy makers
> the best that science has to offer.

Given that humans are diverse, there will always be diverging opinions, and these are valid in science as in other areas. However, what science does provide is a *preponderance of evidence* of what is known. This preponderance of evidence is also called a 'consilience' of evidence, where multiple sets of data (independently derived) support the same explanation (Oreskes, 2007b). It has been pointed out for many years that there is a consensus in the scientific community about the human dilemma in terms of the environmental crisis (Ehrlich and Ehrlich, 1998). All the scientific academies around the world conclude that human-caused climate change is real. Oreskes (2004 and 2007b) studied 928 abstracts of scientific papers published in refereed journals between 1993 and 2003. Seventy-five per cent endorsed human-caused climate change while 25 per cent took no position. None opposed the consensus position that human-caused climate change was real. Doran and Zimmerman (2009) conducted a survey of 3146 earth scientists (a field that includes climate scientists). They asked the question 'Do you think human activity is a significant contributing factor in changing mean global temperatures?'. Overall 82 per cent of the scientists answered yes. However, not all of these were climatologists who actively published research on climate change in peer-reviewed journals. Of those, 97.5 per cent responded yes. This is as good as one gets with scientific consensus. By contrast, only 58 per cent of the general public believed in anthropogenic climate change (Gallup, 2009).

Another problem about certainty is 'absolute proof'. As Paul and Anne Ehrlich (1998) have pointed out, 'if scientists waited for "proof" or perfection, no scientific papers would ever be published'. Over the last two decades there has been an important debate on 'the precautionary principle', which considers the *burden of proof*. Should we wait to have absolute proof in regard to an environmental problem before we act? Alternatively, if there is doubt about some action or process, should the burden of proof be on the proponent to show that the action is harmless to the environment? The precautionary principle is defined by the Rio Declaration (The Earth Summit) and is also included in Article 3 of the UN Framework Convention on Climate Change, where the parties:

> Should take precautionary measures to anticipate, prevent or minimize the causes of climate change and mitigate against its adverse effects. Where there are threats of serious or irreversible damage, lack of full certainty should not be used as a reason for postponing such measures.

One historical example of failure to take a precautionary approach was the use of thalidomide, the morning sickness drug that was eventually proven to cause birth deformities. Although there was suggestive evidence for some years, it was not until the link was conclusively 'proven' that the drug was banned (Knightley et al, 1979). Another example was asbestos, where again its use continued until it was proven to cause several diseases. A third is the classic case of tobacco. There was denial about all of these (and for some there still is). The climate change debate is another excellent example of the precautionary principle, and this may be why some deniers (for example Plimer, 2009) totally refute this principle, even though it is a key foundation of ecological sustainability (Soskolne, 2008; Washington, 2009).

While there is very strong evidence that human-caused climate change is happening, should we wait for absolute proof? Alternatively, given the risks posed of serious environmental damage, should we take precautionary action *before* absolute proof is available? When such proof is finally available it may well be too late to take action to halt climate change. It may have gone into the 'runaway' phase (see Chapter 2). The overwhelming majority of climate change scientists are saying that the preponderance of evidence *is* clear and requires action. This is a precaution, as they point out the risk we run in regard to runaway climate change. 'Risk' is a key aspect in this debate. Risk is the assessment of likely threats. Climate change action is very much about risk assessment and action. Most people understand the idea of risk, even if they are unsure about 'probability'. Insurance companies, banks and other businesses all understand risk. This is why the insurance industry has been one of the first corporate areas to acknowledge human-caused climate change (Dunlap and

McCright, 2010) and in Australia pushed for action on climate change (Kelly, 2007). They know climate change is already costing them money and could cost much more (Pittock, 2009).

So how does science reach a 'preponderance of evidence' through an adversarial system? Scientific papers are sent out for peer review by experts in that field. Any mistakes or wild claims are examined and will respectively have to be corrected or defended. The peer review process is not perfect, but it does generally prevent unsupported views being published. Deniers hate peer review as their arguments fall apart in the light of rational assessment. If the data does not show something, it will generally be questioned or rejected. Of course we are talking here about mainstream peer-reviewed scientific journals. Today the deniers have their own forums and journals in which they publish without the peer review process of the mainstream scientific community. People get confused about peer review, but all it's about is checking the facts and data put forward and testing the logic of the arguments. This has happened right throughout the history of science. It's not the 'thought police' trying to stop divergent views being published, though deniers claim this. After all, Flat Earthers have a right to *believe* in a flat Earth, but not to expect a paper on this to be accepted by a mainstream scientific journal for publication. A flat Earth is a belief system, not a scientific fact. This is not to suggest that science does not have its own dogmas, ideologies or 'sacred cows', for it does (Passmore, 1975; Chalmers, 1976; Worster, 1994). Historian Donald Worster (1994) has shown how the accepted norm in ecology has been influenced by the dominant ideology over time. However, at least science *tries* to be objective, tries to seek the truth, and has a philosophy of challenging its biases and beliefs, not adhering to blind faith or blind denial. Denial does not do this, it is about refusal to believe the truth. Sometimes science may be slow to accept something that challenges the prejudices of key luminaries in that field, but eventually it moves past denial to accept the new evidence. Those in denial do not.

Denial of scientific evidence about the environmental crisis (not just climate change) has been going on for so long, and has become so organized, that it has been called variously 'brownlash' and 'anti-science' (Ehrlich and Ehrlich, 1998), green backlash (McCright and Dunlap, 2000), and anti-environmental backlash (Lahsen, 2008). This denial network is composed of industry, conservative political groups, politicians and sympathetic scientists (Lahsen, 2008). The distinguished scientists Paul and Anne Ehrlich (1998) note that:

> With few exceptions, brownlash writers don't publish their attacks on environmental science in peer-reviewed journals, where their views would be exposed to the rigorous criticism of the scientific community. Nor do they constantly carry out research to test and retest ideas, as most scientists do.

The Ehrlichs also point out that for the most part 'contrarian' (or denial) scientists are notably absent from the ranks of scholars who are also 'systematically seeking solutions'. There is just a small key group of conservative denial scientists (mostly physicists) who have led the denial of climate science (McCright and Dunlap, 2000; Lahsen, 2008; Oreskes and Conway, 2010). Denial, then, is not about solving the world's problems; it is about hiding from them. In fact the denial anti-science is mostly inconsistent and often contradictory, with many denial statements contradicting other denial statements (Enting, 2007). In an uncertain world, the way we try and work out what is most likely or 'proven' is through the slow accretion of observations and theories that explain them. That is mainstream science. It has been noted by Stefan Rahmstorf (2005) that deniers (or some still call them skeptics) come in three types. These are:

1 Trend skeptics: those who deny the warming trend;
2 Attribution skeptics: those who accept the trend and attribute it to natural causes; and
3 Impacts skeptics: those who accept human causation of the warming trend but claim that the impacts will be beneficial or benign.

In terms of the scientific community, biologist Peter Doherty (2009) has argued that there are four types of deniers:

1 Outright deniers: those who suggest that the IPCC is a fraud and climate scientists are fools;
2 Combative confrontationalists: those who automatically adopt a position in opposition to any general consensus;
3 Professional 'controversialists': those who are keen to seek recognition by being part of a prominent public discourse; and
4 Conflicted 'naysayers', who may have worked closely with the mining industry, and feel a strong sense of personal loyalty towards it.

Mathematician Ian Enting (2007) notes that deniers (or skeptics) distort scientific evidence about climate change in several ways, being:

- **Outright lies**: for example the claim that the IPCC ignores the saturation of CO_2 as its concentration increases (in fact it gives a formula for this);
- **Twisting phrasing**: this mostly arises from using correct quotes, but then seeking to mislead readers from these quotes;
- **Removing qualifiers**: as when 'no close correlation' becomes 'no correlation';
- **Bait and switch**: where a true proposition is used to imply a similar sounding but false proposition;
- **Guilt by association**: the most obvious of these is the suggestion that climate scientists are socialists or Marxists;
- **Misrepresenting nature of evidence 'for' vs. 'against'**: the inconclusive nature of some particular evidence for an issue is used to reject the large body of evidence that *supports* the issue;

- **Raising true but irrelevant 'facts'**: for example 'rising sea levels create coral reefs'. Darwin noticed that as volcanic mountains slowly sink, the coral keeps building up to the surface. This is beside the point today in that sea levels are rising faster now, and in any case it is warming water temperatures that cause coral bleaching and thus kill reefs; and
- **Assembling petitions**: the best known being the Oregon Petition denying climate change. This approach goes back a long way; for example there was a group of '100 authors against relativity'. Einstein remarked that if the arguments were valid, 'one would have been enough' (Enting, 2007).

Pascal Diethelm and Martin McKee (2009) organize general denial arguments under five useful headings:

1 **Conspiracy theories**: Deniers won't admit that scientists have independently studied the evidence to reach their conclusions. Instead they claim that scientists are engaged in a complex and secretive conspiracy. For example, the South African government was influenced by conspiracy claims that HIV was not the cause of AIDS.

2 **Fake experts**: These are individuals purporting to be experts but whose views are inconsistent with established knowledge. They have been used extensively by the tobacco industry to counteract the growing evidence on the harmful effects of second-hand (passive) smoke. This tactic is often complemented by denigration of established experts, seeking to discredit their work.

3 **Cherry-picking**: This involves selectively drawing on isolated papers that challenge the consensus, and thus ignores the broader body of research. An example is a paper describing intestinal abnormalities in 12 children with autism which suggested a possible link with immunization. This has been used extensively by campaigners against immunization, even though 10 of the paper's 13 authors subsequently retracted the suggestion of an association.

4 **Impossible expectations of what research can deliver**: Tobacco company Philip Morris tried to promote a new standard for the conduct of epidemiological studies. These stricter guidelines would have invalidated in one sweep a large body of research on the health effects of cigarettes.

5 **Misrepresentation and logical fallacies**: Logical fallacies include the use of 'straw people', where the opposing argument is misrepresented, making it easier to refute. For example, the Environmental Protection Agency in the US determined in 1992 that environmental tobacco smoke was carcinogenic. This was seen as nothing less than a 'threat to the very core of democratic values and democratic public policy' (Gori and Luik, 1999). Oreskes and Conway (2010) explain the ideology that drives some of these logical fallacies on climate (see Chapter 4).

These headings are also useful when applied to climate change denial, and we use them to organize climate change denial arguments in Chapter 3. We should also assess what arguments climate change deniers suggest are the real reasons for climate scientists to publish peer-reviewed papers about human-caused climate change. In terms of the motivations of climate scientists, it has been suggested that they have their 'snouts in the carbon trough', that they are manufacturing the data about climate change so as to receive more research grants (Carbonsense, 2009). This of course is the stuff of conspiracy theories, as noted above. However, a moment's consideration of the adversarial nature of science can demonstrate just how improbable this is. Thousands of scientists would have to be in on such a scam, abandoning any ethical principles just for extra research funds. Moreover, scientists – like many of us – seek glory and fame. The scientist who could convincingly demonstrate that human-caused climate change was not real would be almost as famous as Einstein. Are we to believe that all those ambitious scientists would pass up such a chance for fame? If there is no credible climate scientist that has done this, it is because the data consistently shows the opposite and that no such claim can withstand peer scrutiny. It is therefore not greed that drives the vast majority of climate scientists to warn about the risks of climate change – it is a commitment to the truth.

There is one other claim about climate scientists that is worth dealing with, that of Lyndon LaRouche (2009), the American millionaire who has also claimed that the British royal family runs a drug syndicate. LaRouche received a 15-year sentence in 1988 for conspiracy to commit mail fraud and tax code violations, but was released on parole in 1994 (Monbiot, 2006). He argues that climate scientists or activists are making their statements because they are genocidal and that the 'entire climate change campaign has been a murderous scientific fraud from the very beginning' (LaRouche, 2009). This 'anti-human' argument is promoted by many deniers (Sawyer, 1990; Plimer, 2009). If such claims are to be believed, it would mean that scientists were not only greedy, but also sociopaths. In fact most scientists are well-meaning and often altruistic. That's why they got into science in the first place: they were looking for the truth or trying to help society and nature. Clearly, claims of greed and genocidal intent are ad hominem attacks or 'playing the person and not the ball'. In other words, deniers cannot win on rational arguments based on reliable data; hence they commonly slander the reputation of climate scientists.

To recap this introduction, we need to understand how common denial is. It is everywhere. We also need to understand how science operates and the nature of uncertainty in any scientific issue. We need as well to understand what science can and cannot tell us. For example, we should not hide behind science when difficult ethical choices are called for (Hulme, 2009). We also need to recognize that there is a very strong denial movement about environmental problems in general. As the Ehrlichs (1998) have comprehensively shown, denial of environmental problems is indeed a 'betrayal of science and reason'.

References

ABC (2009) available at www.abc.net.au/news/stories/2009/10/13/2712203.htm

Agarwal, A. and Narain, S. (1991) *Global Warming in an Unequal World: A Case of Environmental Colonialism*, Centre for Science and Environment, New Delhi

Assadourian, E. (2010) 'The rise and fall of consumer cultures', in L. Starke and L. Mastny (eds) *2010 State of the World: Transforming Cultures from Consumerism to Sustainability*, Earthscan, London

Athanasiou, T. and Baer, P. (2002) *Dead Heat: Global Justice and Global Warming*, Seven Stories Press, New York

Baer, P., Harte, J., Haya, B., Herzog, A., Holdern, J., Hultman, N., Kammen, D., Norgaard, R. and Raymond, L. (2000) 'Equity and greenhouse gas responsibility', *Science*, vol 289, no 29, p2287

Beck, U. (1992) *The Risk Society: Towards Modernity*, Sage Publications, London

Bronowski, J. (1978) *Magic, Science and Civilisation*, Cambridge University Press, New York

Bulkeley, H. (2000) 'Common knowledge? Public understanding of climate change in Newcastle, Australia', *Understanding of Science*, vol 9, pp313–333

Carbonsense (2009) http://carbon-sense.com/2009/11/08/snouts-in-carbon-trough (accessed 28 September 2010)

Chalmers, A. (1976) *What Is This Thing Called Science?*, University of Queensland Press, St Lucia, Australia

Cohen, S. (2001) *States of Denial: Knowing About Atrocities and Suffering*, Polity Press, Cambridge, UK

Conisbee, A. and Simms, E. (2003) *Environmental Refugees: The Case for Recognition*, New Economics Foundation, London

Diamond, J. (2005) *Collapse: Why Societies Choose to Fail or Succeed*, Viking Press, New York

Diethelm, P. and McKee, M. (2009) 'Denialism: What is it and how should scientists respond?', *European Journal of Public Health*, vol 19, no 1, pp2–4

Doherty, P. (2009) 'Copenhagen and beyond skeptical thinking', *The Monthly*, no 51

Doran, P. and Zimmerman, M. (2009) 'Examining the scientific consensus on climate change', *Eos Trans, American Geophysical Union*, vol 90, no 3, p22

Dunlap, R. (1998) 'Lay perceptions of global risk: Public views of global warming in cross national context', *International Sociology*, vol 13, no 4, pp473–498

Dunlap, R. and McCright, A. (2010) 'Climate change denial: Sources, actors and strategies', in Lever-Tracy (ed) *Routledge Handbook of Climate Change and Society*, Routledge, London (Chapter 14)

Ehrlich, P. and Ehrlich, A. (1998) *Betrayal of Science and Reason: How Anti-environmental Rhetoric Threatens Our Future*, Island Press, New York/Shearwater Books, Washington, DC

Enting, I. (2007) *Twisted: The Distorted Mathematics of Greenhouse Denial*, Australasian Mathematical Sciences Institute, Melbourne, Australia

Gallup (2009) Poll on environment, see www.gallup.com/poll/1615/Environment.aspx

Giddens, A. (1991) *Modernity and Self Identity: Self and Society in the Late Modern Age*, Polity Press, Cambridge, UK

Gori, G. and Luik, J. (1999) *Passive Smoke: The EPA's Betrayal of Science and Policy*, The Fraser Institute, Calgary, Canada

Halford, G. and Sheehan, P. (1991) 'Human responses to environmental changes', *International Journal of Psychology*, vol 269, no 5, 599–611

Hamilton, C. (2010) *Requiem for a Species: Why We Resist the Truth About Climate Change*, Allen and Unwin, Sydney, Australia

Hansen, J. (2009) *Storms of My Grandchildren: The Truth about the Coming Climate Catastrophe and Our Last Chance to Save Humanity*, Bloomsbury, London

Hellevik, O. (2002) 'Beliefs, attitudes and behaviour towards the environment', in Lafferty et al (eds) *Realizing Rio in Norway: Evaluative Studies of Sustainable Development*, Program for Research and Documentation for a Sustainable Society (Prosus), University of Oslo, pp7–19

Houghton, J. (2008) *Global Warming: The Complete Briefing*, Cambridge University Press, Cambridge, UK

Hulme, M. (2009) *Why We Disagree about Climate Change: Understanding Controversy, Inaction and Opportunity*, Cambridge University Press, Cambridge, UK

IPCC (2007) *IPCC Fourth Assessment Report: Climate Change (AR4)*, Intergovernmental Panel on Climate Change, see www.ipcc.ch/publications_and_data/publications_and_data_reports.htm

Kelly, K. (2007) 'General insurance industry submission regarding the proposed National Emissions Trading Scheme (NETS)', Insurance Council of Australia, Sydney, Australia

Kempton, W., Boster, J. and Hartley, J. (1995) *Environmental Values in American Culture*, MIT Press, Cambridge, MA

Knightley, P., Evans, H., Potter, E. and Wallace, M. (1979) *Suffer the Children: The Story of Thalidomide*, Viking Press, New York

Lahsen, M. (2008) 'Experiences of modernity in the greenhouse: A cultural analysis of a physicist "trio" supporting the backlash against global warming', *Global Environmental Change*, vol 18, pp204–219

Laing, R. D. (1970) *Knots*, Penguin Books, London

LaRouche, L. (2009) 'LaRouche: Copenhagen summit must reject London genocide policy', 24 November, see www.larouchepac.com/node12510, accessed 10 January 2011

McCright, A. and Dunlap, R. (2000) 'Challenging global warming as a social problem: An analysis of the conservative movement's counter-claims', *Social Problems*, vol 47, no 4, pp499–522

Medawar, P. (1984) *The Limits of Science*, Harper and Row, New York

Merton, R. (1973) *The Sociology of Science: Theoretical and Empirical Investigations*, University of Chicago Press, Chicago, IL

Monbiot, G. (2006) *Heat: How to Stop the Planet Burning*, Penguin Books, London

Norgaard, K. (2003) 'Denial, privilege and global environmental justice: The case of global climate change', paper presented at the annual meeting of the American Sociological Association, Atlanta Hilton Hotel, Atlanta, available from www.allacademic.com

Norgaard, K. (2006a) '"People want to protect themselves a little bit": Emotions, denial and social movement nonparticipation', *Sociological Inquiry*, vol 76, no 3, pp372–396

Norgaard, K. (2006b) '"We don't really want to know"', *Organisation and Environment*, vol 19, no 3, pp347–370

Oreskes, N. (2004) 'The scientific consensus on climate change', *Science*, vol 306, p1686

Oreskes, N. (2007a) 'The long consensus on climate change', *Washington Post*, 1 February, see www.washingtonpost.com/wpdyn/content/article/2007/01/31/AR2007013101808_pf.html

Oreskes, N. (2007b) 'The scientific consensus on climate change: How do we know we're not wrong?', in J. DiMento and P. Doughman (eds) *Climate Change: What It Means for Us, Our Children, and Our Grandchildren*, MIT Press, New York, pp65–99

Oreskes, N. and Conway, E.M. (2010) *Merchants of Doubt: How a Handful of Scientists Obscured the Truth on Issues from Tobacco Smoke to Global Warming*, Bloomsbury Press, New York

Passmore, J. (1975) 'The revolt against science', in P. Gardner (ed) *The Structure of Science Education*, Longman, London

Pittock, A. B. (2009) *Climate Change: The Science, Impacts and Solutions*, CSIRO Publishing, Melbourne, Australia

Plimer, I. (2009) *Heaven and Earth: Global Warming: The Missing Science*, Connorcourt Publishing, Ballan, Australia

Rahmstorf, S. (2005) 'The climate sceptics', in Munich Re (ed) *Weather Catastrophes and Climate Change*, PG Verlag, Munich, Germany, pp76–83

Rosa, E. (2001) 'Global climate change: Background and sociological contributions', *Society and Natural Resources*, vol 14, no 6, pp491–499

Sawyer, P. (1990) *Green Hoax Effect: Greenhouse and Other Myths from the Multinational Corporations*, Groupacumen Publishing, Wodonga, Australia

Schneider, S. (2009) 'Mitigation and adaptation to climate change', powerpoint presentation by Prof. Stephen Schneider of Stanford University, University of NSW Institute of Environmental Studies Seminar, 16 March

Shiva, V. (2002) *Water Wars: Privatisation, Pollution and Profit*, South End Press, Cambridge, UK

Slovic, P. (2000) (ed) *The Perception of Risk*, Earthscan, London

Soskolne, C. (2008) (ed) *Sustaining Life on Earth: Environmental and Human Health through Global Governance*, Lexington Books, New York/Plymouth

Specter, M. (2009) *Denialism: How Irrational Thinking Hinders Scientific Progress, Harms the Planet and Threatens our Lives*, Penguin Press, New York

Stern, P. (1992) 'Psychological dimensions of global environmental change', *Annual Review of Psychology*, vol 43, pp269–302

Washington, H. (2009) 'Embedding sustainability in an Australian council', *Journal of Sustainability* (eJournal), vol 2, no 2, 1 August, http://journalofsustainability.com/lifetype/index.php?op=ViewArticle&articleId=63&blogId=1

Worster, D. (1994) *Nature's Economy: A History of Ecological Ideas*, Cambridge University Press, Cambridge, UK

Zerubavel, E. (2006) *The Elephant in the Room: Silence and Denial in Everyday Life*, Oxford University Press, New York

2

Climate Science

This chapter will attempt to cover the key points of climate science. Its coverage will of necessity be brief, as there are many books (for example Flannery, 2005; Houghton, 2008; Pittock, 2009) and articles (for example Hansen et al, 2008) available that discuss climate science in greater detail. But the rest of this book will make greater sense if the reader has a general understanding of the basics of climate science. Concern about climate change has been growing for decades. In 1988 a UN Conference on the Changing Atmosphere concluded:

> Humanity is conducting an unintended, uncontrolled, globally pervasive experiment whose ultimate consequences could be second only to a global nuclear war. (Pittock, 2009)

The IPCC was set up in response to these concerns; it has since produced assessments that are arguably the most comprehensive, carefully written and detailed scientific assessments on any issue (Houghton, 2008; Pittock, 2009). Deniers will tell you that 'climate science' is a contradiction in terms, that it lacks scientific rigour (see, for example, Plimer, 2009). In fact climate science is the same as the rest of science – the slow, steady accretion of knowledge that is considered 'proven' or at least knowledge with a high probability of being correct. Like all science there is some uncertainty involved. Nevertheless, as the climate science becomes more certain, paradoxically public doubt about climate change is increasing. We shall see later that in large part this is due to denial. Climate scientist Barrie Pittock's (2009) comprehensive book on climate change concludes:

> Despite the contrarians, the weight of evidence that global warming is happening, and is in large part caused by human action, is now overwhelming... the real issue now is urgency.

In regard to climate science, first one needs to distinguish between weather and climate. Climate is the long-term averaging of weather. Weather is chaotic and shows great variation, but over time this can be averaged to show climate trends. Climate isn't about if one year was cold or hot, it's about average temperature and precipitation (rainfall and snowfall) over time (Houghton, 2008). While you can't predict with certainty whether a coin will land heads or tails, you can predict the statistical results of a large number of coin tosses. Second, climate has *always changed*, and these changes have been recorded in places such as ice-caps, tree rings, stromatolites and cave deposits (Houghton, 2008). Climate has been very different in the past, both far hotter and far colder. The acknowledgment that climate changes, however, is no reason for us to *create* such changes when we currently live in a stable climate. The fossil record is littered with biodiversity catastrophes, with five major extinction events (Wilson, 1988). Given that the wondrous diversity of life on Earth is ethically a 'good thing', there is no justifiable reason for us to create a sixth mass extinction (Leakey and Lewin, 1998).

Human civilization developed during a benign climate period, a period of remarkable stability over the last 8000 years (Houghton, 2008). While the world experienced the Medieval Warming and the Little Ice Age in the last thousand years, we have not seen major climate shifts in recorded history. Minor climate shifts may have led, however, to the destruction of civilizations in the past (for example in South America, see Bowen, 2005), and Jared Diamond (2005) has shown that environmental stress led to the collapse of past civilizations. How would today's civilizations handle a *major* climate shift, one that could raise sea levels by several metres, possibly send large numbers of species extinct and radically disrupt agriculture in an overpopulated world (Hansen, 2009; Pittock, 2009)? It is hard to say. The rocks are not going to melt, the seas will not boil, nor will *Homo sapiens* go extinct. However, we could be facing a radically different world, where stresses on natural systems – and the human society that nature supports – would be much greater (Lynas, 2007; Pittock, 2009).

The obvious question is whether global warming and climate change are actually happening. The best known quote from the IPCC (2007) is that it has:

> Very high confidence that the global average net effect of human activities since 1750 has been one of warming.

'Very high confidence' means more than 90 per cent. However, elsewhere in the Fourth Assessment Report (Contribution of Working Group I) it states that:

> Warming of the climate system is *unequivocal*, as is now evident from observations of increases in global average air and ocean temperatures, widespread melting of snow and ice, and rising global average sea level. (emphasis added)

Some key climate change findings over the past century from the Fourth IPCC (2007) Assessment Report are shown in the list below, as summarized by Graeme Pearman (2008):

- Global temperatures risen by 0.74 ± 0.18°C;
- Northern hemisphere warmth of the last half century is likely the highest in the past 1300 years;
- Eleven of last 12 years rank in 12 warmest years recorded;
- Snow cover decreased in most regions, especially in spring and summer;
- Summer period extending 12.3 days;
- Arctic sea-ice decline of 2.7 ± 0.6 per cent per decade;
- Sea levels risen 1.9 ± 0.5mm per year 1961–2003 (now rising at 3.4mm/yr); and
- Increasing ocean acidification has caused the pH to drop by 0.1 so far.

The scientific consensus is thus that climate change is happening and that humans are responsible for the increased global temperatures over the last century.

Probability

We have discussed how probability is central to science. Are there uncertainties involved in climate science? Of course there are, just as there are with all science. It therefore becomes a matter of assessing probability and responding to risk. There is a 'cascade of uncertainties' in regard to assessing climate change, as shown in Figure 1 (Pittock, 2009).

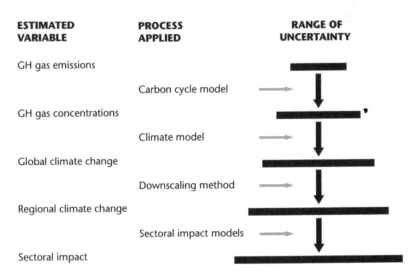

Figure 1 *The cascade of uncertainties around climate change*

Source: Pittock (2009)

Figure 1 demonstrates that as one proceeds down the cascade, the uncertainties become greater. However, the risk of serious impacts also becomes greater. In an essentially uncertain Universe, the suggested uncertainty about climate science needs to be put in perspective. John Houghton (2008) notes:

> No previous scientific assessments on this or any other subject have involved so many scientists so widely distributed both as regards their countries and their scientific disciplines. The IPCC reports can therefore be considered as authoritative statements on the contemporary views of the international scientific community.

It has been pointed out by Mike Hulme (2009) that no matter how strong the consensus may be among scientists about climate change risks, no matter how convincing the analysis by the experts, the ways in which such risks are perceived, ranked and given priority in people's lives are a function of many things not captured by these narrow risk assessments. Knowledge, values, beliefs and culture will all affect how we understand and give importance to climate change risk. There will always be uncertainties, and deniers love to focus on these. The uncertainties can be large – but then so are the *consequences* to the Earth and to humanity.

'Forcing'

Something that changes climate is called a 'forcing'. Forcings can be many-fold, they can be:

- **Volcanic eruptions** – sulphate aerosols and other particulates reflect light and reduce the temperature of the Earth for several years. They thus cool the planet. In past geological eras however it is thought that massive 'flood' volcanic eruptions also released such huge amounts of CO_2 that they later warmed the planet (once the particles settled).
- **Solar variation** – variation in solar output will heat or cool the Earth.
- **Orbital variations** – the Earth varies its elliptical orbit (Milankovitch cycles with a period of 100,000 years), varies the tilt of its axis (period of 41,000 years) and changes the times of year when the Earth is closest to the Sun (period of 23,000 years). These can affect climate, and 60 per cent of past ice ages can be explained by these orbital changes (Houghton, 2008).
- **Changes in greenhouse gases** – greenhouse gases warm the atmosphere by trapping infra-red radiation emitted from the Earth. Sunlight is not absorbed by the greenhouse gases. At certain wavelength bands (4300 and 1500 nanometres for CO_2) greenhouse gases absorb the infra-red radiation (heat) emitted by the Earth that was heated by the incoming sunlight. Greenhouse gases thus alter the *energy balance* of the atmosphere (Houghton, 2008; Pittock, 2009). Increasing greenhouse gas concentrations means increasing temperature, as the energy absorbed has to go somewhere. Greenhouse gases

include water vapour, carbon dioxide, methane, nitrous oxide and halo-carbons (CFCs, HCFCs, HFCs and halons).

Contrary to claims by some deniers, climate scientists are fully aware of the different ways climate can be (and has been) forced through orbital changes, solar output variability and volcanic eruptions (Pittock, 2009). They do not attribute all climate changes to CO_2 (Houghton, 2008; Pittock, 2009; Oreskes and Conway, 2010). Humans cannot affect solar output, volcanic eruptions or the Earth's orbit. However, we can affect the composition of greenhouse gases in our atmosphere and force climate in this way. Houghton (2008) concludes that 'warming over the last one hundred years is very unlikely to be due to natural variability alone' and climates 'cannot be modelled successfully without taking the greenhouse feedback into account'. Climate scientist James Hansen (2009) goes further, claiming that forcing from CO_2 changes is the immediate cause of the large climate swings we have seen over the last 65 million years (Hansen, 2009). Orbital variations initiated global warming, which released CO_2 and methane, which then caused further warming through amplification (Pittock, 2009). Release of greenhouse gases such as CO_2 and methane thus amplified orbital forcing. The ending of past ice ages is therefore partly due to orbital change but *also* due to the greenhouse gases these caused to be released. This tells us that what we are doing by pouring greenhouse gases into the atmosphere will also have an impact.

Temperature in the past has been collated from many sources, such as tree ring growth, corals and cave deposits. The steepening of the temperature curve from the 1950s has led to the temperature curve being described as a 'hockey stick', with the sharp upturn being the head of the stick (Mann et al, 1998). This has led to extensive debate, with deniers alleging poor statistics and claiming the 'hockey stick' does not exist (for example Plimer, 2009). However, the US National Academy of Sciences has affirmed the steepening of the temperature curve (Brumfiel, 2006). Figure 2 below shows both the Mann et al (1998) original climate reconstruction from 1998 and also that of Ammann and Wahl (2007). These agree closely. The actual instrumental temperature data after 1950 agrees closely with both reconstructions. While there is some minor variation, they all show a *steep increase in temperature after the 1950s*. Climate author James Hoggan (2009) notes that if you look at climate reconstructions since Mann's paper 'you could outfit a whole hockey team and still have sticks left over'.

Natural and Human-Caused Greenhouse Effect

No scientist can credibly argue that a greenhouse effect does not exist per se; the question is whether it is accelerating and whether humans are the cause. There has been a greenhouse effect since the Earth's atmosphere first developed. The natural greenhouse effect is why the Earth is not a frozen waste with a surface temperature of minus 18 degrees Celsius (Hansen, 2009; Pittock, 2009). In fact,

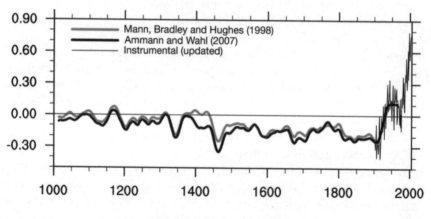

Figure 2 *The 'hockey stick'*

Vertical axis shows global temperature change in degrees Celsius; horizontal shows time since 1000 AD. Original hockey stick graph (Mann et al, 1998) compared to Ammann and Wahl (2007) reconstruction, plus the instrumental record (after 1900). Note strong agreement despite some variation. Note also the steeply rising instrumental temperature after 1900.

Source: Ammann and Wahl (2007, Figure 2); to view related data from Wahl and Ammann (2007) in colour see www.ucar.edu/news/releases/2005/ammann.shtml

due to greenhouse gases, the average temperature of the Earth is 15 degrees Celsius. The natural greenhouse is thus why life as we know it can exist on Earth. So it's not a matter of whether a greenhouse effect 'exists', it's about its *increase* and whether human action is the cause. Compared to a CO_2 molecule, each molecule of the other greenhouse gases traps the following amount of heat (Henderson-Sellars and Blong, 1989; Houghton, 2008; Pittock, 2009).

- Water vapour – ca. 0.03;
- Methane – 21;
- Nitrous oxide – 296;
- CFC 11 and 12 – 10,000;
- HFCs – 12 to 12,000;

So water vapour does not trap much heat per molecule compared to CO_2, but since there is a lot of it, it is the dominant greenhouse gas in the *natural* greenhouse effect, being responsible for two-thirds of the heat retained in the atmosphere in pre-industrial times (Henderson-Sellars and Blong, 1989). Greenhouse gases are like a blanket around the Earth, as they radiate heat back and warm the atmosphere. However, humans are affecting atmospheric chemistry and hence enhancing the greenhouse effect. This is called the anthropogenic, human-caused or enhanced greenhouse effect. For several thousand years before industrialization, CO_2 was remarkably constant at 280 ppm. The CO_2 level is now 387 ppm (NOAA, 2009), an increase of 36 per cent over pre-industrial levels. Isotope research shows that this carbon comes from fossil fuels, and that 45 per cent of human carbon emissions each year stay in the atmosphere, the rest being absorbed by vegetation and oceans (Houghton, 2008). Figure 3 shows the actual observed warming temperatures, plus modelling that shows temperature due to natural forcings (Figure 3a), due to anthropogenic forcings (Figure 3b) and due to natural and anthropogenic forcings combined (Figure 3c). It can be seen that the last figure, where natural and anthropogenic (human-caused) forcings are combined, best explains observed warming over the last 100 years. One cannot explain observed warming since 1960 without adding in anthropogenic forcings (Houghton, 2008). The rapid warming over recent decades has been predominantly caused by human action in burning fossil fuels (and to a lesser extent clearing and burning forests).

The Earth has warmed by 0.7 degrees Celsius due to human-caused greenhouse gases, and 0.6 degrees Celsius of further warming is already in the pipeline at our current CO_2 level due to ocean thermal inertia (Hansen et al, 2008; Pearman, 2008). The table below shows the contribution of various greenhouse gases to the human-caused greenhouse effect.

Gas	Contribution (radiative forcing in W/m²)	Major Sources
CO_2	56.4% (1.66)	Burning of fossil fuels, deforestation and burning of biomass
Methane	16.3% (0.48)	Rice paddies, cattle, biomass burning, gas and coal fields, tundra warming, offshore methane hydrates, fertilizers
Nitrous oxide (N_2O)	5.4% (0.16)	Combustion of fossil fuels and biomass; fertilizers
Halocarbons	11.6% (0.34)	Refrigeration and air-conditioning, fire-fighting systems, horticultural gassing (includes CFCs, HCFCs, HFCs, halons and SF_6)
Ozone*	10.2% (0.3 net)	Photochemical smog

* Note that ozone is not a long-lived greenhouse gas while the other gases are

Source: IPCC (2007) Fourth Assessment Report: Working Group I, Summary for Policy Makers, Figure SPM.2, 'Radiative Forcing Components', and Table 2.1, Chapter 2

The above table uses data from Working Group I of the Fourth Assessment Report. These differ somewhat from other figures given by Working Group III (Introduction 1.1b), largely due to the omission of the short-lived ozone, but also due to different estimates of the importance of halocarbons. However, the table shows that humans are changing greenhouse gas levels in several ways,

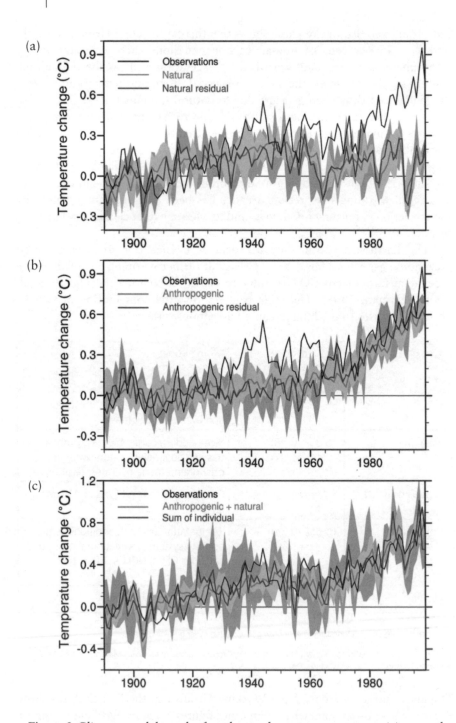

Figure 3 *Climate model results for observed temperature versus (a) natural, (b) anthropogenic and (c) combined forcings compared to observations*

Source: Meehl et al (2004)

with CO_2 increase being responsible for more than half of the recent warming (Houghton, 2008). If the focus of climate scientists has been on CO_2, it is because it is the *major* greenhouse gas in terms of overall effect. Nonetheless, increasing methane is also of concern, as this is an important positive feedback mechanism we will discuss later. We have raised methane levels by over 100 per cent and nitrous oxide by 16 per cent (Houghton, 2008), while halocarbons such as CFCs and halons never previously existed in the atmosphere, and tropospheric ozone is due to human air pollution. Climate scientists often talk of CO_2e or CO_2 *equivalent*, which is what the CO_2 level would be if we converted the other greenhouse gases to an amount of CO_2 that would give the same warming and added this to actual CO_2. Thus the actual atmospheric CO_2 level is now 387 ppm (NOAA, 2009) but CO2e levels are at least 450 ppm due to other greenhouse gases (Houghton, 2008). That is to say, if you look at the heating from the other increased greenhouse gases, then the total heating is equivalent to having a CO_2 level of 450 ppm. Considering CO2e levels is crucial in order to understand what a 'safe' atmospheric concentration of CO_2 might be to avoid 'runaway' greenhouse. Since CO_2 is the major component of the human-caused greenhouse effect, we now turn to consider the carbon cycle.

The Carbon Cycle

Figure 4 below shows the carbon cycle. This is a simplified diagram produced by the Globe Carbon Cycle Project, an inter-agency body of the US government that involves NASA and the National Science Foundation. More detailed diagrams of the carbon cycle are available (for example Sabine et al, 2004). It is important to understand that we are talking about a cycle of carbon moving around the biosphere, from air to water to vegetation to ground. Historically there has been a *balance* operating, which led to a pre-industrial CO_2 level of 280 ppm. This is not to say that CO_2 has not been higher in the past over geological time-spans of many millions of years, for it has (Pearson and Palmer, 2000; Hansen, 2009). However, in human history the CO_2 level has not been this high; we have increased it by 36 per cent and continue to increase it each year by 2 ppm (Hansen et al, 2008).

It is important to realize that oceans and vegetation are both sources *and* sinks for carbon. Currently the oceans emit 90 Gt/yr but absorb 92, thus being a net sink where 2 Gt of carbon are removed from the atmosphere each year. Photosynthesis in plants fixes 120 Gt of carbon a year, which is in balance with 60 emitted in respiration and 60 taken into litter (and thence to soil respiration). Vegetation currently is thus essentially in balance. This may change as climate alters, however (see positive feedbacks later). It can be seen that the atmospheric pool of carbon of 750 Gt is small compared to that in the oceans (38,000 Gt) or in the Earth's crust (100 million Gt). It is also smaller than the carbon locked up in fossil fuels (4000 Gt). It is thus impossible to talk about vegetation or the ocean being only a source of CO_2, as they are also a sink for CO_2 in the carbon cycle. They are both source and sink, and you cannot consider only half of the

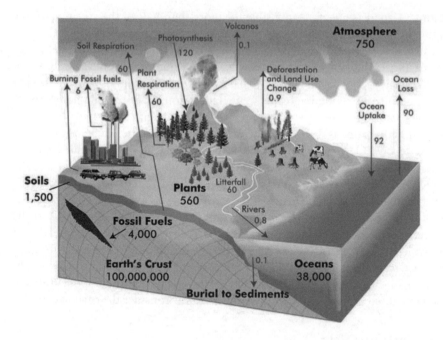

Figure 4 *The global carbon cycle*

Units are in petagrams (10^{15} grams) = gigatonnes (Gt) = billions of tonnes of carbon; note that 1 tonne of carbon = 3.67 tonnes CO_2.

Source: Globe Carbon Cycle Program (University of New Hampshire, funded by inter-agency body involving NASA and US National Science Foundation; see http://globecarboncycle.unh.edu/AdditionalResources.shtml)

equation, as that tells only half the story. However, that is what climate change deniers commonly do. Understanding the carbon cycle (which deniers often seek to confuse) is thus a key step to being able to meaningfully talk about climate change. The emissions from fossil fuels (6 Gt/yr) and deforestation (0.9 Gt/yr, though Pittock, 2009, puts this at 1.6 Gt/yr) may seem small in comparison to the other fluxes of carbon. Yet one needs to remember that these are a perturbation of an existing balance. Around half of these additions are removed, mostly by the oceans and vegetation, but the rest accumulates in the atmosphere, forcing the climate.

Some deniers have also stated that we don't need to be concerned about increasing CO_2 levels, as natural weathering will remove excess CO_2. While this may be true on a *geological* timescale of millions of years, this is not the timescale that is relevant to human civilization today. Over the long term, human changes to atmospheric greenhouse gases will probably eventually be corrected by the natural processes that led to the balance originally. However, if human greenhouse gas emissions should cause a 'runaway' greenhouse effect, then this may take many thousands of years to return to a climate similar to today's.

Modelling

Much has been written about climate change models and their accuracy (or lack thereof). Climate scientist James Hansen (2009) is critical of models, preferring to make use of palaeoclimate data. It has been noted by a statistician that 'all models are wrong, some are useful' (Box and Draper, 1987). Models are not reality; rather they are a projection of probable future reality. We all build models. If we build a house we build a model in the mind, then an architect draws a plan – a model. Using a flow chart is a model. Humans model the future all the time, because we find it useful to plan ahead. It is often said about models that 'garbage in, garbage out', and this has some truth. However, we should not expect models to *be* reality. Depending on the accuracy of the data, they are the best approach we have to projecting future reality. Some of the early climate models undoubtedly had problems. However, the data available has improved immensely with satellite measurements, and the computers themselves are now many times more powerful (Pittock, 2009). Nevertheless, climate change is difficult to model, especially as key aspects such as the probable cloud formation as temperature rises are not well understood (Houghton, 2008). A whole chapter of the IPCC (2007) Fourth Assessment Report is devoted to climate models and their evaluation. Barrie Pittock notes that 'model performance and verification is complex, but is being actively tested and improved' (Pittock, 2009). Climate models provide the best projections of what might happen as we force the climate. They warn us of the risks. There are several climate models that have been developed by climate scientists, and these show good agreement in terms of projected outcomes. Models have also accurately confirmed total climate forcings (natural plus anthropogenic) that agree with observed actual temperatures. In this way the models have been tested and shown to be fairly accurate. The observed temperature increase over the last 100 years can only be explained using both natural and anthropogenic forcings combined (Houghton, 2008; Pittock, 2009).

Feedback

In the climate debate, one often hears of 'positive feedback'. 'Feedback' is when something acts to amplify or reduce something. Negative feedback is when something can lead to reduced global temperature; positive feedback increases temperature further. As Hansen (2009) explains, feedback is the guts of the climate problem. Climate scientists are concerned that there are several positive feedbacks involved with the current warming of the Earth. These are:

- **Increased water vapour:** Many climate scientists (for example Houghton, 2008) believe this is the most important positive feedback. The higher the atmospheric temperature, the more water vapour it can hold (seven per cent more for each 1°C increase). Water vapour is the major component of the natural greenhouse effect. Increasing the amount of water vapour is thus most likely to speed up warming as a positive feedback. Yet this is complicated by cloud formation and precipitation. Clouds act like snow and reflect light back to space, cooling the atmosphere. However, Houghton (2008) explains that water vapour increase overall could *double* the increase in global average temperature that would otherwise occur.

- **Reduced ice cover:** Increased temperature decreases ice cover, which reduces the albedo (reflectivity) of the Earth's surface so that less light is reflected and more is absorbed on land and sea. Reduced ice area thus helps to warm the Earth, especially polar regions. If CO_2 doubled, then the reduced ice albedo could increase temperatures by a further 20 per cent (Houghton, 2008).

- **Warming oceans emit CO_2:** The chemistry of CO_2 is such that cooler seas absorb more CO_2 whereas warmer seas can hold less. As the oceans warm they will first cease to be a sink for CO_2 and then become a source, as they will not be able to retain as much CO_2. Currently they are a net sink absorbing 2 billion tonnes of carbon a year. However, the capacity of the oceans to absorb CO_2 has declined over the last 20 years (Canadell et al, 2007; Le Quéré et al, 2007). With warming of oceanic water, the oceans may thus become a net source of CO_2. Given that 38,000 Gt of carbon are stored in the world's oceans, the potential for outgassing of CO_2 from the oceans is significant.

- **Methane outgassing:** As the North Pole warms, permafrost melts and biological breakdown of carbon sequestered in tundra and peat-bogs speeds up (IASC, 2010). More methane is released as a result, and this could result in increased warming. There is a second more worrying aspect in that huge amounts of methane are locked in methane hydrates (ice/methane lattices) found mainly in the top layers of the continental shelves around the world. As oceans and tundra warm, these methane hydrates will at some stage melt, resulting in large releases of methane. There is geological evidence that this has happened before, radically changing climate by several degrees, and even altering ocean chemistry for 10,000 years (Pearson and Palmer, 1999) or perhaps even 100,000 years (Hansen, 2009). Estimates of carbon stored in methane hydrates are larger than that stored in fossil fuels, ranging from around 5000 Gt (Hansen, 2009) to 10,000 Gt (Kvenvolden, 1988; Pittock, 2009). The potential for methane release accelerating climate change is thus major. Hansen (2009) notes that the 'charge in the methane gun' is now much larger than at the time of the Palaeocene–Eocene Thermal Maximum (55 million years ago), when there was a large methane release. The impact of a methane release today would thus be larger. The temperature point that would trigger such methane eruptions is uncertain, but already warming oceans have triggered some methane release (Science Daily, 2009; Shakhova et al, 2010). There have been several methane outgassings in geological history, and the evidence is that these are a feedback event from previous warming. If global warming continues, it is therefore only a question of time before we get a massive methane eruption (Hansen, 2009). A review by Euan

Nisbet (2002) concluded that the case is open for a major methane release this century. The potential risk is thus large, in fact it remains one of the main ways that climate could be forced into the 'runaway' stage.

- **Biomass becomes carbon source**: As world temperature increases, not only does it increase oxidation of biomass in swamps and bogs but in addition forests will dry out and burn more frequently. The biosphere could become a net source of CO_2 by 2050 (Pittock, 2009). In Australia, climate change will lead to a substantial increase in bushfire risk (Pearman, 2008). If we were to increase global temperatures by up to four degrees, then in Australia we would unleash 'hell on Earth' (Karoly in Hamilton, 2010). In the US, wildfire frequency has increased fourfold in the last 30 years (Schneider, 2009). Modelling of climate change in the Amazon shows large projected dieback of Amazon rainforest and significant release of carbon. Up to 240 Gt of carbon could be released by 2100 from forest decline (Houghton, 2008). Hence vegetation overall could move from being in balance in regard to the carbon cycle to becoming a net source of carbon emissions. The potential release of 240 Gt would be a significant positive feedback.
- **Atmospheric and ocean circulation changes**: These may reinforce adverse changes in the carbon cycle and ice sheet stability (Pittock, 2009).

It is harder to find likely negative feedbacks to climate change. These can be listed as:

- **Increased cloud formation**: Increased water vapour may increase the area of the Earth covered with clouds, which would reflect light and lower temperature. Cloud formation and dynamics are hard to model, so it is difficult to gauge the likelihood of such a negative feedback, but in any case it is likely to be a small one. Cloud formation remains the 'greatest single uncertainty associated with climate sensitivity' (Houghton, 2008). It needs to be remembered that greater cloud formation is due to increased water vapour, and that in itself is a strong *positive* feedback.
- **Increased geological uptake of** CO_2: Plimer (2009) suggests that increased CO_2 would be mopped up by geological processes such as the formation of limestone. However, he does not reference this claim, nor indicate over what time-span it would occur. Geologists tend to think in geological timescales, often not relevant to human history. He does nonetheless note that in past methane spikes it took 10,000 years for climate to come back to normal. Hansen (2009) notes that carbon uptake into geological processes operates at best at scales of thousands of years. This is not going to help us remove the major CO_2 build-up that has occurred over 100 years.
- **CO_2 as fertilizer**: As CO_2 increases the efficiency of photosynthesis up to a 1000 ppm concentration, it has been argued that increased CO_2 will simply be mopped up by vegetation (Plimer, 2009). There is some evidence for this CO_2 fertilization effect (Houghton, 2008). However, humans have cleared a major fraction of the Earth's forests and continue to do so, releasing stored

CO_2 to the atmosphere. Research suggests that as the world warms, biomass may become a net source – not a sink – of CO_2 (Houghton, 2008).

Runaway Climate Change

Runaway climate change is an important term to understand. The best example of runaway climate change is the planet Venus, with a CO_2 concentration of 96 per cent and a surface temperature of 470 degrees Celsius (where lead would melt). Until recently we would have said that what climate scientists mean by runaway climate change on Earth is not that our planet will turn into Venus. However, Hansen (2009) does raise the possibility of a 'Venus syndrome' for Earth if we burn all fossil fuels. Raised temperature may cause a methane spike and thus would mean higher temperatures, which would then put more water vapour in the atmosphere, which would further warm the planet in a spiralling acceleration in temperature. Hansen concludes that if we burned the Earth's tar sands and oil shales then a Venus syndrome would be 'a dead certainty'. Other climate scientists (for example Karoly, 2010) believe it is unlikely the Earth could move towards a Venus scenario. Nevertheless, when one of the world's most eminent climate scientists raises the issue, at the very least one has to acknowledge the worrying possibility.

However, leaving the possibility of the Venus syndrome aside, we have enough to worry about with what the majority of climate scientists believe is most likely. What most climate scientists mean by runaway climate change is that if positive feedbacks are too strong, we may be locked into accelerating temperature that may stabilize some 6–10 degrees Celsius higher than today (Lynas, 2007). Related to this idea is the term 'climate surprises', which refers to abrupt transitions to different states of a climate system (Pittock, 2009). Think of gradually increasing the force you exert on a light switch, at some point the switch will suddenly flick open. Runaway climate change means that past a certain point global warming may be uncontrollable until temperatures settle on the new higher level. The higher the temperature, the greater the impact on the Earth's ecosystems. Science journalist Fred Pearce (in Pittock, 2009) has referred to this as 'waking the sleeping giants'. We need to prevent runaway climate change – no matter what the final temperature might be. Many people think that CO_2 emissions are linked to temperature in a steady linear manner, but this is a false linearity (Lynas in Hamilton, 2010). Runaway climate change would mean that the trend would not be linear. Beyond a certain point, temperature increase will be beyond our control, even if we then drastically reduce emissions.

It has been suggested that warming the world by more than two degrees could push us into the area where we may cause runaway climate change. It may then take thousands of years to get back to current world temperatures. The world has already warmed by 0.7 degrees Celsius (Houghton, 2008; Pittock, 2009) and another 0.6 degrees is in the pipeline (Hansen, 2009). Runaway climate change means that human action would then be unlikely to stop the temperature increase (short of massive geoengineering). Hansen et al (2008) define the 'tipping level' as the climate forcing threat that, *if maintained for a long time*, gives rise to a specific consequence. They define the 'point of no return' as a climate state beyond which the consequence is inevitable, even if climate forcings are reduced. A point of no return can be avoided, even if the tipping level is temporarily exceeded. This has been called an 'overshoot' scenario, where one exceeds the 'safe' CO_2 level but then removes CO_2 to return to that level (Pittock, 2009). Ocean and ice sheet inertia permit overshoot 'provided the climate forcing is returned below the tipping level before initiating irreversible dynamic change' (Hansen et al, 2008). Points of no return are difficult to define. We may be at the tipping level already at 387 ppm CO_2, and it will require strong action to reduce CO_2 levels so that we don't pass the point of no return and can return CO_2 levels below 350 ppm. Hansen et al (2008) note we may need to drop CO_2 below 325 ppm to restore sea ice to the area it had 25 years ago (and so remove this positive feedback).

It can be seen from the above that there are both *more* positive feedbacks than negative feedbacks and that they are better understood. The probability of positive feedback is thus high. The crux of this problem is all about *risk*. How lucky do we think we are? We know that massive methane eruptions have changed climate in the past. Are we happy to gamble the future of the Earth, its ecosystems and the human societies that depend on them? The Millennium Ecosystem Assessment (MA, 2005) noted that runaway climate change would put great stress on already stressed ecosystems. Closed lake systems, coral reefs, freshwater and mangrove coastal areas are all at risk from climate change. Abrupt changes can also occur in ecological systems where the ecosystem suddenly changes and moves to a new stable state (Pittock, 2009). This new state may well be one that humans don't like (MA, 2005).

Is There a Safe Level of CO_2?

Is there a safe level of CO_2 we can increase to, beyond which we may trigger runaway climate change? The Kyoto Protocol referred to avoiding 'dangerous climate change', but this was not defined. Hansen (2009) concluded that the collapse of the ice sheets is the critical event that defines 'danger'. He noted that 'once the ice sheets collapse begins, coastal devastation and their economic impact may make it impractical for humanity to take actions to rapidly reverse climate change'.

Remember we are at an actual CO_2 level of 387 ppm already, which has resulted in 0.7 degrees Celsius of warming. There is at least another 0.6 degrees of warming that is on the way from this current CO_2 level (Hansen et al, 2008). This is the *actual* CO_2 level, but considering the other greenhouse gases the CO2e level is equivalent to 450 ppm of CO_2. A 550 ppm CO_2 level was once considered the 'safe' level beyond which we should not pass (Houghton, 2008). However, as data has come in since the last IPCC report, the suggested 550 ppm level, or even a 450 ppm level, is no longer perceived as a 'safe level'. Brian

O'Neill and Michael Oppenheimer (2002) proposed a 450 ppm CO_2 threshold, which if exceeded would lead to dangerous climate change (mass coral reef bleaching, ice sheet disintegration and the Gulf Stream current stopping). Hansen et al (2008) noted that a CO_2 level below 500 ppm was likely responsible for Antarctic glaciations in the past, so levels beyond this could lead to large-scale Antarctic ice melt. There were earlier suggestions by Hansen et al (2007) that 450 ppm would be a safer level. Now the data 'indicate that that 385 ppm CO_2 is already a threat' (Hansen et al, 2008). Last year Hansen (2009) concluded that a two degree warming (usually tied in to 450 ppm CO_2) is a disaster scenario. Pittock (2009) agrees that 450 ppm is too high and risks passing dangerous tipping points; 350 ppm – less than the current CO_2 level – would be a safer level if we want to avoid 'tragic consequences' (Hansen et al, 2008).

The Spinning 'Greenhouse Gamble' Roulette Wheel

Remember it's all about probability. Oceanographer Wallace Broecker (1987) described continued release of greenhouse gases as like playing:

> Russian Roulette with the climate, hoping that the future will hold no unpleasant surprises. No one knows what lies in the active chamber of the gun.

We don't know the exact CO_2e level that will result in runaway climate change. We only know that runaway climate change gets more likely the higher we raise the levels of greenhouse gases. The safe approach would thus be not to raise CO_2 any higher than it is now, and to actually reduce it as soon as possible to no more than 350 ppm. The most comprehensive modelling yet carried out on the likelihood of how much hotter the Earth's climate will get in this century shows that without rapid and massive action, the problem will be about *twice as severe* as estimated six years ago – and could be even worse than that (MIT, 2009). The Greenhouse Gamble 'roulette wheel' in Figure 5 depicts the MIT Joint Program's estimation of the range of probability of potential global warming to 2100. This looks at two scenarios – a 'no policy' scenario, where no action is taken to try to curb the global emissions of greenhouse gases, and a 'policy taken' scenario. Depicted as a roulette wheel, the image portrays estimations of climate change probability, or the likelihood of potential (global average surface) temperature change over the next hundred years. The face of the wheels are divided into slices, with the size of each slice representing the estimated probability of the temperature change in the year 2100 falling within that range.

Uncertainties still exist (they always do), but the Greenhouse Gamble roulette wheel shows that if we take effective policy action, we move the odds in our favour, so that we have a good chance of avoiding runaway climate change. The real question is your propensity to gamble – so just how lucky do

No policy action

Policy action taken

Figure 5 *The 'Greenhouse Gamble' roulette wheel.*

Source: MIT (2009); see http://globalchange.mit.edu/resources/gamble

you feel? Would *you* bank the future of the world on it? The chance of serious problems arising from climate change is much higher than the risk of your house burning down, yet we all take out fire insurance. Why then, asks Stephen Schneider (2009), do we not take out insurance for climate change?

So we come back to the question of whether there is a safe level of CO_2 and other greenhouse gases? We simply don't know in absolute terms. All we can say is that the more we increase greenhouse gases, the greater the chance will be that we enter runaway climate change. Recent climate science is indicating that things are proceeding *worse* than the worst of the IPCC forecasts (Hansen et al, 2008). If we were going to apply the precautionary principle and 'play it safe', we would not increase CO_2 and other greenhouse gases beyond what they are today. Indeed some believe this is already too high, which is why there is the '350 movement' (www.350.org) that argues we need to return CO_2 levels to no higher than 350 ppm.

So What? Is There Really a Problem?

So if climate change is happening, is there really a problem? What does all this mean? In the next chapter, under the argument 'Global Warming Is Good' we present a table that analyses this question in more detail. Inevitably, there will be some climate changes in some areas which may be seen as positive. The table in Chapter 3 shows there are 10 possible positive changes as opposed to 37 likely negative changes. We shall briefly summarize some of the problems here.

Species and ecosystem loss

Global warming means if we warm the planet too much, then the oceans will release more CO_2, ice cover will decrease and the seas will absorb more sunlight, vegetation is likely to become a net source of CO_2, and the methane hydrates may release large amounts of methane, a greenhouse gas 21 times more powerful than CO_2. The world would then rapidly warm by an amount that we cannot guess (but temperatures may be at least six degrees greater than now). Any major temperature increase would radically alter the Earth's ecosystems, rainfall patterns and agriculture. The world would be a very different place from the benign climate in which we now live. There is also accumulating evidence that ecosystems can reach their own 'point of no return' and flip into an alternative state that humans generally don't like (MA, 2005).

The next concern is the *speed of change* involved in human-caused climate change, which is thought to be happening at a much faster rate than that of previous climate changes, some of which took thousands of years (Houghton, 2008). The difference between the last ice age and today was about five degrees Celsius, and this warming happened over 10,000 years. This is 0.05 degrees per century. In contrast, the observed rate of warming over the last 50 years is 0.7 degrees Celsius (and another 0.6 degrees is in the pipeline, making this 1.3 degrees) and the estimated rate for the next century is more than five degrees, which is 100 times faster than the last glaciations (Pittock, 2009). It is one thing to adapt to changed climate over 10,000 years, but a very different thing to adapt over 100 years. Most plant species cannot migrate faster than one kilometre a year (Houghton, 2008). It is this fast speed of change on the world's already stressed ecosystems (MA, 2005) that is likely to lead to major species extinction. The IPCC (2007) considered the effects of what increased temperatures might be. Mark Lynas (2007) has also considered the effect of rising temperature in his book *Six Degrees*. Hansen (2009) concludes we 'really do have a planet in peril'.

Figure 6 shows some of the projected impacts as the world warms. As temperatures increase, the problems arising from this become more serious. There is reasonable adaptive capacity up to around a two-degree temperature rise. As one moves beyond this, the risk to water supplies, food production and species extinction becomes far greater. As positive feedbacks become greater, the risk of large-scale shifts in climate correspondingly becomes greater. It needs to be remembered that due to human impact, species extinction is already 1000 times (Attenborough, 2009) to 10,000 times (Wilson, 1988) greater than the normal rate, and that (without action) half of the world's species may be extinct by 2100. This is due primarily to clearing and fragmentation of habitat, but also due to introduced species and overharvesting (Wilson, 2003; Pounds and Puschendorf, 2004). The biodiversity crisis will lead to a major reduction in evolutionary pathways and possibilities, and for this reason has rightly been called 'the death of birth' (Wilson, 1988 and 2003). One consequence of mass extinction is the destruction of ecosystem services, and thus a great impact on human wellbeing (Ehrlich and Ehrlich, 1981). As eminent biodiversity expert E. O. Wilson (in Suzuki, 1989) has noted, what we are doing in sending so many species extinct is 'like burning Renaissance masterpieces to cook dinner'.

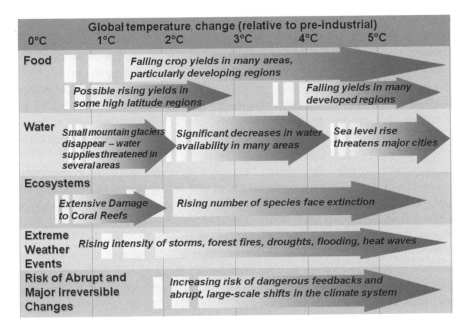

Figure 6 *Projected impacts of climate change*

Source: Stern (2007) 'The economics of climate change', talk given to the World Bank, 23 March; figure based on Figure 2 in Stern (2006)

Ecosystems are thus already severely stressed by human impacts and climate change is an extra stress on top of these. Many plant and animal species are unlikely to survive major climate change. New analyses suggest that 15–37 per cent of a sample of 1103 land plants and animals would eventually become extinct as a result of climate changes expected by 2050 (Pounds and Puschendorf, 2004). Certainly natural systems have never been as fragmented in previous climate changes, making it difficult for species to migrate in response to temperature change. Hansen (2009) notes that a study of 1000 plants, animals and insects in the second half of the 20th century found they could migrate four miles a decade. However, isotherms (areas of the same temperature) have been moving 35 miles a decade in the last 30 years, much faster than living things can move. We thus find ourselves in the process of a major extinction event due to our actions – which climate change makes worse. Such extinction will cause major change in the ecosystems humans rely on for 'ecosystem services' such as clean air, clean water and healthy soil (Ehrlich and Ehrlich, 1981). The answer to the question is that there really is a problem, and it really does matter.

Sea-level rise

Over the last 100 years the sea level has risen by 10–20cm (Houghton, 2008) and it is currently rising by 3.4mm/yr (Hansen, 2009). This is due to both thermal expansion of the oceans and meltwater from glaciers and ice-caps. IPCC estimates are that by 2100 the sea level could rise by 0.9 metres (IPCC, 2007).

However, there are uncertainties involved in this estimate, as we do not know exactly *how* ice-caps disintegrate or at what speeds as the world warms. There remains a possibility that the sea level could rise by six metres this century, as noted by Hansen (2009). An increasing number of scientists agree that sea-level rise may be well above one metre by 2100 (Pittock, 2009). During the warming from the last ice age to the current inter-glacial period, the sea level rose by 3–5 metres each century for many centuries (Hansen, 2009). Andrew Glikson (2008) shows that in past warmings from ice ages, the sea level rose some five metres for each degree Celsius of global warming.

It is therefore hard to be definite as to exactly when (and by how much) the sea level will rise. However, in the warm period before the onset of the last ice age (120,000 years ago), the global average temperature was less than a degree warmer than today. The sea level then was 5–6 metres higher (Houghton, 2008). The equilibrium sea level for today's CO_2 concentration is at least several metres higher, judging from palaeoclimate history (Hansen et al, 2008). Hansen (2009) points out that the climate forcing humans are doing now is far *greater* than that when the last ice age ended. The speed at which the ice sheets disintegrate may thus also be greater. Once started, the collapse of the ice sheets may be irreversible and take centuries to complete (Hansen, 2009; Pittock, 2009). It is notable that there is currently a net loss of ice from the Greenland ice-cap (Wouters et al, 2008; Velicogna, 2009). Recent developments suggest that Greenland and even the West Antarctic Ice Sheet (WAIS) may be destabilized by even a two-degree global warming (Pittock, 2009). There is the equivalent of seven metres of sea-level rise if the Greenland ice-cap was to melt and five metres if the WAIS was to melt (McNeil, 2008).

Some 100 million people live within one metre of the current sea level, while one billion people live within 25 metres (Hansen, 2009; Pittock, 2009). Sixteen of the world's 19 megacities are on coastlines. In Bangladesh alone, 20 per cent of the country (and 15 million people) live within a one-metre sea-level rise zone (Houghton, 2008). Islands such as the Maldives and Tuvalu are similarly at risk of inundation from even small sea-level rises. Given the population and resources tied up in coastal cities, Hansen (2009) points out that to speak of realistically 'adapting' to major sea-level rise is 'insane'.

Climate change, human health, safety and food production

The direct effect of rising temperatures is heat stress – 21,000 people died in 2003 in a heat wave that hit France, Spain, Portugal and Italy (Houghton, 2008). This was the hottest summer since 1500 AD, and very high night-time temperatures were a big reason for the high death rate. By 2040, more than half of Europe's summers are likely to exceed the record temperatures of 2003 (McNeil, 2008). Climate change increases the intensity of droughts by increasing evaporation. It also decreases rainfall in many areas. In Perth, Australia, climate change has already meant a decrease of 10 to 20 per cent in rainfall and a 40–50 per cent reduction in inflow to Perth's water supply (Pittock, 2009). Climate change also puts more water vapour into the atmosphere, which increases extremes in the hydrologic cycle, meaning heavier rains, more extreme floods and more intense storms. This means more rain and snowfall at high latitudes (Pittock, 2009). These storms can also become winter blizzards, so climate change can make winter weather more extreme (Hansen, 2009). Hansen (2009) refers to the 1993 cyclonic blizzard 'superstorm' in the US, and states that this would be eclipsed by the storms of the 21st century due to increasing water vapour levels and stronger frontal cyclones. It does not sound terribly threatening to speak of 'worse storms'. But to put this in perspective one can look at data from the World Disasters Report. Over 30 years, the ratio of the 1990s/1960s non-weather related disasters went up 1.5 times. However, the same ratio of weather-related disasters went up 4.5 times, the ratio of economic losses went up 7.9 times and the ratio of insured losses went up 13.6 times (Pittock, 2009). This shows why the insurance industry was one of the first business groups to become concerned about climate change.

Increasing temperatures also aid the spread of various diseases such as viral encephalitis, malaria, dengue fever and yellow fever (Houghton, 2008; Pittock, 2009). With regard to food production, climate change is likely to exacerbate intense droughts. Food reduction due to climate change could affect 60 million people in Africa alone (Houghton, 2008). A sixth of the world's populations depend on glacier- or snowmelt-fed rivers (Assadourian, 2010).

New factors emerging

The list below shows new factors that are emerging (Pearman, 2008). It suggests we have *underestimated* the changes and new factors that will occur:

- Global CO_2 emissions growth is at the high end of predictions (Raupach et al, 2007);
- Both temperature and sea-level increase have exceeded previous predictions (Rahmstorf et al, 2007);
- The oceans' capacity to absorb CO_2 decreased over the last 20 years (Canadell et al, 2007);
- Observed changes in biological systems – effects on migration/breeding/flowering times/behaviour/fecundity/genetics (Rosenzweig et al, 2008);
- Deglaciation – Arctic sea-ice extent decreased by 20 per cent in summer (NSIDC, 2007); Wilkins Ice Shelf broke up in days (NSIDC, 2007);
- Low productivity areas of the Atlantic and Pacific oceans increasing (Polovina et al, 2008); and
- Political and economic instability caused by climate change now being considered (Borgerson, 2008).

The list above illustrates that we don't know everything about the unplanned experiment we are conducting on the Earth. It shows that research since the IPCC (2007) Fourth Assessment Report indicates things were proceeding *faster and worse* than scientists had previously believed. Unpleasant climate surprises are happening.

Scientific and Ethical Disconnects

We have covered here the basics of climate science. However, all too often there is a failure of the policy living up to the science. There was a 'scientific disconnect' revealed at COP15 in Copenhagen in 2009, where on the one hand parties spoke of limiting CO_2 to 450 ppm and a two-degree temperature rise, while on the other they failed to acknowledge that the proposed targets put on the table by nation states had no chance of delivering this. By disconnecting policy from science, governments are in effect taking a huge risk. The politics of climate change is often well and truly disconnected from the scientific reality and any ethical responsibility to the future. Governments remain in denial about the science of climate change.

References

Ammann, C. and Wahl, E. (2007) 'The importance of the geophysical context in statistical evaluations of climate reconstruction procedures', *Climatic Change*, vol 85, pp71–88

Assadourian, E. (2010) 'The rise and fall of consumer cultures', in L. Starke and L. Mastny (eds) *2010 State of the World: Transforming Cultures from Consumerism to Sustainability*, Earthscan, London

Attenborough, D. (2009) *State of the Planet*, BBC television series hosted by David Attenborough and featuring biodiversity experts such as Professor E. O. Wilson of Harvard University

Borgerson, S. (2008) 'Arctic meltdown: The economic and security implications of global warming', *Foreign Affairs*, vol 87, no 2, pp63–77

Bowen, M. (2005) *Thin Ice: Unlocking the Secrets of Climate in the World's Highest Mountains*, Owl Books, New York

Box, G. and Draper, N. (1987) *Empirical Model-Building and Response Surfaces*, Wiley, London

Broecker, W. (1987) 'Unpleasant surprises in the greenhouse', *Nature*, vol 328, pp123–126

Brumfiel, G. (2006) 'Academy affirms hockey-stick graph', *Nature*, vol 441, 29 June, pp1032–1033

Canadell, C., Ciais, P., Conway, T., Field, C., Le Quéré, C., Houghton, S., Marland, G., Raupach, M., Buitenhuis, E. and Gillett, N. (2007) 'Recent carbon trends and the global carbon budget (updated to 2006). Global Carbon Project', see www.globalcarbonproject.org/global/pdf/GCP_CarbonCycleUpdate.pdf

Diamond, J. (2005) *Collapse: Why Societies Choose to Fail or Succeed*, Viking Press, New York

Ehrlich, P. and Ehrlich, A. (1981) *Extinction: The Causes and Consequences of the Disappearance of Species*, Random House, New York

Flannery, T. (2005) *The Weather Makers: The History and Future Impact of Climate Change*, Text Publishing, Melbourne, Australia

Glikson, A. (2008) 'Milestones in the evolution of the atmosphere with reference to climate change', *Australian Journal of Earth Sciences*, vol 55, pp125–139

Hamilton, C. (2010) *Requiem for a Species: Why We Resist the Truth About Climate Change*, Allen and Unwin, Sydney, Australia

Hansen, J. (2009) *Storms of My Grandchildren: The Truth about the Coming Climate Catastrophe and Our Last Chance to Save Humanity*, Bloomsbury, London

Hansen, J., Sato, M., Ruedy, R., Kharecha, P., Lacis, A., Miller, R., Nazarenko, L., Lo, K., Schmidt, G. A., Russell, G., Aleinov, I., Bauer, S., Baum, E., Cairns, B., Canuto, V., Chandler, M., Cheng, Y., Cohen, A., Del Genio, A., Faluvegi, G., Fleming, E., Friend, A., Hall, T., Jackman, C., Jonas, J., Kelley, M., Kiang, N. Y., Koch, D., Labow, G., Lerner, J., Menon, S., Novakov, T., Oinas, V., Ja, Ju, Rind, D., Romanou, A., Schmunk, R., Shindell, D., Stone, P., Sun, S., Streets, D., Tausnev, N., Thresher, D., Unger, N., Yao, M. and Zhang, S. (2007) 'Dangerous human-made interference with climate: A GISS model E study', *Atmospheric Chemistry and Physics*, vol 7, pp2287–2312

Hansen, J., Sato M., Kharecha, P., Beerling, D., Berner, R., Masson-Delmotte, V., Pagani, M., Raymo, M., Royer, D. and Zachos, J. (2008) 'Target atmospheric CO_2: Where should humanity aim?', *The Open Atmospheric Science Journal*, vol 2, pp217–231

Henderson-Sellars, A. and Blong, R. (1989) *The Greenhouse Effect: Living in a Warmer Australia*, NSW University Press, Sydney, Australia

Hoggan, J. (2009) *Climate Cover Up: The Crusade to Deny Global Warming*, Greystone Books, Vancouver, Canada

Houghton, J. (2008) *Global Warming: The Complete Briefing*, Cambridge University Press, Cambridge, UK

Hulme, M. (2009) *Why We Disagree about Climate Change: Understanding Controversy, Inaction and Opportunity*, Cambridge University Press, Cambridge, UK

IASC (2010) 'Permafrost in the Arctic', in J. Walsh et al (eds) *Arctic Climate Assessment, Section 6.6*, International Project of the Arctic Council and International Arctic Science Committee, see www.eoearth.org/article/Permafrost_in_the_Arctic, accessed 21 July 2010

IPCC (2007) *IPCC Fourth Assessment Report: Climate Change (AR4)*, Intergovernmental Panel on Climate Change, Geneva, Switzerland, www.ipcc.ch/publications_ and_data/publications_and_data_reports.htm

Karoly, D. (2010) Personal communication by email from Prof. David Karoly, climate scientist, University of Melbourne, 3 February

Kvenvolden, K. (1988) 'Methane: A major reservoir of carbon in the shallow geosphere?', *Chemical Geology*, vol 71, nos 1–3, pp41–51

Le Quéré, C., Rödenbeck, C., Buitenhuis, E., Thomas, J., Conway, T., Langenfelds, R., Gomez, A., Labuschagne, C., Ramonet, M., Nakazawa, T. and Metzl, N. (2007) 'Saturation of the Southern Ocean CO_2 sink due to recent climate change', *Science*, vol 316, pp1735–1738

Leakey, R. and Lewin, R. (1998) *The Sixth Extinction: Patterns of Life and the Future of Humankind*, Anchor Books, New York

Lynas, M. (2007) *Six Degrees: Our Future on a Hotter Planet*, Fourth Estate, London

MA (2005) *Living Beyond Our Means: Natural Assets and Human Well-being*, Statement of the Millennium Ecosystem Assessment Board, available at www.maweb.org

Mann, M., Bradley, R. and Hughes, M. (1998) 'Global-scale temperature patterns and climate forcing over the past six centuries', *Nature*, vol 392, pp779–787

McNeil, B. (2008) 'A review of the latest science on climate change', talk presented at NSW Parliament House, Sydney, Australia, by Dr Ben McNeil, Climate Change Research Centre, University of NSW

Meehl, G., Washington, W., Ammann, C., Arblaster, J., Wigley, T. and Tebaldi, C. (2004) 'Combinations of natural and anthropogenic forcings in twentieth-century climate', *Journal of Climate*, vol 17, pp3721–3727

MIT (2009) 'Climate change odds much worse than thought', *MIT News,* 19 May, Massachusetts Institute of Technology, http://web.mit.edu/newsoffice/2009/roulette-0519.html

Nisbet, E. (2002) 'Have sudden large releases of methane from geological reservoirs occurred since the Last Glacial Maximum, and could such releases occur again?', *Philosophical Transactions of the Royal Society of London B,* vol 360, pp581–607

NOAA (2009) Mauna Loa CO_2 annual mean data from NOAA, 'trend' data was used, US National Oceanic and Atmospheric Administration, Washington, DC, www.noaa.gov

NSIDC (2007) National Snow and Ice Data Center, see http://nsidc.org/news/press/2007_seaiceminimum/20070810_index.html

O'Neill, B. and Oppenheimer, M. (2002) 'Dangerous climate impacts and the Kyoto Protocol', *Science,* vol 296, no 5575, 14 June, pp1971–1972

Oreskes, N. and Conway, E.M. (2010) *Merchants of Doubt: How a Handful of Scientists Obscured the Truth on Issues from Tobacco Smoke to Global Warming,* Bloomsbury Press, New York

Pearman, G. (2008) 'Climate change: Transition to sustainability', talk presented to the Climate Change Summit, Sydney, Australia on 23 July by Dr Graeme Pearman, former head of CSIRO Atmospheric Physics, now consultant to GP Consulting Pty Ltd, Monash University, Victoria, Australia

Pearson, P. and Palmer, M. (1999) 'Middle Eocene seawater pH and atmospheric carbon dioxide concentrations', *Science,* vol 284, pp1824–1826

Pearson, P. and Palmer, M. (2000) 'Atmospheric carbon dioxide concentrations over the past 60 million years', *Nature,* vol 406, 17 August, pp695–699

Pittock, A. B. (2009) *Climate change: The Science, Impacts and Solutions,* CSIRO Publishing, Melbourne, Australia

Plimer, I. (2009) *Heaven and Earth: Global Warming: The Missing Science,* Connorcourt Publishing, Ballan, Australia

Polovina, J., Howell, E. and Abecassis, M. (2008) 'Ocean's least productive waters are expanding', *Geophysical Research Letters,* vol 35, doi:10.1029/2007GL031745

Pounds, J. and Puschendorf, R. (2004) 'Clouded futures', *Nature,* vol 427, 8 Jan, pp107–109

Rahmstorf, S., Cazenave, A., Church, J., Hansen, J., Keeling, R., Parker, D. and Somerville, R. (2007) 'Recent climate observations compared to projections', *Science,* vol 316, no 5825, 4 May, p709

Raupach, M., Marland, G., Ciais, P., Le Que, C., Canadell, J., Klepper, G. and Field, C. (2007) 'Global and regional drivers of accelerating CO_2 emissions', *Proceedings of the National Academy of Sciences,* vol 104, no 24, 12 June, pp10,288–10,293

Rosenzweig, C., Karoly, D., Vicarelli, M., Neofotis, P., Wu, Q., Casassa, G., Menzel, A., Root, T. L., Estrella, N., Seguin, B., Tryjanowski, P., Liu, C., Rawlins, S. and Imeson, A. (2008) 'Attributing physical and biological impacts to anthropogenic climate change', *Nature,* vol 453, pp353–358

Sabine, C., Feely, R., Gruber, N., Key, R., Lee, K., Bullister, J., Wanninkhof, R., Wong, C., Wallace, D., Tilbrook, B., Millero, F., Peng, T., Kozyr, A., Ono, T. and Rios, A. (2004) 'The oceanic sink for anthropogenic CO_2', *Science,* vol 305, no 5682, pp367–371

Schneider, S. (2009) 'Mitigation and adaptation to climate change', PowerPoint presentation by Dr Stephen Schneider, Professor of Environmental Biology and Global Change, Stanford University, University of NSW Institute of Environmental Studies Seminar, 16 March

Science Daily (2009) 'Warming of Arctic current over 30 years triggers release of methane gas', *Science Daily*, 16 August

Shakhova, N., Semiletov, I., Salyuk, A., Yusupov, V., Kosmach, D. and Gustafsson, O. (2010) 'Extensive methane venting to the atmosphere from sediments of the east Siberian arctic shelf', *Science*, vol 327, no 5970, pp1246–1250

Stern, N. (2006) *The Economics of Climate Change* (Stern Review), Cambridge University Press, Cambridge, UK, see http://webarchive.nationalarchives.gov.uk/+/http://www.hm-treasury.gov.uk/sternr eview_index.htm

Stern, N. (2007) 'The economics of climate change', talk given to World Bank, Jakarta, 23 March, see www.worldbank.org

Suzuki, D. (1989) *It's a Matter of Survival*, Canadian Broadcasting Corporation radio series

Velicogna, I. (2009) 'Increasing rates of ice mass loss from the Greenland and Antarctic ice sheets revealed by GRACE', *Geophysical Research Letters*, vol 36, doi:10.1029/2009 GL040222

Wahl, E. and Ammann C. (2007) 'Robustness of the Mann, Bradley, Hughes reconstruction of Northern Hemisphere surface temperatures: Examination of criticisms based on the nature and processing of proxy climate evidence', *Climatic Change*, vol 85, pp33–69

Wilson, E. O. (1988) 'The current state of biological diversity', in E. O. Wilson and F. M. Peter (eds) *Biodiversity*, National Academy Press, New York

Wilson, E. O. (2003) *The Future of Life*, Vintage Books, New York

Wouters, B., Chambers, D. and Schrama, E. (2008) 'GRACE observes small-scale mass loss in Greenland', *Geophysical Research Letters*, vol 35, doi:10.1029/2008GL034816

3

The Five Types of Climate Change Denial Argument

This chapter looks at the five types of climate change denial arguments and considers nine key denial arguments as examples within these categories. These five types of denial argument are:

1 Conspiracy theories;
2 Fake experts;
3 Impossible expectations;
4 Misrepresentations and logical fallacies; and
5 Cherry-picking (Diethelm and McKee, 2009).

We list here nine common denial arguments, but there are dozens of others. These can be found at the website www.skepticalscience.com, which is managed by one of us (Cook). We suggest readers may wish to visit the website to examine denial arguments in more detail.

Pascal Diethelm and Martin McKee (2009) observe that the various movements that deny an overwhelming scientific consensus all exhibit common characteristics. Their goal is to convince the public and the media that there are sufficient grounds not to take the action recommended by the consensus position of mainstream science. To achieve this, the vocal minority employ rhetorical arguments that give the appearance of legitimate debate where there is none. The various denial movements employ some or all of the five types of denial described below. Note that these five categories apply to almost all denial, not just climate change denial.

Conspiracy Theories

'Climategate proves conspiracy'

In November 2009, the email servers at the University of East Anglia in Britain were illegally hacked and emails were stolen. When a selection of emails between climate scientists was published on the internet, a few suggestive quotes were seized upon to claim that global warming was all just a conspiracy (Cook, 2010). The incident, dubbed 'Climategate', is symptomatic of a movement that denies the scientific consensus (Delingpole, 2009). If one disagrees with a view held by the great majority of the world's scientists, the most common response is to assume all those scientists are involved in a *vast conspiracy to deceive.*

To determine if there had been any wrongdoing, a series of international investigations independently investigated the Climategate emails and *all cleared climate scientists of any wrongdoing.* The House of Commons Science and Technology Committee found that the criticisms of the Climate Research Unit (CRU) were misplaced and that 'Professor Jones's [of the CRU] actions were in line with common practice in the climate science community' (Willis et al, 2010). The University of East Anglia's Scientific Assessment Panel, in consultation with the Royal Society, assessed the integrity of the research published by the CRU and concluded there was 'no evidence of any deliberate scientific malpractice in any of the work of the Climatic Research Unit' (Oxburgh, 2010). The Independent Climate Change Email Review examined the emails to assess whether manipulation or suppression of data occurred and concluded that 'the scientists' rigor and honesty are not in doubt' (Russell et al, 2010).

Thus independent investigations conclude unanimously that nothing in the Climategate emails actually affected the science. The issue was of isolated quotes taken out of context. The most quoted email was from Phil Jones discussing palaeo-data used to reconstruct past temperatures:

> I've just completed Mike's Nature trick of adding in the real temps to each series for the last 20 years (i.e. from 1981 onwards) and from 1961 for Keith's to hide the decline.

The phrases often repeated from this email are 'Mike's Nature trick' and 'hide the decline', interpreted to reveal nefarious intent. However, the issues discussed in this email are openly published in the peer-reviewed literature. 'Mike's Nature trick' refers to a technique (in other words a '*trick* of the trade') used in a paper published in *Nature* by lead author Michael Mann (Mann et al, 1998). The 'trick' is the technique of plotting recent instrumental data along with the reconstructed palaeo-data. This places recent global warming trends in the context of temperature changes over longer timescales.

The most common misconception regarding this email is to assume that 'hide the decline' refers to declining temperatures. Republican Sarah Palin argued, 'The emails reveal that leading climate "experts" deliberately destroyed records, manipulated data to "hide the decline" in global temperatures' (McCullagh, 2010). The 'decline' actually refers to a decline in tree-ring growth in certain high-latitude regions since the 1960s. This is known as the 'divergence problem', where some tree-ring proxies diverge from modern instrumental temperature records after 1960. This was discussed in the peer-reviewed literature as early as 1995, suggesting a change in the sensitivity of tree growth to temperature in recent decades (Jacoby and D'Arrigo, 1995). When you look at Jones's email in the context of the science discussed, it is not the scheming of a climate conspiracy, but technical discussions of data-handling techniques readily available in the peer-reviewed literature.

The second most cited email is from climate scientist and IPCC lead author Kevin Trenberth:

> The fact is that we can't account for the lack of warming at the moment and it is a travesty that we can't.

This has been interpreted by climate change deniers as climate scientists secretly admitting among themselves that global warming has stopped. Trenberth is actually discussing a paper he'd recently published that discusses the planet's energy budget – how much net energy is flowing into our climate and where it's going (Trenberth, 2009). In Trenberth's paper, he discusses how the planet is continually heating due to increasing CO_2. Nevertheless, surface temperature sometimes shows short-term cooling periods. This is due to internal variability as the ocean exchanges heat with the atmosphere. Trenberth laments that our observation systems can't comprehensively track all the energy flow through the climate system. However, Trenberth expressed this openly and frankly in the peer-reviewed literature. They didn't need to steal his emails.

It's important to put the Climategate emails in perspective. A handful of scientists discuss a few pieces of climate data. Even without this data, there is still an overwhelming and consistent body of evidence, painstakingly compiled by independent scientific teams across the globe. They find that humans are massively emitting CO_2 into the atmosphere, with the result that atmospheric CO_2 levels have increased by 36 per cent from pre-industrial levels. Various lines of evidence find that rising CO_2 levels are causing an energy imbalance and trapping heat. Thousands of lines of evidence find the planet is subsequently warming, with numerous fingerprints of warming unique to an increasing greenhouse effect. A few suggestive quotes taken out of context may serve as a distraction for those wishing to avoid the physical realities of climate change, but they change nothing about our scientific understanding of humanity's role in global warming.

Fake Experts

'There is no consensus'

There have been claims purporting to prove there is no scientific consensus on human-caused global warming. Often you will see statements made with the apparent aura of scientific expertise, but these are misleading. The most prominent is the Petition Project, published in early 2008 by the Oregon Institute of Science and Medicine (OISM, 2008). This petition features a list of over 31,000 people who claim to be scientists and reject the science behind the theory of human-caused global warming. However, anyone with a BSc or higher can be listed. These include graduates of computer science, mechanical engineering, zoology, medicine, metallurgy and other fields unrelated to climate science. Around 0.1 per cent of the signatories were climatologists. Obviously, the OISM were going for quantity, not quality. Their approach raises the question: is a veterinarian or a mechanical engineer qualified to have an authoritative opinion on the complexities of climate science?

Confirmation of a scientific consensus comes from the peer-reviewed scientific literature. A survey of all peer-reviewed abstracts on the subject 'global climate change' published between 1993 and 2003 shows that not a single paper rejected the consensus position that human activities are causing global warming (Oreskes, 2004). Seventy-five per cent of the papers agreed with the consensus position, while 25 per cent made no comment either way (focused on methods or palaeoclimate analysis). A comprehensive survey of 3146 earth scientists asked the question 'Do you think human activity is a significant contributing factor in changing mean global temperatures?' (see Figure 7). Overall, 82 per cent of the scientists answered yes. Of scientists who were non-climatologists and didn't publish research, 77 per cent answered yes. In contrast, *97.5 per cent* of climatologists who actively published research on climate change responded yes (Doran and Zimmerman, 2009).

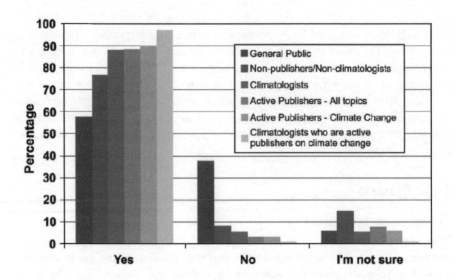

Figure 7 *Response to the survey question 'Do you think human activity is a significant contributing factor in changing mean global temperatures?'*

Source: Doran and Zimmerman (2009); public data from Gallup (2009)

As the level of active research and specialization in climate science increases, so does agreement that humans are significantly changing global temperatures. Especially striking is the divide between expert climate scientists (97.5 per cent) and the general public (58 per cent). The paper concludes:

> It seems that the debate on the authenticity of global warming and the role played by human activity is largely nonexistent among those who understand the nuances and scientific basis of long-term climate processes. The challenge, rather, appears to be how to effectively communicate this fact to policymakers and to a public that continues to mistakenly perceive debate among scientists.

This overwhelming consensus among climate experts is confirmed by an independent study that surveys all climate scientists who have publicly signed declarations supporting or rejecting the consensus (Anderegg et al, 2010). They found that between 97 and 98 per cent of climate experts support the consensus.

Impossible Expectations

'Climate models are unreliable'

The uncertainties of climate models are often used as an excuse to reject them along with all evidence of human-caused global warming. A common denier argument is 'Scientists can't even predict the weather next week, so how can they predict the climate years from now?'. This betrays a misunderstanding of the difference between weather, which is chaotic and unpredictable, and climate, which is weather averaged over time. In weather terms, you can't predict the exact route a storm will take, but the average temperature and precipitation will still be the same for a region over a period of time.

There are various difficulties in predicting future climate. The behaviour of the Sun is difficult to predict. Short-term perturbations like El Niño or volcanic eruptions are difficult to model. Nevertheless, the major forcings that drive climate are well understood. In 1988, James Hansen projected future temperature trends using three different greenhouse gas emission scenarios (Hansen et al, 1988). Scenario A assumed continued accelerating greenhouse gas growth, Scenario B assumed a slowing and eventually constant rate of growth, and Scenario C assumed a rapid decline in greenhouse gas emissions around 2000. Several decades later, we can compare those initial projections with subsequent observations (Hansen et al, 2006).

The greenhouse gas emissions in Hansen's Scenario B (with the triangles in Figure 8) most closely match actual greenhouse emissions. The projected temperature change in Scenario B slightly overestimates the observed warming (darker line) for two main reasons. First, Scenario B slightly overestimated how much greenhouse gas emissions would increase, and second, Hansen's model used a higher climate sensitivity of around four degrees Celsius for a doubling of atmospheric CO_2. In order to accurately predict global warming over the past

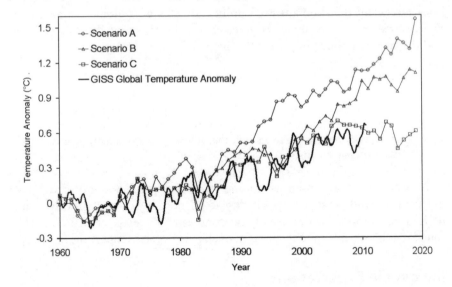

Figure 8 *Global surface temperature computed by Hansen for Scenarios A, B and C, compared with 12-month moving average of observational data*

Source: redrawn from Hansen et al (2006) with GISS updated to August 2010

22 years, Hansen's climate model would have needed a climate sensitivity of just over 3 degrees Celsius. This is consistent with the range of IPCC climate sensitivity values of 2–4.5 degrees Celsius, with a most likely value of 3 degrees Celsius (IPCC, 2007).

When Mount Pinatubo erupted in 1991, the sulphate aerosols thrown into the atmosphere had a dramatic cooling effect as they reflected incoming sunlight back out to space. This event provided an opportunity to test how successfully models would predict the climate response. The models accurately forecast subsequent global cooling of about 0.5 degrees Celsius. Furthermore, the radiative, water vapour and dynamical feedbacks included in the models also matched the observed response (Hansen et al, 2007).

A common misconception is that climate models are biased towards 'exaggerating' the effects from CO_2. But it's worth mentioning that uncertainty can go either way. In fact, in a climate system with net positive feedback, uncertainty means climate change is likely to be greater than expected (Roe and Baker, 2007). For this reason, many of the IPCC predictions have subsequently been shown to *underestimate* the climate response (Freudenburg and Muselli, 2010). Satellite and tide-gauge measurements show that sea-level rise is accelerating faster than IPCC predictions. The average rate of rise for 1993–2008 as measured from satellites is 3.4mm/yr, while the IPCC Third Assessment Report projected a best estimate of 1.9mm/yr for the same period (Allison et al,

2009). Sea-level observations are tracking along the upper range of IPCC projections.

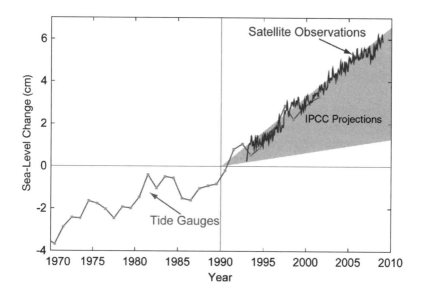

Figure 9 *Sea-level change: Models and observations*

Tide gauge data and satellite data are indicated; the grey band shows the projections of the IPCC Third Assessment Report.

Source: Allison et al (2009)

Similarly, summertime melting of Arctic sea ice has accelerated far beyond the expectations of climate models. The area of sea-ice melt during 2007–2009 was about 40 per cent greater than the average prediction from IPCC AR4 (Fourth Assessment) climate models. The thickness of Arctic sea ice has also been on a steady decline over the last several decades.

Should we wait until climate models are 'completely certain' before acting to reduce CO_2 emissions? Models are in a constant state of development to include more processes, rely on fewer approximations and increase their resolution as computer power develops. The complex and non-linear nature of climate means there will always be a process of refinement and improvement. The main point is we now know enough to *act*. Models have evolved to the point where they successfully predict long-term trends and are now developing the ability to predict more chaotic, short-term changes. They don't need to be exact in every respect to give us an accurate overall trend. If you knew there was a 90 per cent chance you'd be in a car crash, would you get in the car? The IPCC conclude a greater than 90 per cent probability that humans are causing global warming. To wait for 100 per cent certainty would mean society would never act on anything.

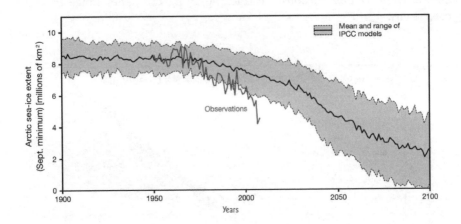

Figure 10 *Observed and modelled September Arctic sea-ice extent
in millions of square kilometres*

Solid black line gives the average of 13 IPCC AR4 models while the grey area represents their range. The 2009
minimum has recently been calculated at 5.10 million km², the third lowest year on record and well below the
IPCC worst case scenario.

Source: Allison et al (2009)

Misrepresentations and Logical Fallacies

'Climate's changed in the past'

One argument is that 'climate has changed naturally in the past and therefore
current climate change must be natural'. This argument is logically flawed, akin
to saying 'forest fires have occurred naturally in the past so any current forest
fires must be natural'. We do not see a movement of 'arson deniers' being seen
as credible. However, the 'past climate change' argument is popular among
climate change deniers, being the major theme in *Heaven and Earth* (Plimer,
2009).

In addition, this argument betrays a lack of understanding of the nature of
climate sensitivity. Our planet is governed by the principle that when you add
more heat to our climate, global temperatures rise. Conversely, when the climate
loses heat, temperatures fall. This energy imbalance is known as radiative
forcing, the change in net energy flow at the top of the atmosphere. When the
Earth experiences a positive energy imbalance, our climate builds up heat and
global temperature warms. As it gets warmer, a number of feedbacks come into
play. What climate scientists are particularly interested in is the net feedback –
the overall result when you add up all the various positive and negative
feedbacks. Another way of expressing this is 'climate sensitivity' – how sensitive
is our climate to a change in energy balance?

Climate sensitivity and net feedback can be empirically determined by
looking at past climate change. One needs to find a period where we have

temperature data and measurements of the various forcings that drove the climate change. Once you have the change in temperature and radiative forcing, climate sensitivity can be calculated. There have been many estimates of climate sensitivity using data spanning the past 150 years. Several studies used the observed surface and ocean warming over the 20th century. Satellite data for the radiation budget has been analysed in various studies. Some recent analyses used the well-observed forcing of major volcanic eruptions. A number of studies examined palaeoclimate reconstructions from the last millennium to millions of years ago (Knutti and Hegerl, 2008).

There are independent studies covering a range of periods, studying different parts of climate and employing various methods of analysis. They all yield a broadly consistent answer, indicating that the net climate feedback is *significantly positive*. There is no credible line of evidence that yields very high or very low climate sensitivity. When past climate change is cited to refute the human influence on global warming, this ignores the science that such changes show net positive feedback that further warms the Earth. Ironically, past climate change actually provides evidence that human actions can affect climate *now*.

Cherry-picking

The human fingerprint on climate change is observed by multiple sets of independent observations. However, science operates in something of an adversarial process. People put forward data and ideas, and these get tested by other scientists to see if the data stands up to scrutiny. Sometimes it doesn't and the authors themselves accept there was an error or another explanation for their data. That is how scientific consensus is achieved. Nonetheless, the papers that *seemed* to show an anomaly were published in peer-reviewed journals and are still out there. To avoid accepting human-caused climate change, climate deniers commonly *select* isolated papers that challenge the consensus – to the neglect of the broader body of research. Similarly, deniers often focus on narrow pieces of data while ignoring other evidence that does not support their viewpoint. Sometimes they publish only part of the data or graph (Oreskes and Conway, 2010). Most denier arguments adopt this technique of 'cherry-picking'.

'Temperature measurements are unreliable'

There is a denial movement seeking to cast doubt on the surface temperature record using photographs of weather stations positioned near car parks, air-conditioners and other warming influences (Watts, 2010). These photos attempt to communicate that the global warming trend is being inflated by poor temperature data. To assess this, you need to compare the trend from the good sites to that from the bad sites. This analysis has been done and the results are surprising.

Poor sites show a *cooler* trend than good sites. All those photographed weather stations near car parks are actually giving cooler readings than pristine weather stations. This is largely due to a change in instruments during the mid

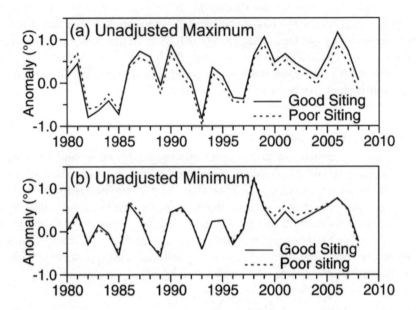

Figure 11 *Annual average maximum and minimum unadjusted temperature change calculated using (a) maximum and (b) minimum temperatures from good and poor exposure sites*

Source: Menne et al (2010)

and late 1980s. When this change is taken into account, as well as other biases such as station relocation and time of observation, the trend from good sites show close agreement with poor sites (Menne et al, 2010; see Figure 11).

However, one needs to take a step back to observe the cherry-picking at play here. Surface temperature is not measured solely by thermometers. It's also measured by satellites, which are not influenced by urban heat islands or nearby car parks. When we compare the satellite temperature data to the surface temperature data, we find consistent results (Figure 12).

So the evidence for the warming trend over the last few decades is based on independent lines of evidence. The campaign to persuade the public with photos of weather stations is an attempt to distract them from the many physical signs of global warming happening all over the globe, such as:

- Ice sheets melting at an accelerating rate, losing billions of tonnes of ice each year (Velicogna, 2009);
- Sea levels rising at an accelerating rate, largely due to diminishing ice sheets (Church and White, 2006);
- Signs of warming being observed in tens of thousands of species all over the world as they respond to earlier springs and migrate towards the poles (Parmesan and Yohe, 2003);

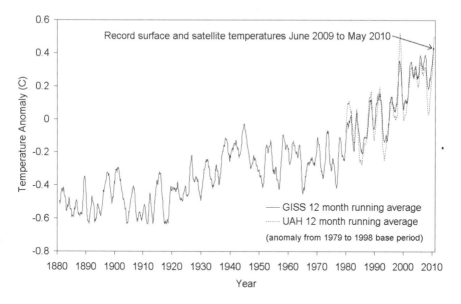

Figure 12 *Annual global temperature from UAH and NASA GISS*

Source: redrawn from UAH (2010) and NASA GISS Temperature Index

- Glaciers retreating, threatening water supplies for millions of people (Kehrwald et al, 2008);
- Arctic permafrost warming at greater depths and degrading, releasing methane (IASC, 2010); and
- Arctic sea ice declining at an accelerating rate (Stroeve et al, 2008).

To get a full understanding of climate, we need to look at all the evidence. What we see are many lines of evidence all pointing to the same conclusion – global warming is a physical reality.

'Global warming stopped in 1998'

A common refrain from deniers is that global warming stopped in 1998. This is based on a temperature record compiled by the Hadley Centre of the UK Met Office and the Climatic Research Unit (CRU), often referred to as HadCRUT. This dataset (Figure 13) shows unusually warm temperatures in 1998, leading to that year being the hottest in the HadCRUT record. These unusually warm conditions were due to the strongest El Niño on record occurring at the time.

It's important to realize that the HadCRUT record is not a truly global temperature record. It doesn't include regions where the fastest warming is occurring. An analysis by the European Centre for Medium-Range Weather Forecasts (ECMWF) calculated global temperature utilizing a range of sources including surface temperature measurements, satellites, radiosondes, ships and buoys. They found recent warming has been higher than that shown by

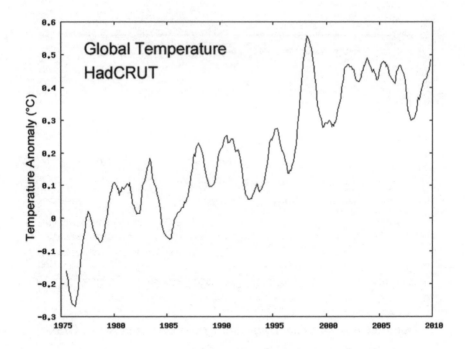

Figure 13 *Twelve-month average of global temperature anomaly from the Hadley Centre*

Source: plotted from HadCRUT, 2010

HadCRUT, as the latter misses out on regions of greatest warming (Simmons et al, 2010).

This is confirmed by NASA GISS, which found that a major contributor to recent warming is the extreme Arctic warming (Hansen et al, 2006). As there are few meteorological stations in the Arctic, NASA extrapolated temperature anomalies from the nearest measurement stations. They found that the estimated strong Arctic warmth was consistent with infrared satellite measurements and record low sea-ice concentrations. According to the NASA GISS global temperature record, the hottest 12 months on record was from June 2009 to May 2010, statistically tied with 2005 (see Figure 14).

However, even this doesn't give the full picture. The surface temperature record tells us only about air temperatures at the Earth's *surface*, which (as Figure 15 demonstrates) is only a small part of global warming. Did this energy imbalance stop in 1998? To determine this, one study measured the Earth's total heat content since 1950 (Murphy et al, 2009). The authors used measurements of ocean heat content to 3000 metres depth. The amount of heat in the atmosphere was calculated using the surface temperature record and the heat capacity of the lower atmosphere.

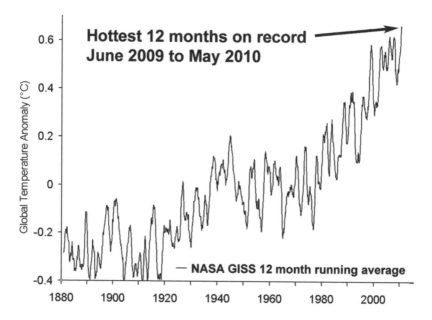

Figure 14 *Twelve-month average of global temperature anomaly from NASA GISS*

Source: plotted from NASA GISS Temperature Index, June 2010

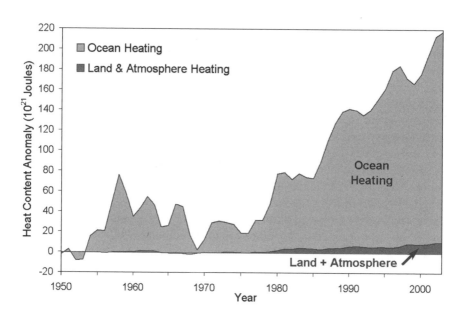

Figure 15 *Total Earth heat content from 1950 to 2003*

Source: redrawn from original data in Murphy et al (2009, Figure 6b)

The results find that the planet is clearly still building up heat *after* 1998. Global warming has not stopped, but most of the warming has gone into the oceans. The heat capacity of the land and atmosphere is small compared to that of the oceans. Consequently, relatively small exchanges of heat between atmosphere and ocean can cause large changes in surface temperature. In 1998 we experienced the strongest El Niño on record, moving massive amounts of heat from the Pacific Ocean into the atmosphere. Conversely, 2007 saw the strongest La Niña conditions in over 20 years, which had a cooling effect on global temperatures. In 2010 the Pacific transitioned back to El Niño conditions, although not as strong as in 1998. Nevertheless, this resulted in the warmest 12 months on record from June 2009 to May 2010.

'The hockey stick was broken'

This issue was touched on in Chapter 2, but we will enlarge on this denial argument. The rejection of the 'hockey stick' figure of global temperature increase over time is another example of wishful cherry-picking. The hockey stick refers to a 1998 reconstruction of temperature over the past 1000 years using tree rings, ice cores, coral and other records that act as proxies for temperature (Mann et al, 1999). The reconstruction by Michael Mann et al (1998) found that global temperature gradually cooled over the last 1000 years with a sharp upturn in the 20th century (the head of the hockey stick). The principal result shown by the hockey stick graph is that global temperatures over the last few decades are the warmest in the last 1000 years.

A critique of the hockey stick was published in 2004 claiming the hockey stick shape was the inevitable result of using a particular statistical method (McIntyre and McKitrick, 2005). However, an independent assessment of Mann's hockey stick was conducted by the National Center for Atmospheric Research. They reconstructed temperatures employing a variety of statistical techniques (with and without principal components analysis). Their results found slightly different temperatures in the early 15th century. Nevertheless, they confirmed the principal results of the original hockey stick – that the warming trend and temperatures over the last few decades are *unprecedented* over at least the last 600 years (Wahl and Ammann, 2007).

While many deniers continue to fixate on Mann's early work on proxy records, the science of palaeo-climatology has moved on. Since 1999 there have been many independent reconstructions of past temperatures, using a variety of proxy data and a number of different methodologies. All find the same result – that the last few decades are the hottest in the last 500 to 2000 years (depending on how far back the reconstruction goes). These include temperature from boreholes (Huang et al, 2000), determining temperature from stalagmites (Smith et al, 2006) and historical records of glacier length (Oerlemans, 2005). Figure 16 illustrates the similarities between the reconstructions for the last 1000 years.

When you combine all the various proxies, including ice cores, coral, lake sediments, glaciers, boreholes and stalagmites, it's possible to reconstruct Northern Hemisphere temperatures (without tree-ring proxies) going back 1300

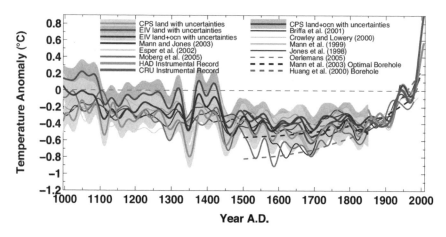

Figure 16 *Composite Northern Hemisphere land and land plus ocean temperature reconstructions and estimated 95 per cent confidence intervals*

Shown for comparison are published Northern Hemisphere reconstructions

Source: Mann et al (2008)

years (see Figure 16). The result is that temperatures in recent decades exceed the maximum proxy estimate (including uncertainty range) for the past 1300 years. When you include tree-ring data, the same result holds for the past 1700 years. Palaeo-climatology draws upon a range of proxies and methodologies to calculate past temperatures. This allows independent confirmation of the basic hockey stick result: that *the past few decades are the hottest in the past 1300 years*. A narrow focus on an early paper from 1998 has no bearing on over a decade's worth of research independently confirming the hockey stick result.

'It's the Sun'

The most common alternative explanation for global warming among deniers is the Sun. This is an intuitive response – it's not hard to imagine the huge, fiery ball on the sky has a significant influence on climate. Indeed it does. As supplier of almost all the energy in the Earth's climate, changes in solar output have an effect on global temperature. A comparison of Sun and climate over the past 1150 years found temperatures closely match solar activity (Usoskin et al, 2005). This correlation is enough for skeptics to conclude that the Sun must be causing global warming. However, this doesn't take into account all the data. After 1975, temperatures rose while solar activity showed little to no long-term trend. Usoskin et al (2005) concluded:

> During these last 30 years the solar total irradiance, solar UV irradiance and cosmic ray flux has not shown any significant secular trend, so that at least this most recent warming episode must have another source.

In fact a number of independent measurements of solar activity indicate the Sun has shown a *slight cooling* trend since 1960, over the same period that global temperatures have been warming (Lockwood, 2008). Over the last 35 years of global warming, Sun and climate have been moving in opposite directions (see Figure 17). The Sun does have an influence on climate, but in recent decades its cooling has been slightly masking the warming from greenhouse gases.

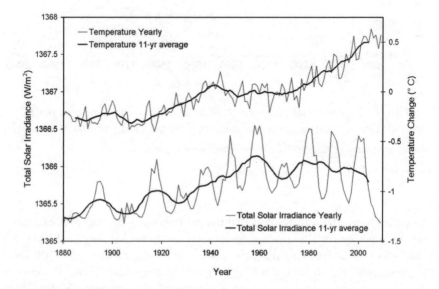

Figure 17 *Change in annual global temperature (top line) and total solar irradiance (TSI; bottom line) with 11-year moving average*

Source: Temperature data from NASA GISS Temperature index. TSI from 1880 to 1978 was reconstructed from sunspot numbers (data from Krivova et al, 2007), while after 1979 the data comes from satellites (data from Frohlich, 2006).

'Global warming is good'

The argument that global warming is good may be used with claims that global warming is either natural or human-caused. Either way deniers argue that warming can only bring good things (see, for example, Plimer, 2009). To do so the denial argument cherry-picks certain data to suggest this. The best way to put this denial argument in perspective is to compare the positives of global warming to the negatives, as in the table on the following pages.

Positives	Negatives
Agriculture	**Agriculture**
• Improved agriculture in some high-latitude regions (Mendelsohn et al, 2006) • Increased growing season in Greenland (Nyegaard, 2007) • Increased productivity of sour orange trees (Kimball et al, 2007)	• Decreasing human water supplies, increased fire frequency, ecosystem change and expanded deserts (Solomon et al, 2009) • Decline in rice yields due to warmer night-time minimum temperatures (Peng et al, 2004; Tao et al, 2008) • Increase of western US wildfire activity, associated with higher temperatures and earlier spring snowmelt (Westerling et al, 2006) • Encroachment of shrubs into grasslands, rendering rangeland unsuitable for domestic livestock grazing (Morgan et al, 2007) • Decreased water supply in the Colorado River Basin (McCabe and Wolock, 2007) • Decreasing water supply to the Murray–Darling Basin (Cai and Cowan, 2008)
Glacier Melt	**Glacier Melt**
	• Severe consequences for at least 60 million people dependent on ice and snow melt for water supply (Kehrwald et al, 2008; Immerzeel et al, 2010) • Contribution to rising sea levels (Pfeffer et al, 2008; Vermeer and Rahmstorf, 2009)
Economics	**Economics**
• Increased cod fishing leading to improved Greenland economy (Nyegaard, 2007)	• Economic damage to poorer low-latitude countries (Mendelsohn et al, 2006) • Billions of dollars of damage to public infrastructure (Larsen et al, 2008) • Reduced water supply in New Mexico (Hurd and Coonrod, 2008)

Positives	Negatives
Arctic Melt	**Arctic Melt**
• An ice-free Northwest Passage, providing a shipping shortcut between the Pacific and Atlantic Oceans (Kerr, 2002; Stroeve et al, 2008)	• Loss of 2/3 of the world's polar bear population within 50 years (Amstrup et al, 2007) • Less compacted ice, hazardous floes and more mobile icebergs posing increased risk to shipping (International Ice Charting Working Group, 2009) • Drying of arctic ponds with subsequent damage to ecosystems (Smol and Douglas, 2007) Warming causes methane to escape from Arctic regions, contributing additional greenhouse warming. The following have been observed: • Melting of Arctic lakes leading to methane bubbling (Walter et al, 2007) • Leakage of methane from the East Siberian Shelf seabed sediments (Shakhova et al, 2008) • Escape of methane gas from the seabed along the West Spitsbergen continental margin (Westbrook et al, 2009)
Health	**Health**
• Winter deaths will decline as temperatures warm (Health Protection Agency, 2007)	• Increased deaths to heatwaves – 5.7% increase to heatwaves compared to 1.5% to cold snaps (Medina-Ramon and Schwartz, 2007) • Increased heat stress in humans and other mammals (Sherwood and Huber, 2010) • Spread in mosquito-borne diseases such as malaria, dengue fever and encephalitis (Epstein et al, 1998) • Increase in occurrence of allergic symptoms due to rise in allergenic pollen (Rogers et al, 2006)

Positives	Negatives
Environment	**Environment**
• Greener rainforests and enhanced plant growth due to higher sunlight levels due to fewer rain clouds (Nemani et al, 2003; Saleska et al, 2007)	• Between 18 and 35% of plant and animal species could be committed to extinction by 2050 (Thomas et al, 2004)
• Increased vegetation activity in high northern latitudes (Zhou et al, 2001)	• More severe and extensive vegetation die-off due to hotter droughts (Breshears et al, 2005)
• Increase in Chinstrap and Gentoo penguins (Ducklow et al, 2007)	• Rainforests releasing CO_2 as regions become drier and burn (Saleska et al, 2007)
• Recent increase in forest growth (McMahon et al, 2010)	• Reduction in area of the Amazon due to reduced rainfall and greater evaporation (Nepstad et al, 2007; Phillips et al, 2009)
	• Extinction of the European land leech (Kutschera et al, 2007)
	• Decrease in Adélie penguin numbers (Ducklow et al, 2007)
	• Disruption to New Zealand aquatic species such as salmonids, stream invertebrates and fishes (Ryan and Ryan, 2007)
	• Oxygen-poor ocean zones are growing (Stramma et al, 2008; Shaffer et al, 2009)
	• Increased mortality rates of healthy trees in western US forests (Pennisi, 2009)
	• Increased pine tree mortality due to outbreaks of pine beetles (Kurz et al, 2008)
	• Increased risk of coral extinction from bleaching and disease driven by warming waters (Carpenter et al, 2008)
	• Decline in lizard populations (Sinervo et al, 2010)
	• In southwest Australia a drop in rainfall of 10–20% and a 40–50% reduction of inflow to Perth's water supply (Sadler, 2003; Pittock, 2009)

Positives	Negatives
Ocean Acidification	**Ocean Acidification**
Note: this is not caused by warming temperatures but by the oceans absorbing more CO_2 (Dore et al, 2009). • Ocean uptake of CO_2 moderates future global warming (Orr et al, 2005)	• Oceans cease to be a sink for CO_2 and become a source, so the moderating buffer aspect of oceans ceases (Canadell et al, 2007) • Substantial negative impacts to marine ecosystems (Orr et al, 2005; Fabry et al, 2008) • Inhibiting of plankton development; disruption of carbon cycle (Turley et al, 2006) • Increased mortalities of sea urchins (Miles et al, 2007)
Sea-Level Rise	**Sea-Level Rise** • Coastal erosion in Nigeria (Okude and Ademiluyi, 2007) • Displacement of hundreds of millions of climate refugees this century (Dasgupta et al, 2007)

In summary, there are both more negative effects than positive, and some of them have far greater impacts. Global warming cannot be seen as a 'good thing' overall. It may indeed benefit certain areas (for example Greenland can now grow potatoes) if temperatures do not rise too much. However, the larger the global warming, the worse the impact. These impacts are already starting to be felt.

Conclusion

The above lists the five categories of denial arguments and gives examples of them. There are many more such climate change denial arguments (see www.skepticalscience.com) and almost all fit under these categories. We are sure that new denial arguments will keep coming. For this reason it is important to consider any denial argument that is put to you. What sort of argument is it? Is it suggesting conspiracy? Is it a fake expert who has no expertise in climate science? Does it demand impossible expectations, such as requiring 100 per cent proof? Is it a logical fallacy? Does it cherry-pick the evidence to support its claims and ignore all other evidence? Remember, true 'skepticism' is a *search for the truth*. We should approach climate change denial arguments with true skepticism. We need to assess what the argument relies on, whether it is logical, and whether it considers *all* the many independent strands of scientific evidence that show climate change is both happening now and is caused by human actions.

References

Allison, I., Bindoff, N. L., Bindschadler, R. A., Cox, P. M., de Noblet, N., England, M. H., Francis, J. E., Gruber, N., Haywood, A. M., Karoly, D. J., Kaser, G., Le Quéré, C., Lenton, T. M., Mann, M. E., McNeil, B. I., Pitman, A. J., Rahmstorf, S., Rignot, E., Schellnhuber, H. J., Schneider, S. H., Sherwood, S. C., Somerville, R. C. J., Steffen, K., Steig, E. J., Visbeck, M. and Weaver, A. J. (2009) *The Copenhagen Diagnosis, 2009: Updating the World on the Latest Climate Science*, The University of New South Wales Climate Change Research Centre (CCRC), Sydney, Australia

Amstrup, S., Marcot, B. and Douglas, D. (2007) 'Forecasting the rangewide status of polar bears at selected times in the 21st century', Administrative report, US Geological Survey, Alaska Science Center, Anchorage, AK

Anderegg, W., Prall, J., Harold, J. and Schneider, S. (2010) 'Expert credibility in climate change', *Proceedings of the National Academy of Sciences*, vol 107, no 27, pp12,107–12,109

Breshears, D. D., Cobb, N. S., Rich, P. M., Price, K. P., Allen, C. D., Balice, R. G., Romme, W. H., Kastens, J. H., Floyd, M. L., Belnap, J., Anderson, J. J., Myers, O. B. and Meyer, C. W. (2005) 'Regional vegetation die-off in response to global-change-type drought', *Proceedings of the National Academy of Sciences*, vol 102, no 42, pp15,144–15,148

Cai, W. and Cowan, T. (2008) 'Evidence of impacts from rising temperature on inflows to the Murray–Darling Basin', *Geophysical Research Letters*, vol 35, L07701

Canadell, J. G., Le Quéré, C., Raupach, M. R., Field, C. B., Buitenhuis, E. T., Ciais, P., Conway, T. J., Gillett, N. P., Houghton, R. A. and Marland, G. (2007) 'Contributions to accelerating atmospheric CO_2 growth from economic activity, carbon intensity, and efficiency of natural sinks', *Proceedings of the National Academy of Sciences*, vol 104, no 47, pp18,866–18,870

Carpenter, K. E., Abrar, M., Aeby, G., Aronson, R. B., Banks, S., Bruckner, A., Chiriboga, A., Cortes, J., Delbeek, J. C., DeVantier, L., Edgar, G. J., Edwards, A. J., Fenner, D., Guzman, H. M., Hoeksema, B. W., Hodgson, G., Johan, O., Licuanan, W. Y., Livingstone, S. R., Lovell, E. R., Moore, J. A., Obura, D. O., Ochavillo, D., Polidoro, B. A., Precht, W. F., Quibilan, M. C., Reboton, C., Richards, Z. T., Rogers, A. D., Sanciangco, J., Sheppard, A., Sheppard, C., Smith, J., Stuart, S., Turak, E., Veron, J. E. N., Wallace, C., Weil, E. and Wood, E. (2008) 'One-third of reef-building corals face elevated extinction risk from climate change and local impacts', *Science*, vol 321, no 5888, pp560–563

Church, J. and White, N. (2006) 'A 20th century acceleration in global sea-level rise', *Geophysical Research Letters*, vol 33, L01602

Cook, J. (2010) 'What do the "Climategate" hacked CRU emails tell us?', *Skeptical Science* website, see www.skepticalscience.com/Climategate-CRU-emails-hacked.htm

Dasgupta, S., Laplante, B., Meisner, C., Wheeler, D. and Yan, J. (2007) 'The impact of sea-level rise on developing countries: A comparative analysis', Research Working Paper No 4136, World Bank, Washington, DC

Delingpole, J. (2009) 'Climategate: The final nail in the coffin of "Anthropogenic Global Warming"?', *Telegraph*, 20 November, see http://blogs.telegraph.co.uk/news/jamesdelingpole/100017393/climategate-the-final-nail-in-the-coffin-of-anthropogenic-global-warming/

Diethelm, P. and McKee, M. (2009) 'Denialism: What is it and how should scientists respond?', *European Journal of Public Health*, vol 19, no 1, pp2–4

Doran, P. and Zimmerman, M. (2009) 'Examining the scientific consensus on climate change', *Eos, Transactions, American Geophysical Union*, vol 90, no 3, pp22–23

Dore, J., Lukas, R., Sadler, D., Church, M. and Karl, D. (2009) 'Physical and biogeochemical modulation of ocean acidification in the central north Pacific', *Proceedings of the National Academy of Sciences*, vol 106, no 30, pp12,235–12,240

Ducklow, H., Baker, K., Martinson, D., Quetin, L., Ross, R., Smith, R., Stammerjohn, S., Vernet, M. and Fraser, W. (2007) 'Marine pelagic ecosystems: The west Antarctic peninsula', *Philosophical Transactions of the Royal Society B: Biological Sciences*, vol 362, no 1477, pp67–94

Epstein, P., Diaz, H., Elias, S., Grabherr, G., Graham, N. and Martens, W. (1998) 'Biological and physical signs of climate change: Focus on mosquito-borne disease', *Bulletin of the American Meteorological Society*, vol 78, pp409–417

Fabry, V., Seibel, B., Feely, R. and Orr, J. (2008) 'Impacts of ocean acidification on marine fauna and ecosystem processes', *ICES Journal of Marine Science*, vol 65, no 3, pp414–432

Freudenburg, W. R. and Muselli, V. (2010) 'Global warming estimates, media expectations, and the asymmetry of scientific challenge', *Global Environmental Change*, vol 20, no 3,pp483–491

Frohlich, C. (2006) 'Solar irradiance variability since 1978: Revision of the PMOD composite during solar cycle 21', *Space Science Reviews*, vol 125, pp53–65, ftp://ftp.pmodwrc.ch/pub/data/irradiance/composite/DataPlots/composite_d41_62_0906.dat

Gallup (2009) Poll on environment, see www.gallup.com/poll/1615/Environment.aspx

HadCRUT (2010) HadCRUT3 global monthly surface air temperatures since 1850, http://hadobs.metoffice.com/hadcrut3/index.html

Hansen, J., Fung, I., Lacis, A., Rind, D., Lebedeff, S., Ruedy, R., Russell, G. and Stone, P. (1988) 'Global climate changes as forecast by Goddard Institute for Space Studies three-dimensional model', *Journal of Geophysical Research-Atmospheres*, vol 93, pp9341–9364

Hansen, J., Sato, M., Ruedy, R., Lo, K., Lea, D. and Medina-Elizade, M. (2006) 'Global temperature change', *Proceedings of the National Academy of Sciences*, vol 101, pp16,109–16,114

Hansen, J., Sato, M., Ruedy, R., Kharecha, P., Lacis, A., Miller, R., Nazarenko, L., Lo, K., Schmidt, G. A., Russell, G., Aleinov, I., Bauer, S., Baum, E., Cairns, B., Canuto, V., Chandler, M., Cheng, Y., Cohen, A., DelGenio, A., Faluvegi, G., Fleming, E., Friend, A., Hall, T., Jackman, C., Jonas, J., Kelley, M., Kiang, N. Y., Koch, D., Labow, G., Lerner, J., Menon, S., Novakov, T., Oinas, V., Perlwitz, Ja., Perlwitz, Ju., Rind, D., Romanou, A., Schmunk, R., Shindell, D., Stone, P., Sun, S., Streets, D., Tausnev, N., Thresher, D., Unger, N., Yao, M. and Zhang, S. (2007) 'Climate simulations for 1880–2003 with GISS modelE', *Climate Dynamics*, vol 29, no 7, pp661–696

Health Protection Agency (2007) 'The health effects of climate change in the United Kingdom', *Health Protection Report*, vol 1, no 19, see www.hpa.org.uk/hpr/archives/2007/hpr1907.pdf

Huang, S., Pollack, H. and Shen, P. (2000) 'Temperature trends over the past five centuries reconstructed from borehole temperatures', *Nature*, vol 403, pp756–758

Hurd, B. and Coonrod, J. (2008) 'Climate change and its implications for New Mexico's water resources and economic opportunities', Agricultural Experiment Station Technical Report 45, New Mexico State University, Las Cruces, NM

IASC (2010) 'Permafrost in the Arctic', in J. Walsh et al (eds) *Arctic Climate Assessment, Section 6.6*, International Project of the Arctic Council and International Arctic Science Committee, see www.eoearth.org/article/Permafrost_in_the_Arctic, retrieved 21 July 2010

Immerzeel, W. W., van Beek, L. P. H. and Bierkens, M. F. P. (2010) 'Climate change will affect the Asian water towers', *Science*, vol 328, no 5984, pp1382–1385

International Ice Charting Working Group (2009) 'National ice services advise of continuing navigation hazards', see http://nsidc.org/noaa/iicwg/IICWG_2009/ IICWG_X_NEWS_RELEASE-2009-10-16.pdf

IPCC (2007) S. Solomon et al (eds) *Climate Change 2007: The Physical Science Basis. Contribution of Working Group I to the Fourth Assessment Report of the Intergovernmental Panel on Climate Change (AR4)*, Cambridge University Press, Cambridge, UK, and New York

Jacoby, G. and D'Arrigo, R. (1995) 'Tree ring width and density evidence of climatic and potential forest change in Alaska', *Global Biogeochemical Cycles*, vol 9, pp227–234

Kehrwald, N., Thompson, L., Tandong, Y., Mosley-Thompson, E., Schotterer, U., Alfimov, V., Beer, J., Eikenberg, J. and Davis, M. (2008) 'Mass loss on Himalayan glacier endangers water resources', *Geophysical Research Letters*, vol 35, L22503

Kerr, R. (2002) 'A warmer arctic means change for all', *Science*, vol 297, no 5586, pp1490–1493

Kimball, B., Idso, S., Johnson, S. and Rillig, M. (2007) 'Seventeen years of CO_2 enrichment of sour orange trees: Final results', *Global Change Biology*, vol 13, pp2171–2183

Knutti, R. and Hegerl, G. C. (2008) 'The equilibrium sensitivity of the Earth's temperature to radiation changes', *Nature Geoscience*, vol 1, no 11, pp735–743

Krivova, N., Balmaceda, L. and Solanki, S. (2007) 'Reconstruction of solar total irradiance since 1700 from the surface magnetic flux', *Astronomy & Astrophysics*, vol 467, pp335–346, www.mps.mpg.de/projects/sun-climate/data/tsi_1611.txt

Kurz, W., Dymond, C., Stinson, V., Rampley, G., Neilson, E., Carroll, A., Ebata, T. and Safranyik, L. (2008) 'Mountain pine beetle and forest carbon feedback to climate change', *Nature*, vol 452, pp987–990

Kutschera, U., Pfeiffer, I. and Ebermann, E. (2007) 'The European land leech: Biology and DNA-based taxonomy of a rare species that is threatened by climate warming', *Naturwissenschaften*, vol 94, no 12, pp967–974

Larsen, P., Goldsmith, S., Smith, O., Wilson, M., Strzepek, K., Chinowsky, P. and Saylor, B. (2008) 'Estimating future costs for Alaska public infrastructure at risk from climate change', *Global Environmental Change*, vol 18, no 3, pp442–457

Lockwood, M. (2008) 'Recent changes in solar output and the global mean surface temperature. III. Analysis of the contributions to global mean air surface temperature rise', *Proceedings of the Royal Society A*, vol 464, pp1–17

Mann, M., Bradley, R. and Hughes, M. (1998) 'Global-scale temperature patterns and climate forcing over the past six centuries', *Nature*, vol 392, pp779–787

Mann, M., Bradley, R. and Hughes, M. (1999) 'Northern Hemisphere temperatures during the past millennium: Inferences, uncertainties, and limitations', *Geophysical Research Letters*, vol 26, no 6, pp759–762

Mann, M., Zhang, Z., Hughes, M., Bradley, R., Miller, S., Rutherford, S. and Ni, F. (2008) 'Proxy-based reconstructions of hemispheric and global surface temperature variations over the past two millennia', *Proceedings of the National Academy of Sciences*, vol 105, no 36, pp13,252–13,257

McCabe, G. and Wolock, D. (2007) 'Warming may create substantial water supply shortages in the Colorado River basin', *Geophysical Research Letters*, vol 34, L22708

McCullagh, D. (2010) 'Sarah Palin on Climategate, Copenhagen: Beware politicized science', *CBS News*, www.cbsnews.com/8301-504383_162-5943590-504383.html

McIntyre, S. and McKitrick, R. (2005) 'Hockey sticks, principal components, and spurious significance', *Geophysical Research Letters*, vol 32, L03710, doi:10.1029/2004GL021750

McMahon, S., Parker, G. and Miller, D. (2010) 'Evidence for a recent increase in forest growth', *Proceedings of the National Academy of Sciences*, vol 107, no 8, pp3611–3615

Medina-Ramon, M. and Schwartz, J. (2007) 'Temperature, temperature extremes, and mortality: A study of acclimatization and effect modification in 50 US cities', *Occupational and Environmental Medicine*, vol 64, no 12, pp827–833

Mendelsohn, R., Dinar, A. and Williams, L. (2006) 'The distributional impact of climate change on rich and poor countries', *Environment and Development Economics*, vol 11, no 2, pp159–178

Menne, M., Williams, C. Jr and Palecki, M. (2010) 'On the reliability of the US surface temperature record', *Journal of Geophysical Research-Atmospheres*, vol 115, D11108, doi:10.1029/2009JD013094

Miles, H., Widdicombe, S., Spicer, J. and Hall-Spencer, J. (2007) 'Effects of anthropogenic seawater acidification on acid–base balance in the sea urchin *Psammechinus miliaris*', *Marine Pollution Bulletin*, vol 54, pp89–96

Morgan, J., Milchunas, D., LeCain, D., West, M. and Mosier, A. (2007) 'Carbon dioxide enrichment alters plant community structure and accelerates shrub growth in the shortgrass steppe', *Proceedings of the National Academy of Sciences*, vol 104, no 37, pp14,724–14,729

Murphy, D S., Solomon, R., Portmann, W., Rosenlof, K., Forster, P. and Wong, T. (2009) 'An observationally based energy balance for the Earth since 1950', *Journal of Geophysical Research-Atmospheres*, vol 114, D17107, doi:10.1029/2009JD012105

NASA GISS Temperature Index (2010) GLOBAL Land–Ocean Temperature Index by the Goddard Institute of Space Studies at NASA, see http://data.giss.nasa.gov/gistemp/tabledata/GLB.Ts+dSST.txt

Nemani, R., Keeling, C., Hashimoto, H., Jolly, W., Piper, S., Tucker, C., Myneni, R. and Running, S. (2003) 'Climate-driven increases in global terrestrial net primary production from 1982 to 1999', *Science*, vol 300, no 5625, pp1560–1563

Nepstad, D., Tohver, I., Ray, D., Moutinho, P. and Cardinot, G. (2007) 'Mortality of large trees and lianas following experimental drought in an Amazon forest', *Ecology*, vol 88, pp2259–2269

Nyegaard, H. (2007) *Climate Change and the Greenland Society*, World Wide Fund for Nature (WWF), Copenhagen, Denmark

Oerlemans, J. (2005) 'Extracting a climate signal from 169 glacier records', *Science*, vol 5722, pp675–677

OISM (2008) Petition Project, Oregon Institute of Science and Medicine, see www.petitionproject.org/

Okude, A. and Ademiluyi, I. (2007) 'Coastal erosion phenomenon in Nigeria: Causes, control and implications', *World Applied Science Journal*, vol 1, no 1, pp44–51

Oreskes, N. (2004) 'Beyond the ivory tower: The scientific consensus on climate change', *Science*, vol 306, p1686

Oreskes, N. and Conway, E. M. (2010) *Merchants of Doubt: How a Handful of Scientists Obscured the Truth on Issues from Tobacco Smoke to Global Warming*, Bloomsbury Press, New York

Orr, J., Fabry, V., Aumont, O., Bopp, L., Doney, S., Feely, R., Gnandesikan, A., Gruber, N., Ishida, A., Joos, F., Key, R., Lindsay, K., Maier-Reimer, E., Matear, R., Monfray, P., Mouchet, A., Najjar, R., Plattner, G., Rodgers, K., Sabine, C., Sarmiento, J., Schlitzer, R., Slater, R., Totterdell, I., Weirig, M., Yamanaka, Y. and Yool, A. (2005) 'Anthropogenic ocean acidification over the twenty-first century and its impact on calcifying organisms', *Nature*, vol 437, pp681–686

Oxburgh, R. (2010) Report of the International Panel set up by the University of East Anglia to examine the research of the Climatic Research Unit, see www.uea.ac.uk/mac/comm/media/press/CRUstatements/SAP

Parmesan, C. and Yohe, G. (2003) 'A globally coherent fingerprint of climate change impacts across natural systems', *Nature*, vol 421, no 6918, pp37–42

Peng, S., Huang, J., Sheehy, J, Laza, R., Visperas, R., Zhong, X., Centeno, G., Khush, G. and Cassman, K. (2004) 'Rice yields decline with higher night temperature from global warming', *Proceedings of the National Academy of Sciences*, vol 101, no 27, pp9971–9975

Pennisi, E. (2009) 'Ecology: Western US forests suffer death by degrees', *Science*, vol 323, no5913, pp447ff

Pfeffer, W., Harper, J. and O'Neel, S. (2008) 'Kinematic constraints on glacier contributions to 21st-century sea-level rise', *Science*, vol 321, no 5894, pp1340–1343

Phillips, O. L., Aragao, L. E. O. C., Lewis, S. L., Fisher, J. B., Lloyd, J., Lopez-Gonzalez, G., Malhi, Y., Monteagudo, A., Peacock, J., Quesada, C. A., van der Heijden, G., Almeida, S., Amaral, I., Arroyo, L., Aymard, G., Baker, T. R., Banki, O., Blanc, L., Bonal, D., Brando, P., Chave, J., de Oliveira, A. C., Cardozo, N. D., Czimczik, C. I., Feldpausch, T. R., Freitas, M. A., Gloor, E., Higuchi, N., Jimenez, E., Lloyd, G., Meir, P., Mendoza, C., Morel, A., Neill, D. A., Nepstad, D., Patino, S., Penuela, M. C., Prieto, A., Ramirez, F., Schwarz, M., Silva, J., Silveira, M., Thomas, A. S., Steege, H., Stropp, J., Vasquez, R., Zelazowski, P., Davila, E. A., Andelman, S., Andrade, A., Chao, K. J., Erwin, T., Di Fiore, A., Honorio, E., Keeling, H., Killeen, T. J., Laurance, W. F., Cruz, A. P., Pitman, N. C. A., Vargas, P. N., Ramirez-Angulo, H., Rudas, A., Salamao, R., Silva, N., Terborgh, J. and Torres-Lezama, A. (2009) 'Drought sensitivity of the Amazon rainforest', *Science*, vol 323, no 5919, pp1344–1347

Pittock, A. B. (2009) *Climate Change: The Science, Impacts and Solutions*, CSIRO/Earthscan, London

Plimer, I. (2009) *Heaven and Earth: Global Warming: The Missing Science*, Connorcourt Publishing, Ballan, Australia

Roe, G. and Baker, M. (2007) 'Why is climate sensitivity so unpredictable?', *Science*, vol 318, no 5850, pp629–632

Rogers, C., Wayne, P., Macklin, E., Muilenberg, M., Wagner, C., Epstein, P. and Bazzaz, F. (2006) 'Interaction of the onset of spring and elevated atmospheric CO_2 on ragweed (*ambrosia artemisiifolia* l.) pollen production', *Environmental Health Perspectives*, vol 114, no 6, June, pp865–869

Russell, M., Boulton, G., Clarke, P., Eyton, D. and Norton, J. (2010) *The Independent Climate Change E-mails Review*, see www.cce-review.org/pdf/ FINAL%20REPORT.pdf

Ryan, P. and Ryan, A. (2007) 'Impacts of global warming on New Zealand freshwater organisms: A preview and review', *New Zealand Natural Sciences*, vol 31, pp43–57

Sadler, B. (2003) 'Informed adaptation to a changed climate: Is South Western Australia a national canary', in *Living with Climate Change*, proceedings of national conference on climate change impacts and adaptation, Australian Academy of Science, Canberra, pp207–217

Saleska, S., Didan, K., Huete, A. and da Rocha, H. (2007) 'Amazon forests green-up during 2005 drought', *Science*, vol 318, no 5850, pp612ff

Shaffer, G., Olsen, S. and Pedersen, J. (2009) 'Long-term ocean oxygen depletion in response to carbon dioxide emissions from fossil fuels', *Nature Geoscience*, vol 2, pp105–109

Shakhova, N., Semiletov, I., Salyuk, A. and Kosmach, D. (2008) 'Anomalies of methane in the atmosphere over the East Siberian shelf: Is there any sign of methane leakage from shallow shelf hydrates?', *Geophysical Research Abstracts*, vol 10, EGU2008-A-01526, 2008, SRef-ID: 1607-7962/gra/ EGU2008-A-01526

Sherwood, S. and Huber, M. (2010) 'An adaptability limit to climate change due to heat stress', *Proceedings of the National Academy of Sciences*, vol 107, no 21, pp9552–9555

Simmons, A., Willett, K., Jones, P., Thorne, P. and Dee, D. (2010) 'Low-frequency variations in surface atmospheric humidity, temperature, and precipitation: Inferences from reanalyses and monthly gridded observational data sets', *Journal of Geophysical Research-Atmospheres*, vol 115, D01110, doi:10.1029/2009JD012442

Sinervo, B., Mendex, F., Miles, D., Heulin, B., Bastiaans, E., Villagran-Santa Cruz, M., Lara-Resendix, R., Martinez-Mendez, N., Calderon-Espinosa, M., Meza-Lazaro, R., Gadsden, H., Avila, L., Morando, M., De la Riva, I., Supelveda, P., Rocha, C., Ibarguengoytia, N., Puntriano, C., Massot, M., Lepetz, V., Oksanen, T., Chapple, D., Bauer, A., Branch, W., Clobert, J. and Sites J. Jr (2010) 'Erosion of lizard diversity by climate change and altered thermal niches', *Science*, vol 328, no 5980, pp894–899

Smith, C., Andy, B., Fairchild, I., Frisia, S. and Borsato, A. (2006) 'Reconstructing hemispheric-scale climates from multiple stalagmite records', *International Journal of Climatology*, vol 26, no 10, pp1417–1424

Smol, J. and Douglas, M. (2007) 'Crossing the final ecological threshold in high Arctic ponds', *Proceedings of the National Academy of Sciences*, vol 104, no 30, pp12,395–12,397

Solomon, S., Plattner, G-K., Knutti, R. and Friedlingstein, P. (2009) 'Irreversible climate change due to carbon dioxide emissions', *Proceedings of the National Academy of Sciences*, vol 106, no 6, pp1704–1709

Stramma, L., Johnson, G., Sprintall, J. and Mohrholz, V. (2008) 'Expanding oxygen-minimum zones in the tropical oceans', *Science*, vol 320, no5876, pp655–658

Stroeve, J., Serreze, M., Drobot, S., Gearheard, S., Holland, M., Maslanik, J., Meier, W. and Scambos, T. (2008) 'Arctic sea ice extent plummets in 2007', *Eos, Transactions, American Geophysical Union*, vol 89, no 2, doi:10.1029/2008EO020001

Tao, F., Hayashi, Y., Zhang, Z., Sakamoto, T. and Yokozawa, M. (2008) 'Global warming, rice production, and water use in China: Developing a probabilistic assessment', *Agricultural and Forest Meteorology*, vol 48, no 1, pp94–110

Thomas, C., Cameron, A., Green, R., Bakkenes, M., Beaumont, L., Collingham, Y., Erasmus, B., Siqueira, M., Grainger, A., Hannah, L., Hughes, L., Huntley, B., Jaarsveld, A., Midgley, G., Miles, L., Ortega-Huerta, M., Peterson, A., Phlllips, O. and Williams, S. (2004) 'Extinction risk from climate change', *Nature*, vol 427, pp145–148

Trenberth, K. (2009) 'An imperative for climate change planning: Tracking Earth's global energy', *Current Opinion in Environmental Sustainability*, vol 1, no 1, pp19–27

Turley, C., Blackford, J., Widdicombe, S., Lowe, D., Nightingale, P. and Rees, A. (2006) 'Reviewing the impact of increased atmospheric CO_2 on oceanic pH and the marine ecosystem', in H. Schellnhuber et al (eds) *Avoiding Dangerous Climate Change*, Cambridge University Press, Cambridge, UK, pp65–70

UAH website (2010) 'MSU global monthly lower troposphere temperatures since December 1978' (MSU = 'microwave sounding units' on satellites), accessed June 2010 see http://vortex.nsstc.uah.edu/data/msu/t2lt/uahncdc.lt

Usoskin, I., Schüssler, M., Solanki, S. and Mursula, K. (2005) 'Solar activity over the last 1150 years: Does it correlate with climate?', in F. Favata, G. Hussain and B. Battrick (eds) *Proceedings of the 13th Cambridge Workshop on Cool Stars, Stellar Systems and the Sun, ESA SP-560*, European Space Agency, Hamburg, Germany

Velicogna, I. (2009) 'Increasing rates of ice mass loss from the Greenland and Antarctic ice sheets revealed by GRACE', *Geophysical Research Letters*, vol 36, L19503, doi:10.1029/2009GL040222

Vermeer, M. and Rahmstorf, S. (2009) 'Global sea level linked to global temperature', *Proceedings of the National Academy of Sciences*, vol 106, no 51, pp21,527–21,532

Wahl, E. and Ammann, C. (2007) 'Robustness of the Mann, Bradley, Hughes reconstruction of Northern Hemisphere surface temperatures: Examination of criticisms based on the nature and processing of proxy climate evidence', *Climatic Change*, vol 85, pp33–69

Walter, K., Edwards, M., Grosse, G., Zimov, S. and Chapin, F. (2007) 'Thermokarst lakes as a source of atmospheric CH_4 during the last deglaciation', *Science*, vol 318, no 5850, pp633–636

Watts, A. (2010) SurfaceStations.org, see www.surfacestations.org/

Westbrook, G. K., Thatcher, K. E., Rohling, E. J., Piotrowski, A. M., Pälike, H., Osborne, A. H., Nisbet, E. G., Minshull, T. A., Lanoisellé, M., James, R. H., Hühnerbach, V., Green, D., Fisher, R. E., Crocker, A. J., Chabert, A., Bolton, C. T., Beszczynska-Möller, A., Berndt, C. and Aquilina, A. (2009) 'Escape of methane gas from the seabed along the West Spitsbergen continental margin', *Geophysical Research Letters*, vol 36, L15608

Westerling, A., Hidalgo, H., Cayan, D. and Swetnam, T. (2006) 'Warming and earlier spring increase western US forest wildfire activity', *Science*, vol 313, no 5789, pp940–943

Willis, P., Blackman-Woods, R., Boswell, T., Cawsey, I., Dorries, N., Harris, E., Iddon, B., Marsden, G., Naysmith, D., Spink, B., Stewart, I., Stringer, G., Turner, D. and Wilson, R. (2010) 'The disclosure of climate data from the Climatic Research Unit at the University of East Anglia', House of Commons Science and Technology Committee, see www.publications.parliament.uk/pa/cm200910/cmselect/cmsctech/ 387/387i.pdf

Zhou, L., Tucker, C., Kaufmann, R., Slayback, D., Shabanov, N. and Myneni, R. (2001) 'Variations in northern vegetation activity inferred from satellite data of vegetation index during 1981 to 1999', *Journal of Geophysical Research-Atmospheres*, vol 106, pp20,069–20,083, doi:10.1029/2000JD000115

4

The History of Denial

The Long History of Denial

Denial is as old as humanity. This book focuses on the history of denial of *environmental* problems, though it has been pointed out how successful creationists have also been in the US in keeping the American public ignorant about evolution. Both evolution and environmental denial feature 'a denial of facts and circumstances that don't fit religious or other traditional beliefs' (Ehrlich and Ehrlich, 1998). Paul and Anne Ehrlich in 1998 tabulated the common themes or claims of denial anti-science, which were:

- Environmental scientists ignore the abundant good news about the environment;
- Population growth does not cause environmental damage and may even be beneficial;
- Humanity is on the verge of abolishing hunger – food scarcity is a local or regional problem and is not indicative of overpopulation;
- Natural resources are superabundant, if not infinite;
- There is no extinction crisis, so most efforts to preserve species are both uneconomic and unnecessary;
- Global warming and acid rain are not serious threats to humanity;
- Stratospheric ozone depletion is a hoax;
- The risks posed by toxic substances are vastly exaggerated; and
- Regulation is wrecking the economy.

These arguments are still being made in virtually the same format (see, for example, Plimer, 2009). It is thus important to realize that today's denial about climate change follows on from a long trend in denial about the environmental crisis. The campaign to deny the need to protect natural areas and wilderness was one of the first great denial issues and continues today (Oelschlaeger, 1991; Washington, 2006). Rachel Carson's (1962) *Silent Spring* raised the problems of synthetic pesticides (especially chlorinated hydrocarbons). This generated the first great environmental denial of the 20th century. DDT was praised by many as a saviour of humanity for reducing malarial mosquito numbers (indeed it still is by some, for example Plimer, 2009). Carson was vilified by the pesticide industry as someone both hysterical and wrong. In fact DDT was abandoned mainly because mosquitoes evolved resistance against it (Oreskes and Conway, 2010), and history and careful biological research have shown that Carson was right (Van Emden and Peakall, 1999; Oreskes and Conway, 2010).

Denial about environmental issues in general was examined in the ground-breaking book by the Ehrlichs (1998), *Betrayal of Science and Reason*. The 'denial industry' around climate change has also been elegantly detailed in George Monbiot's (2006) book *Heat*, in James Hoggan's (2009) *Climate Cover Up*, and in Naomi Oreskes and Erik Conway's (2010) *Merchants of Doubt*. What is apparent when examining the history of denial in these books is that there is far more involved than merely confusion about the science. There is a deliberate attempt to muddy the waters and confuse the public, so that action on these issues is delayed or even stopped. Al Gore (2006) quotes a tobacco company (Brown and Williamson) memo from the 1960s:

> Doubt is our product, since it is the best means of competing with the 'body of fact' that exists in the minds of the general public. It is also the means of establishing a controversy.

The Ehrlichs (1998) have detailed how the 'Wise Use' movement was the leader in the denial of environmental problems in the US. This anti-science denial movement promotes seemingly authoritative opinions in books and the media that 'greatly distort what is or isn't known by environmental scientists'. The Ehrlichs note that this 'brownlash' has produced a body of 'anti-science' that is a:

> Twisting of the findings of empirical science – to bolster a predetermined worldview and to support a political agenda.

Denial anti-science proponents argue that environmental regulation has gone too far, a common conservative theme (Oreskes and Conway, 2010). Even in 1998 the Ehrlichs noted that denial anti-science argued that 'subtle long-term problems like global warming are nothing to worry about'. They noted that this denial anti-science interferes with and prolongs the 'already difficult search for realistic and equitable solutions to the human predicament'.

'Wise Use' opposes efforts to maintain environmental quality in the US, denies the need for national parks or wilderness, opposes environmental regulation, and sees no need for constraints on the exploitation of resources for short-term economic gain (Helvang, 1994; Ehrlich and Ehrlich, 1998). There exists also 'greenscamming', where groups are formed that masquerade as groups concerned about the environment, but actually work against the interests implied in their names. Hoggan (2009) calls these 'astroturf' groups, while Ian Enting (2007) describes them simply as 'front organizations'. Greenscamming is what biologists would call 'aggressive mimicry' (Ehrlich and Ehrlich, 1998). Examples of such sham greenscam groups are the National Wetland Coalition, The Sahara Club, The Alliance for Environment and Resources, The Abundant Wildlife Society of North America, The National Wilderness Institute, The American Council on Science and Health, and the Global Climate Coalition. US Congressman George Miller stated that these groups were seeking to disguise their actual motives, which were driven by profits and greed (Ehrlich and Ehrlich, 1998).

These groups often use code phrases such as 'sound science' and 'balance' – words that suggest objectivity, when in fact 'sound science' means science or views that are interpreted to support denial anti-science (Ehrlich and Ehrlich, 1998). Orthodox science that proceeds by peer review, if it disagrees with the denial anti-science, is labelled as 'junk science'. This is actually a total inversion of reality. There is a 'junk science' website (www.junkscience.com) that promotes denial anti-science. Denial anti-science (with few exceptions) does not proceed through the usual peer review science process. In fact it is this that is actually 'junk science', or rather it is not science at all, merely unsupported statements without proven scientific evidence. PR companies have long been involved in 'spin', in seeking to modify the public's view of reality, and this is certainly the case with the denial industry.

The Ehrlichs (1998) document many of the then denial authors in the US whose views were also quoted around the world. They devote a chapter each to 'fables' about population and food, non-living resources, biological diversity, atmosphere and climate, toxic substances, and economics and the environment. We do not cover these here as our book focuses on denial specifically of climate change. It is, however, important to reiterate that climate change denial is merely the last in a long line of denial anti-science campaigns. This started with DDT, then continued with the nuclear winter, tobacco, acid rain and the ozone hole. Today almost everyone (but not some deniers) accepts that CFCs are responsible for the hole in the ozone layer, yet only 10 years ago this was a hot topic of denial. The reason why denial over this is no longer strongly promoted may be that there is no powerful industry currently funding such denial. The refrigeration industry found economic alternatives to CFCs, and the world has moved on and the ozone hole is now starting to close (ABC, 2007; Hulme, 2009).

Denial books on the environmental crisis continue to emerge, however. Peter Jacques et al (2008) explain that between 1972 and 2005 there were some 141 denial books published, of which 130 came from conservative 'think tanks'. In the 1990s, 56 denial books came out, 92 per cent linked to right-wing foundations or think tanks (Oreskes and Conway, 2010). Probably the best known recent book is that by Bjorn Lomborg (2001) – *The Skeptical Environmentalist*. The Danish Committee for Scientific Dishonesty noted this book had fabricated data, selectively discarded results and misused statistical methods. It concluded that Lomborg was 'out of his depth' in the field of science (Hoggan,

2009). In opening their chapter on 'fables about the atmosphere and climate' the Ehrlichs (1998) note 'there has probably been more nonsense expounded on global warming than on any other topic in environmental science'. They note that Gregg Easterbrook (1998) and Ronald Bailey (1993) seek to exaggerate the differences among climate scientists, when in fact it is not whether warming will occur, but the probable *rate of warming*, and the changes in cloud formation and precipitation that will accompany it (Ehrlich and Ehrlich, 1998). In this way deniers seek to perpetuate the myth that consensus on warming doesn't exist within the scientific community. The Ehrlichs also refer to Fred Singer (1994) who wrote an article entitled 'Climate claims wither under the luminous lights of science'. We shall meet Singer several times in regard to climate change denial. Hoggan (2009) and Oreskes and Conway (2010) enlarge on his denial career, noting that Singer was once a respected physicist. Singer's article argued that the Earth is not warming and that the atmosphere has in fact cooled since 1979. The same claim is made today, but the year has now been moved forward to 1998 (Plimer, 2009).

Monbiot (2006) takes the examination of climate change denial further, through investigation of the professional climate change 'denial industry'. He came to realize that denial stories did not originate with journalists. Deniers make use of otherwise distinguished scholars to bolster their claims. David Bellamy is one of these, with a distinguished career as a botanist and TV presenter. He was arrested at the Franklin River blockade in Tasmania while campaigning to stop the misguided hydroelectric dam, and thus had credibility with environmentalists, but now has become a climate change denial advocate. Monbiot (2006) reports how Bellamy stated that the majority of glaciers around the world were expanding, when in fact they are retreating, as reported by the World Glacier Monitoring Service (Paul et al, 2004, www.wgms.ch). Monbiot traces Bellamy's source to a publication called *21st Century Science and Technology*, associated with Lyndon LaRouche (the denier we discussed earlier), which referred to Singer's website (www.sepp.org) as the source. Singer cited an untraceable paper in *Science* in 1989. In fact Singer's claim is still being made today on climate denial websites, even though the facts regarding glacier retreat are well known (see, for example, Houghton, 2008).

Monbiot (2006) shows that Exxon Oil has funded many organizations that deny climate change. At first glance this may itself sound like conspiracy theory. Hoggan (2009) notes that the idea of a cabal of rich and powerful people conspiring to fool the public about a fundamental point of science strains credulity. Unfortunately this is no joke, and Hoggan shows there are conspiracies aplenty, documented and undeniable. The oil company BP (which now stands for 'Beyond Petroleum') was once a part of the Global Climate Coalition (along with DuPont, Ford, General Motors, Shell, Texaco, the US Chamber of Commerce and of course Exxon). This group lobbied politicians, and sought to discredit the IPCC, and was in large part responsible for the US refusing to ratify the Kyoto Protocol (Diesendorf, 2009). Later, BP resigned from the Global Climate Coalition, most of the others pulled out and it was disbanded. The US did not sign Kyoto, so the Coalition's job was done. Exxon, however, has continued its role as a funder of denial organizations. The Royal Society in the UK has stated that ExxonMobil paid millions of dollars each year to groups that misrepresent greenhouse science (Hoggan, 2009).

Exxon is the world's most profitable corporation and in 2005 made quarterly profits of $10 billion (Monbiot, 2006), most of it from oil. Monbiot details how the Greenpeace website 'Exxon secrets' listed 124 bodies that had taken money from Exxon (see www.exxonsecrets.org/html/listorganizations.php). This list now contains 135 such organizations. Until recently Exxon was paying $20 million to greenscam groups, and in 2008 spent $126 million on political lobbying in the US (Hoggan, 2009). These denial organizations funded by Exxon, in Monbiot's (2006) words:

> Take a consistent line on climate change: that the science is contradictory, the scientists are split, environmentalists are charlatans, liars or lunatics, and if the governments took action to prevent global warming, they would be endangering the global economy for no good reason.

These denial arguments are still being made today (for example Plimer, 2009). Among the bodies funded by Exxon are some well known climate denial lobby groups and websites, such as TechCentralStation, the Cato Institute and the Heritage Foundation. They also include greenscamming organizations such as the Centre for the Study of Carbon Dioxide and Global Change, the National Environmental Policy Institute and the American Council on Science and Health. Of course Exxon is not the only fossil fuel company funding denial. Koch Industries has outspent Exxon on denial funding (Greenpeace, 2010a). The coal industry has also funded the greenscam group Information Council on the Environment (Greenpeace, 2010b; Oreskes, 2010). When money is given to what are found to be greenscam groups, clearly one can apply the famous phrase of the Roman advocate Cicero, '*Cui bono?*' – to whose benefit? At the very least individuals or groups who speak out on climate change, and who receive money from vested interests such as Exxon, should *declare that fact*. However, this is generally not the case. Such fossil fuel industry-funded groups cannot pretend to be unbiased. As novelist Upton Sinclair (1932) has noted 'it's difficult to get a man to understand something when his job depends on him not understanding it'.

By funding these organizations, Exxon creates an impression that doubt about climate change is widespread, and the names of the organizations suggest that serious researchers are challenging the consensus. Monbiot (2006) notes that mostly these groups use 'selection not invention'. They cherry-pick one contradictory study (and remember science operates by people questioning the accepted) and then promote it relentlessly. For example, when one scientific paper stated the troposphere had in fact cooled, these groups promoted this (and still do), even though the author John Christy admitted in 2005 that his figures were incorrect (Merali, 2005). Despite this you will still hear the original (mistaken) paper being circulated and championed by denial groups, and it still appears on denial websites.

When considering the history of climate change denial, we should remember that science (as in all fields) has a broad selection of people – radical, conservative, rational and irrational. Remember also how widespread denial is in the human psyche. There will always be *someone* with a science degree somewhere who will champion almost *any* cause, and sometimes they will have PhDs and can even be professors (we have a couple in Australia). Just because there is a professor of something denying climate change does not mean it is not true, it just means that the professor is in denial. This is why one must make use of the *preponderance of evidence* in science, the collective view. It should also be remembered that having a degree (or several degrees) in another field of science does not make one an expert in climate change. Despite this it is common practice for denial organizations to quote one particular scientist who is in denial. One of the most common of these is the 'Oregon Petition' organized by Frederick Sietz, former chairman of Singer's denial body 'The Science and Environmental Policy Project'. Sietz was a physicist who in the 1960s was President of the US National Academy of Sciences. He wrote the Oregon Petition, which urged the US government to reject the Kyoto Protocol, stating there was:

> No convincing scientific evidence that human release of carbon dioxide, methane or other greenhouse gases is causing or will, in the foreseeable future, cause catastrophic heating of the Earth's atmosphere and disruption of the Earth's climate. (Monbiot, 2006)

Anyone with a degree could sign the petition. It was circulated with a review written by Arthur Robinson, who was not a climate scientist. It was jointly published by Robinson's Oregon Institute of Science and Medicine and the George C. Marshall Institute, the latter of which received $630,000 from ExxonMobil between 1998 and 2005 (Monbiot, 2006). The petition was printed (without permission) in the font and format of the US National Academy of Sciences. The Academy responded by issuing a statement clarifying that the petition was nothing to do with it and that it 'does not reflect the conclusions of expert reports of the Academy' (Monbiot, 2006). Nevertheless, the petition has been circulated widely and has 31,000 signatures, almost all of whom have no background in climate science. Despite this, Bellamy and other deniers have called it a petition by 'climate scientists', and it is trumpeted as evidence that there is no scientific consensus on climate change.

One fascinating twist in denial history is that the corporate campaign to deny human-caused climate change was in fact first initiated by tobacco company Philip Morris (Monbiot, 2006). Philip Morris hired public relations company APCO to consider how to respond to the US EPA's 1992 report on the health effects of passive smoking. APCO warned Philip Morris that the company was not seen by the public as a credible spokesperson on tobacco, and they needed what appeared to be community groups to speak out on this. APCO proposed:

> A national coalition intended to educate the media, public officials and the public about the dangers of 'junk science'. Coalition will address credibility of government's scientific studies, risk assessment techniques and misuse of tax dollars. ... Upon formation of Coalition, key leaders will begin media outreach, for example editorial board tours, opinion articles and brief elected officials in selected states. (Monbiot, 2006)

In 1993 this fake citizen's group was formed with the name 'The Advancement for Sound Science Coalition' (TASSC). APCO stated in 1994 to Philip Morris that it was important that TASSC also comment on 'broader questions about government research and regulations' such as:

- Global warming;
- Nuclear waste disposal; and
- Biotechnology. (Monbiot, 2006)

APCO reported that they would engage in intensive recruitment of 'high-profile representatives from business and industry, scientists, public officials, and other individuals interested in promoting the use of sound science' (Monbiot, 2006). APCO first invented the term 'junk science' for bona fide peer-reviewed mainstream science – science their clients (Phillip Morris and later Exxon) did not like. 'Sound science' meant studies sponsored by the tobacco industry. Singer also worked with APCO (Monbiot, 2006; Hoggan, 2009). Monbiot (2006) details how many conservative 'think tanks' in the US have also been funded by Philip Morris, including the Cato Institute, the Heritage Foundation, the Reason Foundation and the Independent Institute.

Unfortunately, the work of APCO and its greenscam organizations has borne fruit, and denial organizations are often cited as respectable authorities by the media (much of which is also owned by conservative interests). Monbiot concludes that while the denial organizations have been most effective in the US, the same arguments are endlessly repeated in Australia, Canada, India, Russia and the UK. Monbiot (2006) concludes that:

> By dominating the media debate on climate change during seven or eight critical years in which urgent international talks should have been taking place, by constantly seeding doubt about the science just as it should have been most persuasive, they have justified the money their sponsors spent on them many times over. I think it is fair to say that the professional denial industry has delayed effective global action on climate change by several years.

Hoggan (2009) describes it as:

> A story of betrayal, a story of selfishness, greed and irresponsibility on an
> epic scale. In its darkest chapters it's a story of deceit, of poisoning public
> judgement – of an anti-democratic attack on our political structures and
> a strategic undermining of the journalistic watchdogs who keep our social
> institutions honest.

Hoggan is a publicist and due to his trained eye started to notice evidence of the
denial PR campaign and its strategic media manipulation. He started the website
www.desmogblog.com to 'clear the PR pollution that clouds climate science'.
Hoggan notes that nobody used to be confused about climate change in 1988 –
so what happened? As the science got more certain (and alarming), how did the
public 'conventional wisdom' turn more and more to confusion and doubt? A
2009 Gallup Poll showed that 41 per cent thought the seriousness of the global
warming threat was exaggerated (Hoggan, 2009). Other polls in the US show
that 70 per cent of Americans think climate is changing but only 50 per cent
thing humans are the cause. Hoggan (2009) details the reasons why – the clever
use of strong funding and PR tactics, often spearheaded by conservative 'think
tanks'.

One of the most fascinating aspects of 'climate cover-up' is the explanation
by Hoggan (2009) of the new strategy of 'non-denier deniers'. This approach is
described by Enting (2007) as 'greenhouse-lite'. These people put themselves
forward as reasonable interpreters of the science and do not deny climate change
per se or even that humans are the cause. They then argue however that it's too
late to stop warming, so we should adapt, that warming might even be good,
that we must balance action with concern for the economy. One cunning
approach by denier Lomborg (2001) is to argue that there are higher priorities
such as poverty, HIV or malaria (in other words things most people feel should
be acted upon). He concludes that society would be better off spending scarce
funds on these 'higher priorities'. He does not mention, however, that climate
change will make poverty and malaria worse. Hoggan (2009) explains that the
'non-denier denier' is a deliberate PR ploy in the face of overwhelming scientific
evidence. It acknowledges the science but seeks to convince people we just can't
afford to act on it. In reality, of course, it is never an either/or situation. We
need to solve climate change *and* we need to reduce poverty and combat
malaria. The money can be found for each of these. The recent financial bail-
out in the US, and the past history of the Space Race, shows this to be the case
(Pittock, 2009). Hoggan concludes that the denial industry is digging in with
more determination and money than ever before, albeit changing tactics.

Greenpeace (2010b), in their report 'Dealing in Doubt', shows that with
each IPCC Assessment Report there was a concerted effort in denial. They also
show that denial campaigns operate through bad science, fake scientific
conferences, fake scientific support, personal attacks and political influence.
Aaron McCright and Riley Dunlap (2010) detail the involvement of the US

conservative movement in undermining climate science and policy. Oreskes and Conway (2010), in their brilliant book *Merchants of Doubt*, take the history of denial further. They point out that a small group of scientists (mainly physicists with a strong connection to the nuclear industry, see Lahsen, 2008) played a central role in sowing doubt. This was not just about climate change, but started with denial of nuclear winter and went on to include denial about acid rain, tobacco and the ozone hole. They fought the scientific evidence and spread confusion. They seemed to feel that the focus on environmental science had violated their prestige as physicists (Lahsen, 2008). In fact Oreskes and Conway (2010) show that deniers learned from the acid rain and tobacco campaigns the *best way to spread doubt*. They used the same strategy on climate change, though there they did not deny the severity of the problem, rather they denied the science itself. These scientists included Frederick Sietz, Fred Singer, Robert Jastrow and William Nierenberg (Oreskes and Conway, 2010).

Oreskes and Conway (2010) also detail the support that conservative think tanks gave these scientists and ask 'What is going on?'. The link that united the tobacco industry, conservative think tanks and the scientists mentioned above is that they were *implacably opposed to regulation*. They saw regulation as the slippery slope to socialism. They felt that concern about environmental problems was questioning the ideology of laissez faire economics and free market fundamentalism. These conservative bodies equate the free market with liberty, so for them:

> Accepting that by-products of industrial civilization were irreparably damaging the global environment was to accept the reality of market failure. It was to acknowledge the limits of free market capitalism. ... Science was starting to show that certain kinds of liberties are not sustainable – like the liberty to pollute. (Oreskes and Conway, 2010)

So if science impacts on their view of 'liberty', if it shows that regulation of pollution is needed, then science has to be opposed and *denied*. It is of interest that sociology until recently has overlooked the organized conservative opposition to climate change action (McCright and Dunlap, 2000). Sociology and society as a whole can no longer afford to overlook the organized denial industry.

Of course the denial industry has not been limited to America and the UK, it is in full swing in Australia also, and has good access to government. One denial group, the Competitive Enterprise Institute, developed an Australian campaign in 1996, working with the Western Mining Corporation. The Institute of Public Affairs has played a key role leading denial in Australia (Greenpeace, 2010b). Mark Diesendorf (2009) has documented how in 2004 the CEOs of major fossil fuel producers and consumers met the then Prime Minister, John Howard, and discussed ways of limiting the growth of the renewable energy industry. This was later confirmed by Guy Pearse (2007), who for his PhD interviewed captains of carbon-polluting industries. They boasted to him that they were the 'Greenhouse Mafia' and were responsible for writing government policy on greenhouse response (Diesendorf, 2009). The current Labor Government has failed to follow the recommendations of the Garnaut Climate Review and proposed to hand out huge free credits to polluting industries in its planned ETS. Diesendorf (2009) lists four key failings where the Labor Government has failed its election promises regarding renewable energy. These include failing to fund the Energy Innovation Fund, failing to honour its 20 per cent Renewable Energy Target and substantially reducing the subsidies for residential solar electricity.

Heaven and Earth

One of the latest instalments of the climate change denial movement has been the book *Heaven and Earth* by Ian Plimer (2009). Plimer is an Australian professor of geology. His book is much trumpeted by the deniers as scientific proof that human-caused climate change does not exist. As a summary of denial, this book is important enough to discuss here, as it has become something of a 'bible' for climate change deniers (especially in Australia). It is tempting to dismiss the work out of hand, yet this is what Plimer himself does with the IPCC reports and mainstream climate science. To respond in the same way would be to come close to slipping into denial ourselves. James Hansen (2009) notes Gandhi's saying that 'those who we regard as wicked as a rule return the compliment'. It is better to subject his arguments to rational analysis in the light of mainstream science. Plimer's book is denial on a grand scale, so we have used mainstream science to respond to what he has stated. A more detailed treatment of the points in the book can be found in Enting (2009), available at the RealClimate website (www.realclimate.org).

Plimer has been very selective in cherry-picking his references, citing only those that support denial. Indeed Monbiot (2006) notes that quoting each other's papers is common among deniers. Other parts of the book (and far too many key statements) are *not referenced at all*, or referenced only from denial organisations such as the Cato and Marshall Institutes. It is thus very uneven in terms of backing up its statements. Plimer's book was not reviewed by climate scientists, and all its figures have *no source or reference provided*. Given Plimer's scathing comments on how others are 'unscientific', the omission of any sources for his diagrams is a major omission, contrary to the scientific norm. Where did he get his diagrams that purport to show no warming? What data sets is he using? We cannot know as he does not tell us. Enting (2009) shows in detail how many of Plimer's references, given in support of his claims, do not in fact do so.

Those who do not agree with his claims are variously described by Plimer as 'lacking the scientific understanding', 'alarmists', 'catastrophists', 'rabid environmentalists', 'thuggish', 'on the take' and 'fraudulent'. We are led to believe that all climate scientists are suspect and only geologists are to be trusted, even though the American Geophysical Union and the Geological Society of Australia endorse the reality of human-caused global warming (Enting, 2009;

THE HISTORY OF DENIAL

GSA, 2009). Plimer insists that environmentalism is a religion that embraces 'anti-human totalitarianism'. His view of human interaction with the land is that 'humans have burned and eaten the environment since Adam was a boy'. He decries the 'precautionary principle', a fundamental part of ecological sustainability (Rio Declaration, 1992). Plimer states that the use of the term precautionary principle 'abandons scientific proof'. Plimer's environmental stance is summarized as 'sustainability creates a miserable existence, poverty, disease, depopulation and ignorance'. He thus denies the whole thrust of the emerging world paradigm that seeks a sustainable future (Rio Declaration, 1992; Berry, 1999; Soskolne, 2008).

Like many in denial, Plimer does not believe that other environmental problems exist, such as overpopulation, agricultural decline or the biodiversity crisis. Environmentalists, he says, have 'loathing of population increase'. In a world of massive deforestation, he makes the claim that 'the area of forests is expanding'. He (along with denial physicist Nierenberg, see Lahsen, 2008) says that CFCs do not cause the hole in the ozone layer. For Plimer, extinctions have always happened and thus extinction is 'normal' as 'the process of speciation requires extinction'. The concern about this is just 'emotional'. He is content to make pronouncements on biodiversity extinction *without* referencing any of the experts in the field, such as Professor Raven (1987), Professor Soule (Soule and Orians, 1991), Dr Myers (1992) or Professor Wilson (2003). Because extinction is 'normal', it is seen as acceptable for humans to speed this up hugely and thus deprive thousands of species of existence and the ability to further evolve.

Plimer argues that warming would 'bring more species diversity'. His reference is not from respected biologists, but from a book by the Marshall Institute, a conservative think tank. Plimer seeks to bolster his arguments by citing another denier, Lomborg (2001). In this case (as in so much in this book) the real experts in these fields of science are deemed to be fools who don't know what they are doing. On page 23 Plimer summarizes his views on climate change thus:

a) The Earth's climate has always changed with cycles of warming and cooling long before humans appeared on Earth.

Scientific consensus: this is not under debate, and climate scientists do not argue against this (see, for example, Houghton, 2008; Pittock, 2009).

b) Measured global warming in the modern world has been insignificant in comparison with these natural cycles.

Scientific consensus: in the past there have been large changes in global temperature, but these did not happen at the speed we may be currently changing the climate, with consequent major impacts. Currently, global warming is the most significant for the last 10,000 years (Houghton, 2008).

c) Although manmade increases in atmospheric CO_2 may theoretically make some contribution to temperature rise, such links have not been proven and there is abundant evidence to the contrary.

Scientific consensus: the vast majority of climate scientists accept that CO_2 is a greenhouse gas, that humans have increased the levels by more than a third, and that warming in the last 100 years can only be explained by both natural and anthropogenic forcings (Houghton, 2008; Pittock, 2009). It is not just theoretical, it is theory supported by multiple, independent sources of research data.

d) Contrary to nearly two dozen different computer models, temperature has not increased in the last decade despite an accelerated input of CO_2 into the atmosphere by human activities.

Scientific consensus: temperature increases are tracked over time and there is some variation. The long-term trend of global warming is continuing. The oceans continue to warm (Murphy et al, 2009).

e) Other factors, such as major Earth processes, variable solar activity, solar wind and cosmic rays, appear to have a far more significant factor on Earth's climate than previously thought. The IPCC has not demonstrated that the Sun was not to blame for recent warmings and coolings.

Scientific consensus: climate science is the branch of science set up to consider climate changes. Solar variation has changed very little in the past decades (Hansen, 2009). Climate scientists do not argue these other processes do not exist, but say that the best explanation for recent warming is the rapid increase in greenhouse gases added by humans (Houghton, 2008; Pittock, 2009).

f) Humans have adapted to live at sea level, at altitude, on ice sheets, in the tropics and in deserts. As in the past, humans will again adapt to any future coolings or warmings.

Scientific consensus: humans are adaptable, but our societies are far less so (Diamond, 2005). Human civilization arose in a period of 8000 years of benign climate (Houghton, 2008). Few climate scientists argue that global warming will send humans extinct, but that it could lead to major water and food shortages and vastly impoverish the world we share with other species. Human adaptability is thus not the issue. Human rationality and ethics are.

Plimer's arguments boil down to the manifesto that all things bad happen in cold times, whereas 'life blossoms and economies boom in warm times'. This seems to be argued as true no matter at what temperature one starts and how much one increases this temperature. Runaway climate change due to positive feedback is denied. Presumably as all warming is good, runaway climate change would be seen as even better? Plimer states many times that climate is 'driven by the Sun'. In fact there has been little variation in solar output, and we have been at a solar *minimum* (Hansen, 2009). Carbon dioxide is described accurately as a 'trace gas' (as in percentage terms it *is* a trace) without any statement of the amount humans have increased this trace gas or the radiative forcing it is causing. In fact for most of the book, Plimer does not acknowledge the physical and measurable reality that CO_2 absorbs infrared radiation and hence is a *greenhouse gas*. This is as strong as 'facts' get and can be tested in any physics laboratory. Nor does he explain where this extra absorbed energy *goes* – if it doesn't warm the atmosphere. He does note on page 132 that greenhouse gases 'act only as amplifiers' of solar activity. However, either these gases are greenhouse gases and warm the atmosphere or they are not. Having repeatedly denied that CO_2 is a significant greenhouse gas, on page 366 he finally admits that 'in the atmosphere, CO_2 is a highly effective trap of energy in the infra-red wavelength band'. He then states that 'all the CO_2 does is slows down heat loss'. This is what a greenhouse gas is: it slows down heat loss and thus warms the atmosphere. However, later he turns this logic around by saying 'the role of greenhouse is to cool the atmosphere through radiating energy to space'.

Plimer seems to think that climate scientists have somehow *forgotten* other drivers of climate change, when this is not the case. However, humans are not changing orbital mechanics or the output of the Sun, but we *are* currently increasing greenhouse gases. Given that most deniers are strongly anthropocentric (human-centred), it is ironic that Plimer notes, 'If we humans, in a fit of ego, think we can change these normal planetary processes, then we need stronger medication.' In other words the effect of 6.8 billion humans on planet Earth is discounted, and he seems to believe humans don't affect the atmosphere or climate. He fails to note that humans are *already* appropriating more than 40 per cent of the world's net primary productivity and more than 45 per cent of the world's freshwater (Ehrlich and Ehrlich, 1998), and have cleared and fragmented so much habitat that by the end of the century up to half the world's species face extinction (Wilson, 2003). He doesn't mention the 75 billion tonnes/year loss of agricultural soil (Bates and Hemenway, 2010), nor the rapid loss of rainforests around the world. Indeed, so extensive have human impacts on the world's ecosystems become that atmospheric chemist and Nobel Prize-winner Paul Crutzen has coined the term 'the Anthropocene' for the era we live in (Hulme, 2009). Given the unprecedented impact that humans are having all around the planet on natural ecosystems, why is it so inconceivable that we could affect atmospheric processes and climate?

Plimer says that CO_2 is just 'plant food'. The fact that CO_2 is indeed used by plants does not mean any increase is harmless, just as plants use water but we don't want floods. Plants also produce oxygen, which all eukaryotic organisms rely on to survive, yet increasing oxygen levels further would result in devastating wildfires. That CO_2 is used by plants has not been forgotten by climate scientists. It is its effect as a greenhouse gas that climate scientists are concerned about. The repeated dismissal of CO_2 as 'plant food' is thus a red herring. Plimer also ignores recent research that indicates that higher CO_2 levels will in fact favour weeds rather than the food crops and timber trees humans rely on. The US National Oceanic and Atmospheric Administration (NOAA) found in the comprehensive report 'Global climate change impacts in the United States' that 'increased temperatures and carbon dioxide concentrations also favour weeds and insect pests' (Karl et al, 2009).

However, the IPCC is Plimer's main target. The IPCC Assessment Reports – which John Houghton (2008), has called the most comprehensive review ever of any scientific issue – are said to contain many authors who were 'environmental activists' (and hence, by implication, suspect). According to Plimer, expert evidence on the health effects of global warming was ignored – though no reference is given to substantiate this claim. Plimer insists the IPCC is related to environmental activism, politics and opportunism and is 'unrelated to science'. Later he states that the IPCC Summary for Policymakers has been 'underpinned by fraud'. Plimer's conclusion is:

> The IPCC is clearly an ascientific political organization in which environmental activists and government representatives are setting the agenda for a variety of reasons including boosting trade, encouraging protectionism, adding costs to competitors and pushing their own sovereign barrow.

Given the history of the professional denial industry demonstrated earlier, it is interesting that yet again mainstream science is depicted as unscientific, whereas those in denial are seen as the only true scientists. Plimer's key claim seems to revolve around the argument that because past climate changes had other causes (such as orbital mechanics), then our current climate change cannot be due to an increase in greenhouse gases. Plimer thus sets up a 'straw man' to knock down, seeking to portray climate scientists as arguing that all climate change is due to CO_2. Climate scientists know that this is not so, but that doesn't mean that the climate change today is not due to a CO_2 level that humans have increased.

Plimer's other argument is that global warming 'stopped in 1998'. He provides no references to prove this but seeks to make use of the natural variability in climate (2008 being a cold year) to dismiss the steady long-term trend that is the concern of climate scientists. Plimer dismisses the idea that in the past runaway greenhouse occurred. Tipping points or runaway climate change and positive feedback are dismissed as 'non-scientific myths'. Plimer provides no reference as to why these should be dismissed. There is, however, substantial evidence (Hansen, 2009) of methane spikes and very rapid warming (5–9 degrees Celsius) in the Earth's climate history, as Plimer himself notes (p166). Plimer dismisses the many positive feedback processes that could accelerate global warming (see, for example, Pittock, 2009). He argues that a thermostat 'regulates Planet Earth such that there is no permanent icehouse and no permanent runaway greenhouse'. There is, however, no reference for what would seem a critically important argument in the book. Even if this were to be the case, the shortest timescale over which this operates may be thousands of years (Hansen et al, 2008) – not much use to humanity today.

The carbon cycle is confused in the book (no diagram is provided), with emissions from forests and oceans being referred to without referring to the sinks in these same areas. In fact currently the oceans absorb more CO_2 than they emit (Houghton, 2008). Such confusion about the carbon cycle is common among climate change deniers. Plimer also denies that coral bleaching and ocean acidification are increasing, though this is in direct denial of research by marine experts which shows that ocean acidification and thermal stress have led to a 10 per cent decline in growth rate of massive corals in the Great Barrier Reef (www.oceanclimatechange.org.au). He also raises conspiracy theory in regard to the Mauna Loa infrared spectroscopy CO_2 measurements, which replaced the less reliable chemical testing. Plimer suggests that with such 'savage editing of raw data, whatever trend one wants to show can be shown' and he asks if we have 'absolute proof that CO_2 has risen over the last 50 years'. We are thus meant to believe that there was a conspiracy since 1959 to falsify records to show a steady increase decade by decade in CO_2 at many different recording stations around the world. The rate of CO_2 as measured by surface stations is also the same as that measured by multiple satellites, so all of these would have to be falsified also. We know that humanity burns huge amounts of fossil fuels each year. Where does this go if it doesn't increase atmospheric CO_2 levels? Such conspiracy theory claims over 50 years surely stretch credibility.

Plimer's (2009) concluding chapter states that the 'greatest global threat ... is from policy responses to perceived global warming and the demonising of dissent'. He complains that climate deniers have been compared to Holocaust deniers. He describes his own denial as 'critical thinking' and promotes the mistaken view that renewable energy is 'unreliable, far too expensive and adds little base-load power'. He conveniently ignores examples of successful renewable energy systems (Diesendorf, 2007; Pittock, 2009). Climate scientists are said to have 'overplayed their hand'; green movements use blackmail and 'take place in a science-free zone'. Climate scientists are implied to be corrupt. Apparently it is still seen as workable to 'kick the communist can', as environmentalists are portrayed as neo-Marxists who are 'anti-trade, anti-globalization and anti-civilization'. Plimer calls for the Kyoto Protocol to be abandoned. He also calls for society to abandon carbon trading and carbon footprints and all types of mitigation. Plimer makes the demonstrably false statement that 'to reduce per capita energy consumption can only reduce the standard of living', when countless studies have shown that the two are not linked and that energy use can be massively reduced (at least halved) without affecting lifestyle (for example Houghton, 2008).

There is an irony in Plimer's book, given his own vehement denial of science he doesn't wish to believe. He says that advocates of human-induced warming 'dismiss this data in a defiant act of cognitive dissonance' – which of course is what Plimer himself is doing. Apparently all climate and environmental scientists 'have no interest in improving life on Earth, they just demonstrate a complete denial of reality'. This is the ultimate irony, a total reversal of truth, where mainstream science is described as denying reality, when it is the deniers of course who do this. He argues (again ironically) that those who advocate long-delayed action on climate change have 'a maniacal desperation to stamp out contrary views' and 'defend their political dogma with religious zeal'. He also dismisses any concern about fossil fuel companies such as Exxon funding denial organizations, saying that 'the source of the funding matters not, because evidence is evidence'.

Like Paul Ehrlich's (1968) book *The Population Bomb*, Plimer finishes his book with a section 'What if I am wrong?'. He immediately says 'this is not a question asked by warmers'. Yet in fact he does not answer his question. Plimer does not analyse the severe damage to the world's ecosystems and human societies that will occur if mainstream climate science is right and he is wrong. He does not investigate the dangers in further procrastination (economic as well as environmental).

However, Plimer does make one interesting statement (p457):

> This irrationality of destructive delusions costs communities dearly.

The 'destructive delusion' of denial has indeed cost the Earth's biodiversity and human communities dearly. It will cost even more if we stay in rampant denial. Are we never to accept that humanity is faced with problems that need solutions?

References

ABC (2007) 'Hole in ozone shrinking, scientists say', www.abc.net.au/news/stories/2007/11/16/2093586.htm
Bailey, R. (1993) *Eco-scam: The False Prophets of Ecological Apocalypse*, St Martins Press, New York
Bates, A. and Hemenway, T. (2010) 'From agriculture to permaculture', in L. Starke and L. Mastny (eds) *2010 State of the World: Transforming Cultures from Consumerism to Sustainability*, Earthscan, London
Berry, T. (1999) *The Great Work*, Belltower, New York
Carson, R. (1962) *Silent Spring*, Houghton Mifflin, Boston, MA
Diamond, J. (2005) *Collapse: Why Societies Choose to Fail or Succeed*, Viking Press, New York
Diesendorf, M. (2007) *Greenhouse Solutions with Sustainable Energy*, UNSW Press, Sydney, Australia
Diesendorf, M. (2009) *Climate Action: A Campaign Manual for Greenhouse Solutions*, UNSW Press, Sydney, Australia
Easterbrook, G. (1998) *A Moment on the Earth: The Coming Age of Environmental Optimism*, Penguin Books, New York
Ehrlich, P. (1968) *The Population Bomb*, Buccaneer Books, New York
Ehrlich, P. and Ehrlich, A. (1998) *Betrayal of Science and Reason: How Anti-Environmental Rhetoric Threatens Our Future*, Island Press, New York/Shearwater Books, Washington, DC
Enting, I. (2007) *Twisted: The Distorted Mathematics of Greenhouse Denial*, Australasian Mathematical Sciences Institute, Melbourne, Australia

Enting, I. (2009) 'Ian Plimer's *Heaven and Earth* – Checking the claims', ARC Centre of Excellence for Mathematics and Statistics of Complex Systems, The University of Melbourne, see www.realclimate.org

Gore, A. (2006) *An Inconvenient Truth*, Bloomsbury Publishing, New York

Greenpeace (2010a) 'Koch industries secretly funding the climate denial machine', www.greenpeace.org/usa/press-center/reports4/koch-industries-secretly-fund

Greenpeace (2010b) *Dealing in Doubt: The Climate Denial Industry and Climate Science*, Greenpeace International, Amsterdam (or see Greenpeace website)

GSA (2009) Position Statement and Recommendations, 'Greenhouse gas emissions and climate change', 15 July, Geological Society of Australia Inc, www.gsa.org.au/pdfdocuments/management/GreenhouseGasEmissions&ClimateChange_GSAPositionStatement_July2009.pdf

Hansen, J. (2009) *Storms of My Grandchildren: The Truth about the Coming Climate Catastrophe and Our Last Chance to Save Humanity*, Bloomsbury, London

Hansen, J., Sato, M., Kharecha, P., Beerling, D., Berner, R., Masson-Delmotte, V., Pagani, M., Raymo, M., Royer, D. and Zachos, J. (2008) 'Target atmospheric CO_2: Where should humanity aim?', *Open Atmospheric Science Journal*, vol 2, pp217–231

Helvang, D. (1994) *The War Against the Greens: The 'Wise Use' Movement, the New Right, and Anti-environmental Violence*, Sierra Club Books, San Francisco, CA

Hoggan, J. (2009) *Climate Cover Up: The Crusade to Deny Global Warming*, Greystone Books, Vancouver, Canada

Houghton, J. (2008) *Global Warming: The Complete Briefing*, Cambridge University Press, Cambridge, UK

Hulme, M. (2009) *Why We Disagree about Climate Change: Understanding Controversy, Inaction and Opportunity*, Cambridge University Press, Cambridge, UK

Jacques, P., Dunlap, R. and Freeman, M. (2008) 'The organization of denial: Conservative think tanks and environmental scepticism', *Environmental Politics*, vol 17, no 3, June, doi:10.1080/09644010802055576

Karl, T., Jerry, M., Melillo, J. and Peterson, T. (2009) (eds) *Global Climate Change Impacts in the United States*, Cambridge University Press, Melbourne, Australia

Lahsen, M. (2008) 'Experiences of modernity in the greenhouse: A cultural analysis of a physicist "trio" supporting the backlash against global warming', *Global Environmental Change*, vol 18, pp204–219

Lomborg, B. (2001) *The Skeptical Environmentalist: Measuring the Real State of the World*, Cambridge University Press, Cambridge, UK

McCright, A. and Dunlap, R. (2000) 'Challenging global warming as a social problem: An analysis of the conservative movement's counter-claims', *Social Problems*, vol 47, no 4, pp499–522

McCright, A. and Dunlap, R. (2010) 'Anti-reflexivity: The American conservative movement's success in undermining climate science and policy', *Theory, Culture and Society*, vol 27, nos 2–3, pp100–133

Merali, Z. (2005) 'Skeptics forced into climate climbdown', *New Scientist*, vol 2513, 12 August, p10

Monbiot, G. (2006) *Heat: How to Stop the Planet Burning*, Penguin Books, London

Murphy, D., Solomon, S., Portmann, R., Rosenlof, K., Forster, P. and Wong, T. (2009) 'An observationally based energy balance for the Earth since 1950', *Journal of Geophysical Research-Atmospheres*, vol 114, doi:10.1029/2009JD012105

Myers, N. (1992) *The Primary Source: Tropical Forests and our Future*, Norton and Company, New York

Oelschlaeger, M. (1991) *The Idea of Wilderness: From Prehistory to the Age of Ecology*, Yale University Press, New Haven, CT/London

Oreskes, N. (2010) 'My facts are better than your facts: Spreading good news about global warming', in M. Morgan and P. Howlett (eds) *How do Facts Travel?*, Cambridge University Press, Cambridge, UK, pp135–166

Oreskes, N. and Conway, E. M. (2010) *Merchants of Doubt: How a Handful of Scientists Obscured the Truth on Issues from Tobacco Smoke to Global Warming*, Bloomsbury Press, New York

Paul, F., Kaab, A., Maisch, M., Kellenberger, T. and Haeberli, W. (2004) 'Rapid disintegration of alpine glaciers observed with satellite data', *Geophysical Research Letters*, vol 31, 12 November, doi:10.1029/2004GL020816

Pearse, G. (2007) *High and Dry: John Howard, Climate Change and the Selling of Australia's Future*, Penguin Books, Sydney, Australia

Pittock, A. B. (2009) *Climate Change: The Science, Impacts and Solution*, CSIRO Publishing, Melbourne, Australia

Plimer, I. (2009) *Heaven and Earth: Global Warming: The Missing Science*, Connorcourt Publishing, Ballan, Australia

Raven, P. (1987) 'The scope of the plant conservation problem world wide', in D. Bramwell et al (eds) *Botanic Gardens and the World Conservation Strategy*, Academic Press, New York

Rio Declaration (1992) Rio Declaration on Environment and Development, produced at the United Nations 'Conference on Environment and Development' (UNCED), informally known as the Earth Summit, see http://en.wikipedia.org/wiki/Rio_Declaration_on_Environment_and_Development

Sinclair, U. (1932) 'The jungle', in *American Outpost: A Book of Reminiscences*, Farrar & Rinehart, New York

Singer, S. (1994) 'Climate claims wither under luminous lights of science', *Washington Times*, 29 November, pA18

Soskolne, C. (2008) *Sustaining Life on Earth: Environmental and Human Health through Global Governance*, Lexington Books, New York

Soule, M. and Orians, G. (2001) *Conservation Biology: Research Priorities for the Next Decade*, Island Press, New York

Van Emden, H. and Peakall, D. (1999) *Beyond Silent Spring: Integrated Pest Management and Chemical Safety*, UNEP/ ICIPE, Chapman & Hall, London

Washington, H. (2006) *The Wilderness Knot*, PhD thesis, University of Western Sydney, Australia

Wilson, E. O. (2003) *The Future of Life*, Vintage Books, New York

5

Do We Let Denial Prosper?

We have examined denial as opposed to skepticism, we have examined the nature of science and the importance of probability, we have covered the basics of climate science, we have looked at the types of denial arguments, and we have looked at the history of denial of environmental problems such as climate change. Now we should address another question: Why do we let denial prosper?

Fear of Change

Of course many of us are not in denial about environmental problems, but it seems that many people, organizations and governments are. It is essential to ponder just why this is. Why has there been a failure in urgency in regard to solving the environmental crisis (Washington, 2009a)? One reason why many of us don't take action is the *fear of change*. When struggling with the trauma of change, segments of society can turn away from reality 'in favour of a more comfortable lie' (Specter, 2009). The fear of change is related to denial and is a strong trait in humanity, indeed it is the hallmark of conservatism. Many conservatives just don't trust scientists (and certainly not environmentalists) as they think they are too 'liberal' (and hence suspect). This was the conclusion of one of us (Cook), who developed the website www.skepticalscience.com examining climate change denial arguments. This site concluded that in reality many climate change deniers wouldn't accept the facts as they didn't like the political views held by those advocating action on global warming. As the site noted, one climate change denier stated 'the cheerleaders for doing something about global warming seem to be largely the cheerleaders for many causes of which I disapprove' (Orthodoxnet, 2007). Studies have consistently found conservatism to be negatively related to pro-environmental attitudes, especially among political elites (McCright and Dunlap, 2000).

Conservatives see environmental regulation as threatening core elements of conservatism such as the primacy of individual freedom, private property rights, laissez faire government and promotion of free enterprise (McCright and Dunlap, 2000). A binding treaty and carbon price are seen as a direct threat to sustained economic growth, the free market, national security and sovereignty, and the continued abolition of government regulations – key conservative goals. McCright and Dunlap (2000) show that the conservative movement has three counter-claims regarding global warming. These are first that the evidence is weak or even wrong, second that it would be beneficial if warming occurred, and third that global warming policies would do more harm than good. They point out that conservatives also tend to believe that 'radical environmentalists' are socialists 'who want to take over the world'. Naomi Oreskes and Erik Conway (2010) make a similar observation. James Hoggan (2009) points out that in the US, among highly educated people, 75 per cent of Democrats believe humans are causing climate change but among Republicans the figure is only 19 per cent.

Historically, fear of change probably made sense, as change was often bad news. However, today the change is happening whether we like it or not, due to our actions as a society. There is an irony here, for fear of change should actually make one seek to *solve* the problems causing the change. Professor Garnaut (2008) noted that 'conservatism may in fact require erring on the side of ambitious mitigation'. In other words, those who fear change should become environmental activists working to solve climate change. However, what seems to actually happen is twofold. First is the refusal to believe (= denial) that climate change is happening. Second comes a fear of the *solutions* proposed to the changes happening. So there is fear and denial of renewable energy, changed farming practices, new technology and so on. The solutions are generally dismissed off-handedly as too expensive or impractical. Fear of change is a key cause of denial, and it is perhaps no surprise that the strongest climate change denial is found in the most conservative organizations, some of the most active being right-wing think tanks (McCright and Dunlap, 2000; Monbiot, 2006; Hoggan, 2009; Oreskes and Conway, 2010). Conservatism at its root is about the preservation of established customs, and hence involves a fear of change. 'Laissez faire' politics leads inevitably to little action being taken. If you are afraid of changing society to solve environmental problems, then you would not feel the urgency to take action – in fact you would oppose it.

Failure in Values

Another reason why denial prospers is a failure in values. There is little discussion of ethics or values in modern society. When one of us taught as a casual lecturer at university, he asked students 'Does Nature have intrinsic value – a right to exist for itself, not just for human use?'. One worried student later came and asked, 'Why is it that I have never thought about this, never been asked about this before?' Do humans have the right to make half the world's species extinct? For some this is the stuff of nightmares, but to others it doesn't seem to be of concern. This is likely due to the failure of our society to believe in the *intrinsic value* of nature to exist for itself (Oelschlaeger, 1991; Smith, 1998; Washington, 2006). It is interesting when talking to primary school children (even farmers' children in the Australian bush) that they are horrified when they hear that half of the world's species may go extinct by 2100. Yet somehow their 'sense of wonder' at nature seems to be buried in the transition to the adult, as many adults (at least in Western society) do not show this same concern (Washington, 2002). It is a truism that if you don't know where you are coming from you don't know where you are going. If we don't actually strongly *value* the natural world that is in crisis and threatened (not just by climate change but by many other environmental problems), then we probably won't feel the urgency to save it.

Fixation on Economics and Society

Another reason we fail to act on climate change is to do with our fixation on economics and society. Our society looks firstly to economics and secondarily to social issues. It is resourcist (nature is just a resource), modernist (or sometimes postmodernist), consumerist, utilitarian and anthropocentric (Oelschlaeger, 1991; Washington, 2006). Mike Hulme (2009) suggests that a confident belief in the human ability to control nature is a dominant, if often subliminal, attribute of the international diplomacy that engages climate change. The intelligentsia in our society has mainly focused on social justice. Environmental justice is rarely given equal time or prominence. Under these circumstances it is hard for many people to feel a sense of urgency, as ecological degradation is just not *real* to them. Partly this is due to the fact that our society in the West is now more isolated from the natural world than were preceding generations. People don't spend as much time out in nature and spend less time in 'witness' of nature (Tredinnick, 2003).

Our society is also fixated on growth economics, to the extent that there is rarely any discussion of a future 'steady state' economy (Daly, 1991). Indeed the recent recession has only served to re-embed the idea that our economy must keep growing *forever*. It was pointed out by Edward Abbey (1977) that perpetual growth is the ideology of the cancer cell. There is the question also of arguments of false economic expediency. The UK Stern Review (2006) showed that failing to act on climate change would end up costing us *more* than acting now. Professor Ross Garnaut (2008) of the Garnaut Climate Review argued that:

> Prudent risk management would suggest that it is worth the sacrifice of a significant amount of current income to avoid a small chance of a catastrophic outcome.

Given that climate change action is a key part of reaching sustainability, the fixation on economics is one reason why ecological sustainability has become the critical leg of the sustainability tripod, the one closest to breaking. Yet even in sustainability circles, many do not acknowledge the critical importance of ecological sustainability (Washington, 2009b). If you don't put ecological sustainability first, and instead just focus on economy and society, you are not going to feel a sense of urgency regarding the environmental crisis or the climate change emergency.

Ignorance of Ecology and Exponential Growth

Another key reason why we let denial prosper is our lack of an 'ecological grounding'. Most people don't understand how the world works in terms of ecosystems. They don't understand how energy moves through ecosystems, how minerals are cycled, how ecosystem services maintain the landscapes we take for granted (Ehrlich and Ehrlich, 1981). They do not understand about 'keystone' species (which support many other species), or that ecosystems under pressure can collapse and flip to a less productive state, one humans don't like (MA, 2005). Nor do they comprehend the enormity of the looming extinction crisis, where (without action) half the world's species may be extinct by the end of this century (Wilson, 2003). They don't understand how massive extinctions may cripple ecosystems, nor do some of them seem to worry about the crucial ethical questions about what human impacts are doing to the world. The ecological grounding of our society has improved over the last 30 years, but many decision-makers are still woefully ignorant. Some of them still think environmental issues are just about 'tree hugging'. For this reason they feel no urgency to act on environmental issues such as the climate emergency.

Another reason why people don't feel an urgency to act is our inability to really understand exponential growth (Brown, 1978). Part of the urgency of the environmental crisis is that there are so many environmental problems escalating at exponential rates, yet humans generally do not think exponentially. This is highlighted by the French riddle about a water lily in a pond, where the lilies double in size every day. On the 30th day the pond is full, so when is it half full? When asked, many people reply 'the 15th day', when of course the answer is the 29th day (Brown, 1978). Many environmental problems are getting worse exponentially. In regard to climate change, a growing population means increased energy use, exacerbated by increased energy demand per person in developing countries. An exponentially increasing rate of non-renewable energy use is very bad news for climate change. Failure to understand exponential growth means a failure to act urgently on environmental problems and aids denial.

Gambling on the Future

Another aspect that delays us taking action is gambling on the future. Many of us are gamblers at heart. Some people are willing to accept a staggeringly high percentage of risk. For instance, one can put forward the scenario of no policy action on climate change where there is a 50:50 chance that the world will warm five degrees celsius or more (MIT, 2010) and the Earth could go into runaway climate change. Some people, however, are not concerned. The reason they are happy to accept these odds is because there is a 50 per cent chance that the Earth might not. That 50 per cent chance was what they were happy to gamble on. Climatologist Professor Stephen Schneider (2009) has noted that the public does not understand probability, whereas scientists do. This is a serious problem, for some people are happy to gamble on their children's and the planet's future. Schneider asked who in the room had fire insurance and everyone put up their hand. He then said that the risk of your house burning down was far less than the risks inherent with climate change. If people were willing to act on the risk of fire, then why were they not willing to act on climate change risk? Hulme (2009) points out that scientists and campaigners get frustrated as the public does not seem to respond to their scientific assessment of risk. As a result risk communicators tend to 'shout louder', and the public is faced with an increasingly distraught alarm call. This in itself can turn some people off, as they respond negatively to perceived 'alarmist' statements (whether they are true or not). However, if you are a gambler, then you don't feel the sense of urgency, as you will always be gambling that things will turn out fine – or, as we say in Australia, 'she'll be right, mate!'.

The Media

Another aspect that assists denial is the media. First, the media has poorly communicated the reason why climate is warming. Hoggan (2009) explains that in Canada in 2006 the majority of people blamed global warming on the ozone hole. Clearly the media has failed to educate the public on the causes of climate change. James Hansen (2009) notes that 'scientific reticence' may hinder communication with the public. Scientists may be more worried about being accused of 'crying wolf' than they are about being accused of 'fiddling while Rome burns'. To put it another way, scientists are in a double-bind, for the demands of objectivity suggest that they should keep aloof from contested issues, but if they do then the public will not know what an objective view looks like (Oreskes and Conway, 2010). Hansen (2009) asks whether future generations might not wonder how we could have been so stupid and do nothing today. He suggests that this accusation would include scientists who did not adequately communicate the danger.

Second, the media loves controversy and will seek to provoke argument. This is often justified as being 'balanced' reporting, when in fact it shows major bias. A situation where the judgement of the vast majority of the scientific community is given equal space with denial advocates is anything but 'balanced'. In fact 'balance' has become a form of bias in favour of extreme minority views (Oreskes and Conway, 2010). If one examines the newspapers, one could be forgiven for thinking that science is split evenly about whether human-caused climate change is real, rather than 97.5 per cent of climate scientists saying this. The reason is that controversy sells papers and raises TV ratings. Maxwell and Jules Boykoff (2004) analysed four US papers between 1998 and 2005. They found that while scientific papers in peer-reviewed journals came down 928 to 0 (Oreskes, 2004) in accepting climate change, 53 per cent of stories about climate change in the US prestige press gave equal coverage to views that it was due to humans or was natural. Boykoff and Boykoff (2004) describe this as 'balance as bias'. Hoggan (2009) also notes that often people from greenscam organizations (or think tanks) will be invited to write articles in newspapers, without acknowledging their organizations' links and funding (often from Exxon). They are frequently presented as 'independent' scientists, when in fact often they are either not scientists or come with a strong bias.

It seems today that any factually wrong and one-sided article can be published by papers in the name of 'freedom of speech' and putting forward all sides of an issue. However, journalists are not meant to be proponents of just one side of a debate, they are meant to put both sides and to also check their sources. Some journalists will baldly deny climate change exists and claim either that the world is not warming or that it has nothing to do with humans. They will happily quote denial anti-science put forward by the greenscam organizations we met earlier, and are fervent in describing mainstream peer-reviewed science as 'junk science'. They will also latch on to whatever seems to bolster their denial argument, no matter how slender the evidence or ridiculous the argument.

In 2007 the purported results of an 'important new scientific paper' were reported on the internet. It claimed that under-sea bacteria were responsible for the build up of CO_2 in the atmosphere. Within hours this supposed study was reported on denial blogs and circulating around the world as evidence to show that humanity did not cause climate change. Of course it was a hoax, one created by journalist David Thorpe (see Hulme, 2009). Thorpe did this to show that some people will use anything that supports their argument, whether it's true or not and whether they had checked up on it or not. Hoggan (2009) argues that it is past time for the media to check their facts and start sharing them 'ethically, and responsibly, with a public that is hungry for the truth'. Hulme (2009) notes that rather than there just being facts about climate change, the circuitry of the media offers spaces for people to 'filter, amplify and rhetoricize these "facts" in multiple ways'. Newspapers frame climate change risk 'through each newspaper's preferred ideological world-view' (Carvalho and Burgess, 2005). For example, six different climate change 'frames' have been identified as being used by the media, such as the 'scientific uncertainty' frame, the 'national security' frame and the 'catastrophe' frame (Shanahan, 2007). Hence no message about climate change is 'neutral', as certain aspects are emphasized over other aspects, while others are down-played or ignored. These factors in the media make it easier for people to deny climate change, or at least ignore it. In fact, Oreskes and Conway (2010) argue that in the US 'this divergence between the state of the science and how it was presented in the major media helped make it easy for our government to do nothing about global warming'.

Despair, Apathy and Confusion

Another trait in humanity that delays action is despair. The opposite of being in denial can sometimes lead to despair. People who understand the scale of the environmental crisis can see the problems in detail, but often not the solutions. There is so much negative data out there about environmental problems that it is easy to become overwhelmed – and hope is a casualty. It is certainly an occupational hazard for environmentalists, and Joanna Macy (1996) has written eloquently about seeking to counteract environmental despair and grief. The key problem with despair is that you don't in fact take action, you do nothing as you have given up hope. In some ways those in despair do *believe* in the urgency of solving the environmental crisis, it's just they do nothing to actually solve it.

Other common problems that delay action are apathy and confusion. Often when discussing environmental problems, one hears 'yeah, I know'. Some even have commented that they are 'so over that'. They are just apathetic. Partly this is from confusion, as there is so much information out there and they don't know what to believe (in part due to the denial industry). Partly it is apathy stemming from the belief that what they do cannot 'make a difference', and this is common in young people. Many blame governments and business without acknowledging the role their own lack of action takes in perpetuating the problems. Mostly, of course, this is an excuse not to spend the energy and make the effort. Those who are apathetic often know there is a problem, but they don't feel the urgency as they just switch off. Thus they let denial prosper.

Denial within Our Governments

Let us then turn from problems within society in general that assist denial, and consider the denial within our governments. Philosopher Erich Fromm (1976) provides a classic quote in regard to why action is not taken by governments:

> The almost unbelievable fact is that no serious effort is made to avert what looks like a final decree of fate. While in our private life nobody except a mad person would remain passive in view of a threat to his total existence, those who are in charge of public affairs do practically nothing, and those who have entrusted their fate to them let them continue to do nothing. How is it possible that the strongest of all instincts, that for survival, seems to have ceased to motivate us? One of the most obvious explanations is that the leaders undertake many actions that make it possible for them to *pretend* they are doing something effective to avoid a catastrophe: endless conferences, resolutions, disarmament talks, all give the impression that the problems are recognized and something is being done to resolve them. Yet nothing of real importance happens; but both the leaders and the led anaesthetize their consciences and their wish for survival by giving the appearance of knowing the road and marching in the right direction. (emphasis added)

Note that Fromm is careful to say 'both the leaders and the led', so it is not just a problem with our governments, but also a problem with the public also – as we let our governments get away with denial. However, the truth in the above lies partly in the nature of liberal democracies. To take strong action on any problem will mean upsetting somebody, sometimes a lot of somebodies. If a government was to take strong action on an environmental issue – which might slow the economy or cost jobs – it may well be voted out of office. Liberal democracies by their nature tend to work on the long to medium timescale, as to take rapid and strong action may mean political suicide. Being politically ethical and sticking to your principles may thus also mean being out of government. The problem has been that we did not take action 20 or 30 years ago when it could have required only moderate action to solve these problems. Now we are faced with far more serious problems that need more serious solutions.

It has been argued that the combination of libertarian individualism, the hegemony of the market and the unchallenged pre-eminence of liberal democratic ideology makes it impossible to drive forward the political, economic and social reforms needed to respond to climate change (Hulme, 2009). Clive Hamilton (2010) argues that our political institutions are 'too slow, too compromised and too dominated by old thinking to mandate the energy revolutions we must have to guarantee our survival'. When one realizes that acting from a sense of urgency may throw one out of government, one can start to appreciate why many governments slip into denial about climate change. Instead, one often hears of what is 'politically feasible', as if nature will change the laws of physics to meet the desires of the political spin-doctors. Hoggan (2009) makes the point that confusion and denial have a big impact on politics. Seventy per cent of Americans think climate is changing but only 50 per cent believe humans are the cause. This is just not enough politically – 'no one is going to get elected by promising to solve a problem that half the people don't even acknowledge' (Hoggan, 2009). George Monbiot (2006) has also independently come to a conclusion as to why the public and governments *pretend* to take action. Monbiot believes that when people start to realize how serious the science is, their response will be:

> To demand that the government acts, while hoping that it doesn't. We will wish our governments to pretend to act. We get the moral satisfaction of saying what we know to be right, without the discomfort of doing it. My fear is that the political parties in most rich nations have already recognized this. They know that we want tough targets, but that we also want those targets to be missed. They know that we will grumble about their failure to curb climate change, but that we will not take to the streets. They know that nobody ever rioted for austerity.

Monbiot concludes that it reinforces his belief that we have to make the necessary changes 'as painless as possible'. Hansen (2009) refers to 'government greenwash' as the vast disparity between government words and reality. Politicians talk about environmentalism, but their actions are inconsistent with the talk. He feels that politicians are happy if scientists provide information 'and then go away and shut up'. Politicians adopt policies that are convenient, even if not scientifically grounded in terms of what is needed. Hansen (2009) believes the biggest obstacle to solving global warming is the role of money in politics, and the undue sway of special interests. He notes that President Obama and his advisors believe in compromise, but that unfortunately nature and the laws of physics cannot compromise – they are what they are. David Spratt and Philip Sutton (2008) note that we have to break from the 'politics of failure-inducing compromise'. McCright and Dunlap (2010) note that political decisions develop a 'mobilization of bias', where some issues are excluded. The political rules of the game operate to the benefit of some groups at the expense of others. 'Non-decision-making' occurs, where any challenges to the system are suppressed or thwarted. Most political systems currently show a 'mobilization of bias' against climate change action.

Psychological Types of Denial

It has been suggested that the main problem with denial is that information is the limiting factor in public non-response to this issue, an approach that has been characterized as the 'information deficit model' (Bulkeley, 2000; Norgaard, 2003). Climate change is a complex issue and difficult to understand, so people get confused and do not act. For example, in his comparative study of six nations, Dunlap (1998) found the public to be 'poorly informed about global warming'. Effective public response is limited because the layperson's mental models of global climate change suffer from several basic misconceptions (Stern, 1992; Bell, 1994; Bostrom et al, 1994; Dunlap, 1998). Psychologists have described the power of 'faulty' decision-making powers such as 'confirmation bias' (Halford and Sheehan, 1991). Researchers have also asserted that part of the difficulty is that knowledge of global warming requires a complex grasp of scientific knowledge in many fields (Johansen, 2002). Confusion about the issue is clearly one factor in denial.

In a fascinating study in Norway (Norgaard, 2003, 2006a and 2006b) on climate change denial, sociologist Kari Norgaard (2003) asks:

> The public may lack information, but is this fact the limiting factor behind greater public interest, concern or political participation?

Daniel Read et al (1994) have pointed out that only two simple facts are critical to understanding climate change. First, if significant global warming is occurring it is primarily the result of an increase in the concentration of CO_2 in the Earth's atmosphere. Second, the single most important source of CO_2 addition to the Earth's atmosphere is human use of fossil fuels. At the deepest level, large-scale environmental problems such as climate change threaten individual and community senses of *continuity of life*, which has been called 'ontological security'. This is the 'confidence that most human beings have in the continuity of their self-identity and the constancy of the surrounding social and material environments of action' (Giddens, 1991). As Norgaard (2003) notes, 'People work hard to verify and maintain the self-concepts or identities they already hold, and do not easily change them.' Global warming was difficult to think about because it was threatening to the individual and collective sense of identity, raising questions about whether people were really 'good', and disrupted the collective sense of identity as to who they were.

Stanley Cohen (2001) describes three varieties of denial:

1 **Literal denial** – the assertion that something did not happen or is not true. With respect to the issue of global warming, this form of denial is akin to the generation of counter-claims by oil companies that climate change is not happening (Gelbspan, 1997; McCright and Dunlap, 2000).

2 **Interpretive denial** – in which the facts themselves are not denied, but they are given a different interpretation. Euphemisms, technical jargon and word-changing are used to dispute the meanings of events – for example, military generals speak of 'collateral damage' rather than the killing of citizens. Interpretive denial is what we commonly call 'spin'.

3 **Implicatory denial** – where what is denied are 'the psychological, political or moral implications. ... Unlike literal or interpretive denial, knowledge itself is not at issue, but doing the "right" thing with the knowledge' (Cohen, 2001). This is not negation of information about climate change per se, rather a failure to incorporate this knowledge into everyday life or transform it into social action. People have access to information, accept this information as true, yet for a variety of reasons *choose to ignore it* (Norgaard, 2006a and 2006b).

These three types of denial are useful when considering the broad range of denial around climate change. The first, literal denial, is a key topic of this book, being the arguments of the climate deniers and the denial industry. However, the second type, interpretive denial, is generally what we see from government and business. This is what Fromm (1976) described as the way governments make lots of speeches but in fact do little. This seems to be what has happened so often about climate change, most recently at the COP15 conference in Copenhagen.

The third type of denial, implicatory denial, is the type of denial most common in the public. We can all fall prey to implicatory denial. Implicatory denial is about bridging the moral and psychic gap between what you know and what you do (Cohen, 2001). Much of the knowledge about climate change is accepted but fails to be *converted into action*. We are vaguely aware of choosing not to look at the facts, but not quite conscious of just what it is we are evading (Cohen, 2001). The people in Norway believed in climate change, expressed concern about it, yet lived their lives as though they did not know (Norgaard,

2003). Indeed for those interviewed, paying serious attention to climate change raised fears of the future, fears about the government's ability to adequately respond. It was an issue that many people preferred to avoid: 'We don't really want to know'. In the words of one person who held his hands in front of his eyes as he spoke, 'people want to protect themselves a bit'. They had feelings of helplessness and feelings of guilt, and also their self-image of Norwegians as 'close to nature' was in conflict with them being a major greenhouse gas emitter, due to the North Sea oilfields (Norgaard, 2006a and 2006b).

'Distraction' is also an everyday form of denial. If we are worried about something we tend to 'switch off' about the information and shift our attention to something else. We can also tend to 'de-problematize' it by rationalizing that 'humanity has solved these sort of problems before' (Hamilton, 2010). We can also 'distance ourselves' from the problem by rationalizing that 'it's a long way off'. There is also 'hairy-chested denial', where people deny climate change as it will impact on pleasures such as big fast cars (Hamilton, 2010). Blame-shifting is another part of implicatory denial, where we shift the blame onto others, such as the US, China, captains of industry or developing countries.

Implicatory denial is related to questions of social movement non-participation. Why is involvement in environmental groups actually *declining*, along with involvement in community groups in general (Putnam, 2000)? There is an irony in that at a time of deepening political and social fragmentation, climate change is demanding coordinated planetary-scale governance and management (Hulme, 2009). Since members of the community in Norway did know about global warming but did not integrate this knowledge into everyday life, they experienced what has been called a state of 'double reality' (Kellstedt et al, 2008). In one reality was the collectively constructed sense of normal everyday life. In the other reality existed the troubling knowledge of increasing impacts of climate change (Norgaard, 2006a and 2006b). In the words of Kjersti, a Norwegian teacher: 'We live in one way and we think in another. We learn to think in parallel. It's a skill, an art of living.' (Norgaard, 2003).

Cohen (2001) notes:

> We are vaguely aware of choosing not to look at the facts, but not quite conscious of just what it is that we are evading. We know, but at the same time we don't know.

Not knowing certain things can be strategic (Norgaard, 2006a and 2006b). To 'not know' too much about climate change maintains the notion of the innocence of those involved and the sense that if one did know one would have acted more responsibly. In 2004 a large survey of American citizens was carried out regarding climate change. They found that 'more scientifically informed' respondents not only felt less personally responsible for global warming, but also showed less concern about it (Kellstedt et al, 2008). The 'information deficit model' is thus inadequate to understand how people respond to scientific controversies. Much more is involved in people's personal denial.

Because emotions, beliefs, identities and 'cultures of talk' are all themselves socially organized, individual denial is socially organized (Zerubavel, 1997 and 2002). To the extent that individual acts of denial stem from contradictions between political economic reality and social values, denial is a product of material reality. Norgaard (2003) found that her denial study agreed with the work of Eviatar Zerubavel (2002), who outlined the social dimension of 'ignoring' as the sociology of denial, where many people in society take part in co-denial. She noted that denial involves self-censoring or 'knowing what not to know'. Denial is the elephant in the room that we don't see. By avoiding it we thus do nothing to solve the problems it represents. Zerubavel (2006) notes:

> 'Elephants' rarely go away just because we pretend not to notice them. Although 'everyone hopes that if we pretend not to acknowledge their existence, maybe they will go away', even the proverbial ostrich that sticks its head in the sand does not really make problems disappear by simply wishing them away. Fundamentally delusional, denial may help keep us unaware of unpleasant things around us but it cannot ever actually make them go away.

The reason it is so difficult to talk about the elephant in the room is that 'not only does no one want to listen, but no one wants to talk about not listening' (Zerubavel, 2006). We thus deny our denial. This is a particular form of self-deception made famous by George Orwell (1949) in his novel *Nineteen Eighty Four* as 'double-thinking'. Zerubavel (2006) notes that silence like a cancer grows over time, so that a society can collectively ignore 'its leaders' incompetence, glaring atrocities and impending environmental disasters'. The silence now is not that we don't 'talk' about climate change, but that *we deny our denial of it*. Zerubavel (2006) notes that the longer we pretend not to notice the elephants, the larger they loom in our minds. However, one can break the silence of denial, and our strong need to deny things is counter-balanced by our equally strong need to expose denial. This desire to expose and confront denial is indeed the driving force behind the writing of this book. As soon as we acknowledge the elephant, it starts to shrink. One of us can remember speaking to a room of councillors in local government about the environmental crisis, only to have someone say, 'What environmental crisis? It's news to me!'. Thankfully a number of people in the room muttered, 'Where have you been for the last 30 years?'. Zerubavel (2006) explains that breaking conspiracies of silence implies foregrounding the elephant in the room and 'calling a spade a spade'. Zerubavel notes that denial can have its own tipping point where 'increasing social pressure on the remaining conspirators to also acknowledge the elephant's presence eventually overrides the social pressure to keep denying it'. This is one tipping point we do need, to get society to acknowledge its denial about climate change.

Norgaard (2006a and 2006b) concludes that denial of the issue of climate change serves not only to manage negative emotions and preserve our sense of self-identity, but to maintain global economic interests and perpetuate global environmental inequalities. This of course is not limited to Norway, it is relevant to the whole world. Australia is the world's biggest exporter of coal and also the world's biggest emitter of CO_2 per person (Diesendorf, 2009). It is thus easier for many of us to slip into implicatory denial, rather than face the need for change. Hamilton (2010) argues that many of us have constructed a personal identity through shopping and consumerism. Erik Assadourian (2010) shows that the consumer ethic, seen as 'natural' by consumers, is actually a cultural teaching. Thus asking such people to change their consumerism is like asking them to change their identity. William Rees (2008) argues that in times of stress the brain's 'reptilian brain stem' will override the rational cortex. Thus our dedication to growth comes from these survival instincts. However, if we are to survive today, Rees concludes we must assert our capacity for 'consciousness, reasoned deliberation and willpower' to 're-write the "myths we live by" and articulate the necessary conditions for sustainability'. The latest State of the World Report examines our addiction to consumerism, noting that consumer cultures exaggerate the forces that have allowed human societies to outgrow their environmental support systems (Assadourian, 2010).

There is a complexity to the question around why we let denial prosper. Hulme (2009) does not use the word 'denial', as he seeks to see all sides of the climate change issue as competing narratives in what seems to be a post-modernist framework. He makes a distinction between climate change the 'scientific process' (which he accepts) and Climate Change the 'idea', which has many narratives and 'myths' constructed around it. Hulme notes that the climate change controversy is allegedly about science, but that often such disputes are a proxy for 'deeper conflicts between alternative visions of the future'. In this way climate change is altering our physical world but the idea of Climate Change is altering our social worlds. Hulme refers to a view of climate change 'as a manifestation of a free market, consumption-driven, capitalist economy'. He came to see that Climate Change (the idea) meant different things to different people and that the idea was appropriated in support of many different causes. People had different views about climate change because of the things they valued, different expectations about what science can or should tell us, the things they believed, the things they feared, how they understood risk, what they felt about 'progress' or sustainability, and how they thought the world should be governed. Hulme (2009) notes that climate change violates fundamental principles of sustainable development, intergenerational stewardship and fairness, and therefore violates the inalienable rights of future generations. Economist Michael Toman (2006) argues that improved scientific and economic understanding about climate change can 'mask deeper and more complex disagreements about social values. Neither science in general nor economics in particular can resolve the fundamentally moral issues posed by climate change.'

A major study of public views on climate change in the US found that the perception of climate risks goes well beyond basic issues of scientific literacy, analytical reasoning and technical knowledge. Risk perception and policy preferences are strongly influenced by cultural and personal factors, and both individual and social psychology are at work in public risk perceptions of climate change (BBC, 2007). As Hulme (2009) notes, 'When scientific assessments clash with deeply held values or outlooks, it may not always be science that triumphs.'

A critical question arises from the comments on politics by both Fromm (1976) and Monbiot (2006). This is whether the public is going to be passive and let them get away with it. Where are the marches of the magnitude of the protest around the Vietnam War? We do not seem to see today mass rallies about climate change of the size that occurred in the '70s and '80s on other issues. Despite the excellent youth groups and actions happening around the world (for example www.350.org), we still have a long way to go to push our politicians into strong action. This section started by asking 'Do we let denial prosper?'. The answer is clearly '*Yes we do!*'. We let it prosper at various levels. We let it prosper by ignoring the majority of climate scientists and listening to climate change deniers. We let it prosper in our governments by letting them get away with procrastination and endless speeches that don't lead to action. This is the process that led to Copenhagen and its failure to take strong action. We also let it prosper *within ourselves*, through a sort of self-interested sloth. We like flying around the world, big cars, air-conditioning in summer, big houses and so on. We in the West have become used to living like princes and princesses. We have experienced in the West prosperity unmatched in human history and feasted to our heart's content. But the lunch was not free (Oreskes and Conway, 2010). It is so much easier to give lip service to the need for climate change action without actually changing our lives. In fact one report noted that a Greenpeace activist flew around the world to go diving for his holidays. Another scientist from the Antarctic Survey flew long distances for skiing holidays 'because my job is stressful' (Realclimate, 2009). One of us (Washington) also worked as a Director of Sustainability in local government. One staff member was a keen environmentalist who was deeply concerned about climate change, yet she commonly flew overseas for her holidays (without buying carbon offsets). Her answer when asked about this was to reply, 'But everyone does it!'. Denial can thus operate within even the most environmentally aware.

Given that psychologists and sociologists talk about a 'double reality', we urgently need a reality check – and even an ethics check. Do you or I have a responsibility to the future, whether it be to our children and relatives, the whole of humanity, or the whole of nature itself? If we do, then we may need to make small sacrifices and change the way we live. Unlike what the deniers claim, however, climate change action will not mean going to live in caves and dress in skins. Nor will it mean a drastic drop in the *real* quality of life. We waste so much in our society, both energy and materials. So a denial reality check would not cause our lives to come crashing down around our ears. Rather it would be a self-awakening to live responsibly on the Earth.

References

Abbey, E. (1977) *The Journey Home*, Dutton, New York

Assadourian, E. (2010) 'The rise and fall of consumer cultures', in L. Starke and L. Mastny (eds) *2010 State of the World: Transforming Cultures from Consumerism to Sustainability*, Earthscan, London

BBC (2007) 'Most ready for "green sacrifices"', *BBC World Service* survey on climate change attitudes, 9 November, see http://news.bbc.co.uk/2/hi/7075759.stm, accessed 11 April 2009

Bell, A. (1994) 'Climate of opinion: Public and media discourse on the global environment', *Discourse and Society*, vol 5, no 1, pp33–64

Bostrom, A., Morgan, M., Fischhoff, B. and Read, D. (1994) 'What do people know about global climate change? I. Mental models', *Risk Analysis*, vol 14, no 6, pp959–970

Boykoff, M. and Boykoff, J. (2004) 'Balance as bias: Global warming as the US prestige press', *Global Environmental Change*, vol 14, pp125–136

Brown, L. (1978) *The 29th Day*, Norton and Co, Washington, DC

Bulkeley, H. (2000) 'Common knowledge? Public understanding of climate change in Newcastle, Australia', *Understanding of Science*, vol 9, pp313–333

Carvalho, A. and Burgess, J. (2005) 'Cultural circuits of climate change in the UK broadsheet papers, 1985–2003', *Risk Analysis*, vol 25, no 6, pp1457–1470

Cohen, S. (2001) *States of Denial: Knowing About Atrocities and Suffering*, Polity Press, New York

Daly, H. (1991) *Steady-State Economics: Second Edition with New Essays*, Island Press, Washington, DC

Diesendorf, M. (2009) *Climate Action: A Campaign Manual for Greenhouse Solutions*, UNSW Press, Sydney, Australia

Dunlap, R. (1998) 'Lay perceptions of global risk: Public views of global warming in cross national context', *International Sociology*, vol 13, no 4, pp473–498

Ehrlich, P. and Ehrlich, A. (1981) *Extinction: The Causes and Consequences of the Disappearance of Species*, Random House, New York

Fromm, E. (1976) *To Have or to Be*, Abacus Books, New York

Garnaut, R. (2008) *The Garnaut Climate Change Review*, Garnaut Review Australia, www.garnautreview.org.au/domino/Web_Notes/Garnaut/garnautweb.html

Gelbspan, R. (1997) *The Heat is On: The High Stakes Battle Over Earth's Threatened Climate*, Addison-Wesley Publishing Company, Reading, MA

Giddens, A. (1991) *Modernity and Self Identity. Self and Society in the Late Modern Age*, Polity Press, Cambridge, UK

Halford, G. and Sheehan, P. (1991) 'Human responses to environmental changes', *International Journal of Psychology*, vol 269, no 5, pp599–611

Hamilton, C. (2010) *Requiem for a Species: Why We Resist the Truth about Climate Change*, Allen and Unwin, Sydney, Australia

Hansen, J. (2009) *Storms of My Grandchildren: The Truth about the Coming Climate Catastrophe and Our Last Chance to Save Humanity*, Bloomsbury, London

Hoggan, J. (2009) *Climate Cover Up: The Crusade to Deny Global Warming*, Greystone Books, Vancouver, Canada

Hulme, M. (2009) *Why We Disagree about Climate Change: Understanding Controversy, Inaction and Opportunity*, Cambridge University Press, Cambridge, UK

Johansen, B. (2002) *The Global Warming Desk Reference*, Greenwood Press, Westport, CT

Kellstedt, P., Zahran, S. and Vedlitz, A. (2008) 'Personal efficacy, the information environment, and attitudes towards global warming and climate change in the United States', *Risk Analysis*, vol 28, no 1, pp113–126

MA (2005) *Living Beyond Our Means: Natural Assets and Human Well-being*, Statement of the MA Board, available at www.maweb.org

Macy, J. (1996) *World as Lover, World as Self*, Parallax Press, Berkeley, CA

McCright, A. and Dunlap, R. (2000) 'Challenging global warming as a social problem: An analysis of the conservative movement's counter-claims', *Social Problems*, vol 47, no 4, pp499–522

McCright, A. and Dunlap, R. (2010) 'Anti-reflexivity: The American conservative movement's success in undermining climate science and policy', *Theory, Culture and Society*, vol 27, nos 2–3, pp100–133

MIT (2010) 'The Greenhouse Gamble', http://globalchange.mit.edu/resources/gamble from Massachusetts Institute of Technology

Monbiot, G. (2006) *Heat: How to Stop the Planet Burning*, Penguin Books, London

Norgaard, K. (2003) 'Denial, privilege and global environmental justice: The case of global climate change', paper presented at the annual meeting of the American Sociological Association, Atlanta Hilton Hotel, Atlanta, GA, available from www.allacademic.com

Norgaard, K. (2006a) '"People want to protect themselves a little bit": Emotions, denial and social movement nonparticipation', *Sociological Inquiry*, vol 76, no 3, pp372–396

Norgaard, K. (2006b) '"We don't really want to know"', *Organisation and Environment*, vol 19, no 3, pp347–370

Oelschlaeger, M. (1991) *The Idea of Wilderness: From Prehistory to the Age of Ecology*, Yale University Press, New Haven, CT/London

Oreskes, N. (2004) 'The scientific consensus on climate change', *Science*, vol 306, p1686

Oreskes, N. and Conway, E. M. (2010) *Merchants of Doubt: How a Handful of Scientists Obscured the Truth on Issues from Tobacco Smoke to Global Warming*, Bloomsbury Press, New York

Orthodoxnet (2007) Post 14 by 'Augie' on 10 June at Orthodoxnet website, see www.orthodoxytoday.org/blog/2007/06/03/they-call-this-a-consensus/#comment-95231

Orwell, G. (1949) *Nineteen Eighty Four*, Secker and Warburg, London

Putnam, R. (2000) *Bowling Alone: The Collapse and Revival of American Community*, Simon and Schuster, New York

Read, D., Bostrom, A., Morgan, M., Fischhoff, B. and Smuts, T. (1994) 'What do people know about global climate change? II Survey studies of educated lay people', *Risk Analysis*, vol 14, pp971–982

Realclimate (2009) http://climatedenial.org/2009/07/24/why-we-still-dont-believe-in-climate-change/

Rees, W. (2008) 'Toward sustainability with justice: Are human nature and history on side?', Chapter 6 in C. Soskolne (ed) *Sustaining Life on Earth: Environmental and Human Health through Global Governance*, Lexington Books, New York

Schneider, S. (2009) 'Mitigation and adaptation to climate change', Powerpoint presentation at UNSW Institute of Environmental Studies (IES) Seminar, 16 March

Shanahan, M. (2007) 'Talking about a revolution: Climate change and the media', COP13 Briefing and Opinion Papers, IIED, London

Smith, M. (1998) *Ecologism: Towards Ecological Citizenship*, Open University Press, Buckingham, UK

Specter, M. (2009) *Denialism: How Irrational Thinking Hinders Scientific Progress,*

Harms the Planet and Threatens Our Lives, Penguin Press, New York

Spratt, D. and Sutton, P. (2008) *Climate Code Red: the Case for Emergency Action*, Scribe Publishing, Melbourne, Australia

Stern, N. (2006) *The Economics of Climate Change* (Stern Review), Cambridge University Press, Cambridge, UK

Stern, P. (1992) 'Psychological dimensions of global environmental change', *Annual Review of Psychology*, vol 43, pp269–302

Toman, M. (2006) 'Values in the economics of climate change', *Environmental Values*, vol 15, pp365–379

Tredinnick, M. (2003) *Writing the Wild: Place, Prose and the Ecological Imagination*, PhD thesis, University of Western Sydney, Richmond, Australia

Washington, H. (2002) *A Sense of Wonder*, Nullo Books, Sydney, Australia

Washington, H. (2006) *The Wilderness Knot*, PhD thesis, University of Western Sydney, Richmond, Australia

Washington, H. (2009a) 'Sustainability – The failure in urgency', *Journal of Sustainability*, vol 2, no 3 (e-journal), 15 September, http://journalofsustainability.com/lifetype/index.php?op=ViewArticle&articleId=66&blogId=1

Washington, H. (2009b) 'Embedding "sustainability" in an Australian Council', *Journal of Sustainability*, vol 2, no 2 (e.journal), 1 August, http://journalofsustainability.com/lifetype/index.php?op=ViewArticle&articleId=63&blogId=1

Wilson, E. O. (2003) *The Future of Life,* Vintage Books, New York

Zerubavel, E. (1997) *Social Mindscapes: An Invitation to Cognitive Sociology*, Harvard University Press, Cambridge, MA

Zerubavel, E. (2002) 'The elephant in the room: Notes on the social organization of denial', in K. Cerulo (ed) *Culture in Mind: Toward a Sociology of Culture and Cognition*, Routledge, New York

Zerubavel, E. (2006) *The Elephant in the Room: Silence and Denial in Everyday Life*, Oxford University Press, New York

6

Rolling Back Denial:
The Big Picture

We are confronted with the fierce urgency of now. In this unfolding conundrum of life and history there is such a thing as being too late. ... We may cry out desperately for time to pause in her passage but time is deaf to every plea and rushes on. Over the bleached bones and jumbled residues of numerous civilizations are written the pathetic words: Too late. (Martin Luther King, 1968, quoted in Pittock, 2009)

Because We Let It

These words by Martin Luther King were not written about climate change, but they are true for it nevertheless. There is a real urgency to climate change, and time is rushing by as we fail to recognize and act on this urgency (Spratt and Sutton, 2008; Pittock, 2009). Denial is one of the key things holding back solutions. So how do we roll back denial about climate change – or indeed about the environmental crisis in general?

Well the simple answer is 'Accept reality!'. It has been noted by Nobel Prize-winner Richard Feynman that 'reality must take precedence over public relations, for nature cannot be fooled' (Pittock, 2009). This chapter will focus on the big picture of how we roll back denial. This chapter was started during the Copenhagen COP15 conference in December 2009. If any event is likely to focus the mind on denial, this one was. How did humanity get itself in such a fix? Climate change is, in one way, just a symptom of the denial of the overall environmental crisis. It is not the only environmental issue that needs solutions. Overpopulation, land degradation, biodiversity loss, simplification of eco-systems, overharvesting of forests, pollution, overfishing – they are all serious problems that need solutions (Washington, 1991). But climate change is something of an over-arching problem and exacerbates many of the others (such as biodiversity loss and land degradation). Climate change is thus not the only issue that needs to be solved on the path to a sustainable future, but it is arguably the *key* one for which the solutions need to be put in place immediately.

We originally thought this chapter would focus on the 'literal denial' of the denial industry, as this has been a key focus of this book, as it has been for other books on this issue (for example Monbiot, 2006; Hoggan, 2009). Literal denial is a huge problem. There is a denial industry funded by fossil fuel companies to the tune of tens of millions of dollars. Indeed the denial industry on climate change has worked incredibly well for the fossil fuel lobby. The denial statements made are not supported by the most comprehensive scientific study ever carried out by humanity – the work of the IPCC (Houghton, 2008; Pittock, 2009). In fact deniers state that the IPCC's output is both non-scientific and a fraud perpetuated by Marxist sympathisers. This seems to be on the principle that if you are going to tell a lie, then tell a big one. Thus the deniers seek to deny everything in the comprehensive IPCC assessments. The denial statements repeated endlessly in the media are not supported by the vast majority (97.5 per cent) of actual *practising* climate scientists around the world (Doran and Zimmerman, 2009). Of the 1000 to 2000 peer-reviewed mainstream science papers on climate change published each year, none seriously contradict the IPCC (Karoly, 2009). Climate change denial is not supported by a single academy of science. To some extent the science is 'basic', as noted by Nicholas Stern (of the Stern Review, 2006) at COP15. We know that the CO_2 level is increasing, we know it is coming from fossil fuels being burned by humans and we know CO_2 is a greenhouse gas. This means there is an energy imbalance in the atmosphere. Where does that energy go? It stays in the atmosphere and heats our world. It may not heat it uniformly in a nice straight line (for water and air are chaotic systems), but the energy is here and temperatures will continue to rise until the energy imbalance is fixed.

And yet the seed of confusion and denial has been sown and has sadly reaped a bumper crop. The denial industry has been responsible for two decades of prevarication and inaction on climate change. It is still hard at work, seeking to stop or slow effective action. It was there at Copenhagen,` seeking to push denial. Our governments have also prevaricated, created committees, held conferences, made promises, but 'nothing of real importance happens' (Fromm, 1976). The urgency to act has been acknowledged and promoted, but enlightenment has not arrived (Hulme, 2009). Greenhouse gases emissions have gone up 16 per cent in the decade since the Kyoto Protocol was first negotiated. One argument is that climate change has become the 'mother of all problems', and attached to itself many other environmental problems such as energy, poverty, food security, hyper-consumption, tropical deforestation and biodiversity loss. This can be seen as creating a log-jam that is 'not only insoluble, but one that is perhaps beyond our comprehension' (Hulme, 2009). However, we do not agree with this appraisal. No problem is unsolvable – just complex and difficult.

So the denial industry has been incredibly successful, and we are sure Exxon considers its $20 million annual funding of greenscam denial groups a fantastic investment. But why? Why was it so effective? Why did it so effectively sow confusion? *Because we let it.*

The fossil fuel industry has much to answer for in seeking to confuse the public in order to continue to reap massive profits. Governments have much to answer for too – 20 years of interpretive denial, of pretending to know the path and marching in the right direction, when in fact they did almost nothing. Nonetheless, we are compelled to conclude that *we the people* also have something to answer for. We as a society let denial prosper. We let our politicians get away with endless discussion and reports, with policies that do nothing and conferences that set no meaningful targets, or set ones designed to fail. As sociologist Eviatar Zerubavel (2006) notes, only when we all keep our mouths, eyes and ears tightly shut will the proverbial elephant actually stay in the room. James Hoggan (2009) believes we have been living a lie, ambling along as if everything is going to turn out fine with the climate and the future. Many of us let ourselves be deluded by the siren song of denial. After all, if you deny something, you no longer have to worry about it. We seem to think we can deny the bad thing and it will go away, like the Bogeyman in the dark. Except now the Bogeyman is *not* going away. Climate change is real, and for 20 years we have been fiddling as Rome started to burn. It is indeed a siren song we have been listening to – denial is a delusion (Zerubavel, 2006) and in some ways is one of the great dangers in the human psyche. When we worry about something, if it makes us afraid, if it makes us feel helpless, if it clashes with our self-image, then we have this capacity to ignore reality and move into denial. Then we convince ourselves we don't have to worry. But when denial threatens society, the Earth's ecosystems and a sustainable future, it has become not only a delusion, but a *dangerous pathology.*

As a society, we have all let denial flourish for too long in regard to the environmental crisis. Possibly some Romans did the same as Attila the Hun marched into Rome, or some Chinese may have sipped tea as Genghis Khan charged his Mongol hordes into their cities. Some people can analyse changes and threats rationally and bite the bullet and plan for the future. But some of us will not do this, and instead seek refuge in denial. In a recent interview between climate change author George Monbiot and climate change denier Professor Ian Plimer, it was noted that Monbiot had recently written: 'There's no point in denying it: we're losing. Climate change denial is spreading like a contagious disease.' (Monbiot, 2009a). Monbiot (ABC Lateline, 2009) went on to say in the interview:

> This is profoundly ironic because at the same time the evidence has hardened up to a startling degree. And the science of man-made global warming is now as solid as the science linking smoking with lung cancer and HIV with AIDS. And it seems to me that the harder the science becomes, the more people fall into denial because they simply don't want to face the writing that's now on the wall.

The science is thus showing us with greater certainty, through many independently verified lines of inquiry, that climate change is real and caused by humans. At the same time, paradoxically, more and more of us are slipping into denial. The paradox is one of 'implicatory' denial, the type of denial which many of us individually fall into. This may be due to fear, worry about being a 'bad person', conflict with self-image, or simply because we find it easier to stick our heads in the sand and take refuge in denial. So to some extent we have met the enemy – and it is us.

But now this has to change, as things are getting worse rapidly in terms of the climate science. For our own sakes. For the sake of our children. For the sake of their children and future generations. For the sake of our brother and sister species – the incredible diversity of life we share this world with. Ostriches don't *actually* stick their heads in the sand, though they do eat sand and grit for their digestion. Historian Pliny the Elder got it wrong. But if they did stick their heads in the sand, it would be a stupid thing to do if a lion was attacking them. Similarly, if the vast majority of the scientific scholars who actually study the changes in the Earth's climate tell you that we risk major and damaging changes to the Earth's ecosystems (and Barrie Pittock, 2009, points out we can validly use the term 'catastrophe'), then you would be equally foolish to deny this and do nothing. Yet en masse – as the human species overall – that is *exactly what we have done.*

Now both of us authors have been active in seeking change on environmental issues, one of us since 1974. However, we are aware ourselves that sometimes denial has operated in our own lives. We are human and we thus share this capacity for denial. So while the big corporations who support denial (and the politicians who do the same) deserve the strongest condemnation for what they have done, we all collectively need to admit to being part of the problem as well. It was easier to think that things could go on forever in the West as they had for the past 60 years – wasteful electrical devices, big houses, big cars, overseas holidays and profligate lifestyles. We let big business get away with climate change denial, we let our governments get away with climate change denial, and we let ourselves and each other get away with climate change denial, in an orgy of hedonistic sloth. We in the West were living like princes and princesses, and it was easier to believe we could all do this and do it *forever.*

But we can't, and we need to accept that we can't. The most crucial question of our times is 'Can we step aside from denial and accept the reality of climate change – and not only of climate change, of the environmental crisis overall?'. If we can roll back denial and face reality, then these problems – climate change, loss of biodiversity, loss of agricultural soil, population growth – *are all still solvable.* We can still reach a sustainable future where these problems are solved and we live in balance with the natural ecosystems that sustain us. If we can't kick the denial habit, then any rational scientific assessment of the future is grim. It won't mean the end of the world, but it will mean we pass on a much impoverished world to those who come after us.

Now, we do not make this last statement because we enjoy scaring people.

Nor do we like to promote catastrophe because we like catastrophe movies. Unlike what deniers state about environmental activists (for example Plimer, 2009), we are not 'anti-human', nor, as the Citizens Electoral Council in Australia suggests about climate activists, do we connive at the collapse of Western civilization and the death of billions (CEC, 2009). We do not see the future as a world of doom and gloom – *it doesn't have to be*. We know that others (for example Hamilton, 2010) have looked at these issues and concluded that 'it's too late', but we do not agree. If we take this approach, then it will become a self-fulfilling prophecy. We understand that when people are afraid they switch off, they push away the thing that scares them, they go into denial. As several studies have shown, fear is *not* a good motivator for people to take action and can even be counterproductive (Norgaard, 2006a and 2006b; Hulme, 2009). However, as an environmental scientist, one of us (Washington) has been frustrated at times when people have said 'let's not focus on the doom and gloom', as if we should ignore the seriousness of the situation we face.

We first and foremost *have to face reality*. Yet the future is not fixed and can be changed by our actions. To say it's too late means that people will slip into despair and apathy – and fail to act. Facing reality is not despair, for despair (like denial) means you do nothing creative or productive to improve the world and the future. Are things serious? Yes indeed they are, and time is running out. Are things hopeless? Never. It has been argued that there is a new 'eco-political pessimism', which climate change and our attempts to govern global climate have fostered (Hulme, 2009). Nevertheless, there is a difference between realism and pessimism. Pessimism ignores all the positive and creative actions people can take to make things better. We do not advocate *unreasoning* optimism, but a realism that accepts the urgency to act. Whatever the future brings, acting for sustainability can only make things better than they would have been otherwise. We would go so far as to say that this is a matter of honour, this is our pact with the future, that we acted to improve the environmental crisis and reduce climate change impacts.

However, the friends who do not like to focus on 'doom and gloom' had a point. Martin Luther King galvanized American society by saying 'I have a dream!'. He would not have galvanized them by saying 'I have a catastrophe!'. Some have suggested that hope can be a lie, a positive illusion (Hamilton, 2010). We do not agree, for if we accept reality and act then there *is* still hope. Many of us know in our hearts that there is something wrong with the natural world and what humans are doing to it. We may deny it out of fear, confusion, or not knowing what to do, or because it conflicts with our self-image. Nonetheless, if you focus on the *solutions*, on what can be done, then you can inspire people with a *dream of Earth repair*. This is the 'Great Work' that visionary philosopher Thomas Berry (1999) wrote of in his last book. It is neither uneconomic or physically impossible to solve these problems, to solve climate change. Books such as Mark Diesendorf's (2007) *Greenhouse Solutions with Sustainable Energy*, Ben McNeil's (2009) *The Clean Industrial Revolution* and Pittock's (2009) *Climate Change: The Science, Impacts and Solutions* demonstrate this. The solutions exist. The issue is whether collectively we have the guts to take up this task. Do we have the deep beliefs that will provide the impetus to solve these problems? If we don't collectively have these, then why not?

What Stops Us Accepting Reality?

So what impedes us accepting reality? Many things, some of which we touched on in the previous chapter. You can't get away from *values*. If you believe in the intrinsic value of nature, then you will value nature for itself. If you don't, then your values will only apply to the human species (and perhaps not all of humanity). Mike Hulme (2009) raises some interesting points as to why there is (and will always be) disagreement about climate change in terms of people's values. In the foreword to Hulme's (2009) book *Why We Disagree about Climate Change*, Professor Rayner of Oxford notes that:

> Our recognition of climate change as a threat to the ways of life to which we are accustomed and which we value depends on our views of Nature, our judgements about scientific analysis, our perception of risk, and our ideas about what is at stake – economic growth, national sovereignty, species extinction, or the lives of poor people in marginal environments … and whether it is ethically, politically or economically justifiable to make trade-offs between these.

We will return to this later when we discuss humanity's 'worldview'. Ethics are related to values, and Zerubavel (2006) has an interesting quote about the silence of denial about ethics:

> 'The best way to disrupt moral behaviour', notes political theorist C. Fred Alford, 'is not to discuss it and not to discuss not discussing it.' 'Dont talk about ethical issues', he facetiously proposes, 'and don't talk about our not talking about ethical issues.' As moral beings we cannot keep non-discussing 'undiscussables'. Breaking this insidious cycle of denial calls for an open discussion of the very phenomenon of undiscussability.

Ideologies also stop us from accepting reality. These can be capitalism, socialism, resourcism, consumerism – they are all based on the idea of nature being just a resource for human use. We cannot discuss here all of these in detail, for reasons of space, but together you could lump them as 'modernism' (Oelschlaeger, 1991) or 'modernity' (Hamilton, 2010). Modernism operates through science, technology and liberal democracy. It consists of several aspects that intertwine, these being the Renaissance, the Reformation, the Enlightenment, and the democratic, industrial and scientific revolutions (Oelschlaeger, 1991). Calls to delay action on climate change because it will have a 'negative effect on the economy' show just how powerfully the modernist ideology can drown out reality. You can't have an economy without an ecology (in other words functioning ecosystems), yet those who are wedded to the ideological view of eternal growth and exploiting nature are blind to the realities of ecosystem limits and carrying capacity. They simultaneously don't understand and are not listening to or learning from the mistakes of the past. When ideology blinds you to reality, surely it is time to abandon that ideology?

One prevalent ideology that developed in response to modernism was postmodernism, the intellectual revolt against modernism. We realize that by examining the impact of postmodernism on climate change action we may be treading on some sacred cows. This is especially true within academia, where postmodernism (and the related poststructuralism) are often dominant ideologies. However, action on climate change and the environmental crisis is too important to shy away from discussing any ideology which may foster denial or inaction. Academia trains the academics that teach many of the people who will need to take action on climate change. Postmodernism is a 'geography of ideas' that developed in opposition to modernism and is not readily defined; in fact it appears resistant to being defined, as noted by Professor Butler (2002) of Oxford University. Instead of espousing clarity, certitude, wholeness and continuity, postmodernism commits itself to 'ambiguity, relativity, fragmentation, particularity and discontinuity' (Crotty, 1998).

We shall not discuss here all the themes within postmodernism, but some relevant themes in terms of denial are:

- The denial of grand narratives (theories organizing overall meaning) (Lyotard, 1992);
- The suggestion that reason (or rational thought) is suspect (Derrida, 1966; Foucault, 1979; Barry, 1995);
- The questioning of the *real*, that it is impossible to prove the real from a 'simulacra' (Baudrillard, 1993); and
- Concern for the 'Other' (Levinas, 1989; Kristeva, 1992).

Denial is answered by rational thought, so to abandon *reason* is to let denial flourish. Postmodernists dislike 'grand narratives'. The denial of grand narratives leaves us with no overall *dream* of fixing things, so we fritter away our energies on irrelevancies. The questioning of reality obviously aids the denial of reality. Postmodernists often speak of 'co-creating reality', when actually there is a real reality which humans just interpret differently. Presumably some postmodernists would argue that the actual scientific view of climate change and the denial view are equally 'valid'. All counter-claims about the denied reality are seen as just manoeuvres in 'endless truth games' (Cohen, 2001). It seems to us that this leads to more fiddling as Rome burns. Weather is real, climate is real and human actions are really changing climate, with real effects on the ecosystems that support real human societies. Stanley Cohen (2001) notes that some postmodernist statements, such as that morality and values are relativistic, culturally specific and lacking universal force, are 'simply ludicrous'. He argues that while they stayed in academia such statements were harmless fun, but when they circulate in mass culture they supplement the inventory of denials available to the powerful. The crudest deniers can exploit this intellectual malaise to claim they are 'simply offering an alternative version of history'. Cohen (2001) notes about denial of historical atrocities that there are not two 'points of view', as one position is 'simply a fanatical rejection of evidence and a refusal to abide by the rule of rationality and logic'. That same rejection of evidence, along with refusal to apply logic, are also found in climate change denial.

It has been pointed out that, until recently, social scientists did not focus on denial or the organized denial movement, but sought to 'deconstruct' the claims of environmentalists and scientists (McCright and Dunlap, 2000). Arguably the postmodernist penchant to accept that everything is 'relative' and that we 'co-create reality' has meant that much of academia has defended the right of climate change deniers to create their own distorted view of climate science. It has increased skepticism about the existence of objective truth. Cohen (2001) notes that this 'epistemic relativism turns scientific facts into mere "social constructions"'. Just as evolution has been portrayed as a grand narrative (Docherty, 1992), so too climate science can be seen as just another 'grand narrative'. The postmodernist suspicion of rational thought means that the irrational statements of climate change deniers are not exposed as delusions, but accepted as valid alternate realities. This aspect of postmodernism does not fight climate change denial, it assists it.

The concern for the 'Other' in postmodernism could lead one to believe that it demonstrates a welcome questioning of the anthropocentrism inherent in modernism. However, the common focus on the Other in postmodernism is generally limited to our human species (Washington, 2006). Nobody could ethically argue against compassion for everybody within our species. Nonetheless, surely it is time for us to extend our compassion *beyond* our species to care for the Earth as a whole? Postmodernism en masse remains as anthropocentric as its predecessor, modernism. Traditional postmodernism would thus seem to offer little in terms of helping us abandon denial and accept reality. It, like many other ideologies, does not equip us with a way to move beyond denial. We hope it might evolve to do so.

Hulme (2009) proposes what seems to be a postmodernist approach of focusing on four 'myths' of climate change, where myths are stories that 'embody fundamental truths underlying our assumptions about everyday or scientific reality'. His myths are 'lamenting Eden' (human concern about changing Nature), 'presaging apocalypse' (dealing with the catastrophe view of climate change), 'constructing Babel' (human hubris and desire to dominate in regard to climate change action) and 'celebrating jubilee' (using ethics and justice to discuss climate change). These 'myths' may prove useful to some but less useful to others. Arran Gare (1995) has observed that postmodernism has demonstrated many problems with modernism, while it has been *powerless to oppose them*. Postmodernism is thus good at analysing the problems modernism has caused, but very poor at finding solutions to them. As an ideology it (like its predecessor modernism) is therefore not aiding us to roll back denial and solve the environmental crisis. We need something more. We need a dream of the 'Great Work' of repairing the Earth (Berry, 1999).

Population

In terms of moving beyond denial, there is another huge elephant standing in the room. Possibly also there is nothing harder for us collectively to see. Perhaps the only problem more 'wicked' than climate change is overpopulation. Perhaps nothing else raises such passion and pushes people into set positions they will defend to the death. Into it come issues such as religion, racism, social and environmental justice, equity, and poverty. There is also no more taboo issue politically than population. It is possibly the one issue that rivals climate change in terms of consequences. Collectively, the public and governments have been shying away from facing up to it for decades. Yet Hulme (2009) points out that if there is a 'safe' level of greenhouse gases to avoid runaway climate change, then 'is there not also a desirable world population?'.

Some people may criticize us for raising the population issue. Possibly some may even call us 'racists', though we do not believe in the concept of 'race' and the ethnic origins of people is not the point. Rather the point is total numbers of people and their impact on the Earth's carrying capacity. The world is finite. We know that human numbers have grown exponentially (though the rate of growth is now slowing) and that they are now larger than ever before, at more than 6.8 billion people. Various projections indicate that by 2050 the population will grow to between 8 and 10.5 billion people (UN, 2009). In 1968 Paul Ehrlich published *The Population Bomb*, which alerted the world to the dangers of exponentially growing population. He was later involved (Ehrlich, Ehrlich and Holdren, 1977) in coining the simple equation:

$$I = PAT$$

Impact equals population × affluence × technology. Our impact on the Earth is thus the number of people times their affluence (consumption of resources) times the technology we use: 6.8 billion people living simply in a rural economy would have less impact than if everyone lived in cities; 6.8 billion people living at the level of the average person in India would have less impact than the same number living at the Australian or US standard. Technology can be both positive and negative: 6.8 billion people who use a car powered by fossil fuels would have a huge impact compared to the same number using renewable energy vehicles and public transport. The truth of this equation is self-evident. Of course we accept that most of the carbon emissions are *currently* coming from consumers in the developed world (Monbiot, 2009b). However, the developing world is rapidly seeking to increase their affluence to reach the level of the developed world. It wants to catch up. And if this is done using traditional carbon-polluting industry, then the result will be steeply accelerating global carbon emissions. The technology used will thus be the critical factor. Yet improving technology or reducing affluence can only reduce our impact so far. In the end the numbers of people themselves count. A big population has a big impact, especially as the developing world expands its economy. Despite a 30 per cent increase in resource efficiency, global resource use has expanded by 50 per cent over 30 years (Flavin, 2010). This is mainly due to increasing affluence for the large populations in the developing world. This is why China is now the world's biggest carbon polluter, while India now ranks number six (Assadourian, 2010). Accordingly, as Hulme (2009) notes, we need to target all three components of I = PAT if we want to reduce human impact on climate – containing population, limiting affluence and cleaning technology.

Why is population such a diabolical policy issue? Because it cuts at the heart of the received wisdom of two million years of human evolution, where *more* people was always better (Washington, 1991). 'More' meant we could gather more food, cut down more forest, hunt more animals, defend ourselves better, gather more taxes for the State – the list goes on and on. 'More people' as a concept was always seen until the last 100 years as a good thing for society. It is very hard for us to understand in our hearts that now 'more' is no longer better. Add to this the religious bans against birth control methods (for example by the Catholic Church). Add to that the fundamental desire of governments to have more citizens, to have greater power and gather more taxes. Population ecologist Frederick Meyerson (see Hartmann et al, 2008) notes:

> Conservatives are often against sex education, contraception and abortion and they like growth – both in population and in the economy. Liberals usually support individual human rights above all else and fear the coercion label and therefore avoid discussion of population growth and stabilization. The combination is a tragic stalemate that leads to more population growth.

Population exacerbates all the other environmental problems, including climate change. It means cutting more forest for farmland, over-farming land so that it erodes, killing more 'bush meat' (wild animals) for food, over-fishing the rivers and seas. It means burning more fossil fuels as a way of fuelling development. Some climate scholars mention population as an important issue (for example Hulme, 2009), but Hulme notes that one recent popular book on global warming (*The Hot Topic*, Walker and King, 2008) mentions population only once, and not in a policy context. As Chris Rapley, the Director of London's Science Museum notes about population:

> So controversial is the subject that it has become the 'Cinderella' of the great sustainability debate – rarely visible in public, or even in private. In inter-disciplinary meetings addressing how the planet functions as an integrated whole, demographers and population specialists are usually notable by their absence. (BBC, 2006)

Brian O'Neill et al (2001) concluded, after a lengthy study of the relationship between population and climate change, that reducing population reduces greenhouse gas emissions in the long run and improves the resilience of vulnerable populations to impacts. Policies to reduce population therefore qualify as 'no regret policies of the sort identified for priority by the IPCC' (O'Neill et al, 2001). If we are going to accept reality then *we need to accept all of it*. Population growth is an important contributor to rising carbon emissions, one that assumes greater importance as developing countries increase their use of fossil fuels. We need to stop denying this and develop rational, ecologically based population policies. More people is no longer better; in fact it could be very bad indeed. To deny this just exacerbates denial of climate change.

The 'Tragedy of the Commons' Continues

Environmental scientist Garrett Hardin (1968) coined the term 'the tragedy of the commons' for how humans can abuse a resource in common. It describes a situation in which people consider their own self-interest and deplete a shared resource, even when it is clear that it is not in anyone's long-term interest. Hardin describes a hypothetical situation of herders sharing a common where they graze cows. It is in each herder's interest to put on an extra cow, but if others follow suit then the carrying capacity of the common is exceeded and it is damaged for all. This is a story of selfishness and greed, where people put their own interest above the rest of society and ecological sustainability. To profit individually they degrade the resource as a whole. Many native peoples and traditional societies (presumably having learned from past mistakes) developed lore and 'law' to prevent this happening (Knudtson and Suzuki, 1992). However, collectively the tragedy of the commons is what humanity has brought to many resources such as fisheries.

Today a variant of the tragedy of the commons is playing out with climate change action. Nobody wants to make cuts *unless everyone makes them*. People gain benefit from producing greenhouse gases, so they ignore the common good. This is like being in a leaky boat that is sinking and saying 'I am not going to bail any faster than the rest of you!'. Despite research that shows that not acting on climate change will cost us far *more* in the long run (Stern, 2006), we still hear that making cuts would 'adversely affect our economy' – unless everyone else is penalized equally.

If we were really serious about confronting reality, then countries should be vying with each other to be the first to impose strong emission reductions. Yet China and India don't seem to want to limit emissions, as it may impact on their economic growth. They want the historical emitters of much of the problem – the West – to impose greater cuts to redress this (Pittock, 2009). Some will see this as a question of justice, while for others it will be seen as a function of greed and selfishness. In fact, after COP15 in Copenhagen the Indian Environment Minister, Jairam Ramesh, boasted that he had scuttled any binding targets at Copenhagen, so that India's economy would not be affected (*Asian*

Correspondent, 2009). To turn around climate change requires a certain *generosity of spirit*, a concern for the whole rather than for short-term parochial gain. Political scientist Andrew Dobson (2008) argues that rather than 'I won't if you won't', we need a new social logic for the governance of the atmosphere – 'I will even if you won't'. Is this generosity of spirit possible? Can politicians actually set aside the parochial interests of centuries? Some argue not. One could point to Copenhagen as a case in point. However, the real answer is that *they can if we make them*. It is not good enough to blame inaction on politicians. If they haven't acted, it is because we did not lobby them strongly enough to make them act. The world is now our commons, and the tragedy will be one for the future of our planet. The boat is sinking – surely we all need to bail as fast as we possibly can?

How Do You Go about Solving Climate Change?

Worldview and ethics

When faced with the possibility of climate catastrophe, climate scientist Barrie Pittock (2009) argues there are three broad psychological reactions – nihilism (it's hopeless so let's enjoy ourselves), fundamentalism (God or the 'market' will save us) or activism (we can solve this). We espouse the latter, as together we can indeed solve this problem. Humans are intelligent and when committed can – and have – solved huge problems. The Second World War, the Marshall Plan to rebuild Europe after that war and the Space Race are excellent examples of successful major actions that some would have said were impossible. The situation we face is a serious problem, but it is also a major *opportunity*, an opportunity to build a sustainable future. Even in narrow economic terms it is a major opportunity. The actions that are needed to solve climate change are essentially the actions we need to take to solve the environmental crisis in general. We should be doing them anyway. For example, we need to stabilize population for many other reasons (not least of which is finding food and water for the future). We need to stop the biodiversity extinction crisis we are in, as we depend on other species for the ecosystem services that support our society. We need to also stop burning polluting coal and oil for health reasons. The climate crisis is in fact a symptom of an unsustainable worldview and an unsustainable society. Solving climate change will thus mean we solve many other urgent environmental problems, assuming we do it in an appropriate way.

However, this is not a chapter about how to become a climate change activist. Such books exist, notably Diesendorf's (2009) *Climate Action: A Campaign Manual for Greenhouse Solutions*. Rather, we look here at the main ways of solving the climate emergency. Professor Garnaut (2008), in his report to the new Labor Government in Australia, described climate change as a 'diabolical' policy issue. He was right: climate change is far harder than just controlling CFCs to stop the hole in the ozone layer, which was carried out via the Montreal Protocol. Climate change is a response to the way society obtains its energy, but also to our profligacy in wasting stored fossil energy. Almost everything we do today produces greenhouse gases. Climate change also impacts on almost everything we do – whether it's water use, food production, forestry, house-building or industry. If we accept the reality of the problem, then how do we go about solving it? Hulme (2009) refers to what have been called 'wicked' problems, a term deriving from cultural theory. Wicked problems have no one simple solution. He suggests 'clumsy' solutions, where you tackle the problem from many aspects, some of which may even be contradictory. Rather than just one 'silver bullet' to solve the problem, he suggests *silver buckshot*. No single solution is sufficient (Pittock, 2009). The silver buckshot are the multiple solutions one applies to the problem. We agree that solving climate change – and the underlying environmental crisis it is a symptom of – will require several different approaches, a number of 'silver buckshot'.

First we need to change society's *worldview*, the way we see the world. As Naomi Oreskes and Erik Conway (2010) conclude, 'science has shown us that contemporary industrial civilization is not sustainable'. So do we keep a human-centred approach, one that has been called the 'Dominant Social Paradigm' or 'Manifest Destiny' (McCright and Dunlap, 2000)? Or do we adopt an eco-centric approach? Do we value nature for itself? Do we see nature just as a group of resources that only have value for human use? Alternatively, do we see the natural world as something sacred, of spiritual significance? For those who believe in the intrinsic value of nature, then what we are doing with climate change is ethically appalling. As Hulme (2009) notes, what we value will determine how we relate to climate change. Are we ego-centric or eco-centric – is the Universe just about us and our consumption, or is it about sharing our planet with the wondrous evolved diversity of life? The 'wisdom of the elders' of traditional societies enabled them to live in harmony and balance with the land for thousands of years (Knudtson and Suzuki, 1992). Western consumerism and resourcism have impoverished the natural world we share in the last 200 years, and brought us to the brink of tremendous further loss. 'Catastrophe' as a term may switch people off, but it is not too strong a term to describe what we face (Pittock, 2009) – for both the natural world and human society. The ethical dimensions of climate change are at last being recognized. Anglican Bishop David Atkinson (2008) argued:

> Climate change is ... opening up for us ... questions about human life and destiny, about our relationship to the planet and to each other, about altruism and selfishness, about the place of a technological mindset in our attitude to the world, about our values, hope and goals, and about our obligations for the present and for the future. These are moral and spiritual questions.

So people are acknowledging the fundamental *ethical* questions involved in what we are doing to the world, especially with climate change. Indeed people are reconsidering their worldview, and have been revolting against the narrow focus of modernism for decades. One approach divides humanity into three 'personal identities'. These are the 'independent self-construal' identity or Western individualist; the 'interdependent self-construals', who define themselves through connections to other humans (whether family or society); and the 'meta-personal self-construal' (Hamilton, 2010). The last is a self connected to all living things and the cosmos. The first two focus on either ourselves or other humans, while the third approach extends our focus *outside* humanity to the rest of the world. It is the concept of an expanded self that underpins Buddhism (and also some native cultures) (Hamilton, 2010). However, Western society tends to encourage the first two approaches but not the third, and it is for this reason that it is so essential that we change our consumerist worldview. There are many practical and useful things that can be done without changing our worldview (see, for example, McNeil, 2009), but if we don't also change our worldview, we are likely to get ourselves re-entangled in the same messes we are in now. We have to tackle the worldview of consumerism. Climate change can thus be seen as an *opportunity* where we need to reveal the creative, psychological, spiritual and ethical work that climate change can do (and is doing) for us (Hulme, 2009).

So the modernist and consumerist approach of Western society has failed: in fact it has got us into the mess of the environmental crisis, of which climate change is a key part. We now need an eco-centric ethic, an ethic based not just on enlightened self-interest, but one that considers the rest of nature too (Assadourian, 2010). In contrast to Hulme's (2009) postmodernist approach of four 'myths' of climate change is Berry's (1999) eco-centric vision of the 'Great Work' of Earth repair. This is in fact a 'grand narrative', perhaps the grandest of them all! It is an over-arching worldview, a theory that provides meaning at a time when we desperately need it to foster the deep beliefs that will allow us to solve these problems. It is a dream that people can believe in. It is a dream that can inspire young and old alike. It is a dream that can lead to a sustainable future. Given the urgency involved in our predicament, this grand narrative, this Great Work, is precisely what we need to move forward to a sustainable future. There will be many parts to the Great Work (we discuss some here) and they will change over time. However, the big shift is accepting this new worldview – this Great Work of Earth Repair.

Ultimately we cannot roll back denial of climate change unless we roll back our consumer worldview, as the 2010 State of the World Report explains in detail (Starke and Mastny, 2010). Preventing the collapse of human civilization requires nothing less than a wholesale transformation of dominant consumer culture (Flavin, 2010). Consumption has gone up sixfold since 1960, but population numbers have only grown by a factor of 2.2. Consumption expenditure per person has almost tripled (Assadourian, 2010). Humanity now uses the resources and services of 1.3 Earths – an unsustainable situation. If all the world were to adopt American lifestyles, we would need four more planets to supply them (Graff, 2010). Assadourian (2010) suggests three goals to tackle consumerism. First, consumption that undermines wellbeing has to be discouraged. Second, we need to replace private consumption of goods with public consumption of services (libraries, public transport and so forth). And third, necessary goods must be designed to last and be 'cradle to cradle' recyclable. Aaron McCright and Riley Dunlap (2010) note that society needs 'reflexivity', a form of critical self-evaluation, a 'self-confrontation with the unintended and unanticipated consequences of modernity's industrial capitalist order'. This would be a first step to changing our worldview.

Can we change our worldview? Some people feel threatened by this question. However, things are happening, a clean industrial revolution is on the way (McNeil, 2009; Pittock, 2009). Similarly, people's views of how humans relate to nature are changing. Many people may not put it into words, but they *care* about the Earth; they care about cherishing the natural world that cherishes us. This is where the environment and conservation movements came from; this is where the desire to buy 'green' things comes from. This is where the deep belief comes from that we need to make big changes in how we live on Earth. This is where the drive to sustainability comes from, which has swept across the community (and some businesses and governments). This is why international lawyer Polly Higgins (2009) calls for an International Declaration of Planetary Rights. This is why there is a move towards 'Earth jurisprudence' and Ecuador in 2008 put 'rights for the planet' into its Constitution (Flavin, 2010). The shift to sustainability will depend on powerful networks of pioneers and champions (Assadourian, 2010). This process is already happening. Assadourian (2010) suggests the change can be made by six powerful institutions – education, business, government, the media, social movements and sustainable traditions.

So the groundswell for change is there, though it will take decades to make the change to a new worldview (Assadourian, 2010). It's a question of whether people can abandon denial and use their new worldview to *force* action. Now deniers hate the idea of changing our worldview. They espouse the same modernist, consumerist worldview that has got us into this mess. They see any call for a change of worldview as a Marxist conspiracy – without actually doing their research to discover that Karl Marx himself had a resourcist approach to Nature, similar to capitalism. Both capitalists and Marxists see nature as just a resource for human use (Eckersley, 1992; Hay, 2002). An eco-centric approach does not sit well with either traditional capitalism or Marxism, for Marxists don't generally relate to an eco-centric worldview either. What we are talking about goes *beyond* these limited political ideologies. And in some ways that is the rub, as neither capitalists nor Marxists 'get it'. They can only espouse more consumption, more growth – forever.

Changing our economy

Changing our worldview means changing our economy also. It has become a truism for most political parties to support a *growth economy* based on consumerism and a growing population. Growth has become a fetish, even a god for both the Left and the Right. There has been a total victory of free-market economics, far more of a victory than economists such as John Maynard Keynes ever actually originally intended (Hamilton, 2010). However, growth for growth's sake is in the end meaningless. Loss of species, coral reefs or glaciers and inundation of coastlines cannot be compensated for by growth in consumption or by monetary transfers (Hulme, 2010). Eric Neumayer (2007) argues that classical economics is insufficient to grapple with climate change as it:

> Violates fundamental principles of sustainable development, intergenerational stewardship and fairness and therefore violates the inalienable rights of future generations.

Hulme (2009) notes there is a paradox at the heart of economic analyses of climate change – the presumption of growth. Is the presumption of endless growth compatible with plans to control climate? Why do future analyses make growth a cardinal assumption? Ecological economist Clive Spash (2007) argues:

> Traditional pro-growth policies fail to address the problems humanity faces, the necessary transition or the nature of widespread environmental change we are undertaking. All these realizations raise the question of economic activity 'for what?'.

Many believe that the fixation on growth and the assumption that increasing consumption is the way to wellbeing is precisely why greenhouse gas emissions continue to rise (Hulme, 2009). Economist Richard Layard (2005) notes:

> Economic growth is indeed triumphant, but to no point. For material prosperity does not make humans happier: the 'triumph of economic growth' is not a triumph of humanity over material wants; rather it is the triumph of material wants over humanity.

Usually the rationale for growth and development is that it helps people such as the poor (even if it is only due to the 'trickle down' effect). Some even argue that 'green fatalism' holds back improving the lot of the poor (Claire Fox in Hulme, 2009) and that growth is the solution to environmental decline. However, Chris Sneddon et al (2006) note that the primary drivers of environmental degradation – energy and material use – have increased hugely, yet inequalities in access to economic opportunities have also dramatically increased within and between most societies. The mantra of development and growth is thus not helping the poor. Growth is continuing but the poor get less and less of the benefits (Layard, 2005).

A 'steady state' economy was proposed by Nicholas Georgescu-Roegen (1971) and Herman Daly (1973 and 1980) that operates on the basis of:

- Constant human population;
- Constant stock of artefacts or goods;
- Levels of these goods sufficient for a 'good life'; and

- The throughput of matter and energy (to maintain artefacts and population) being kept as low as feasible; products must be long-lasting.

Such a steady-state economy makes sense in a climate change world. We also need to integrate the ideologies of ecology (the 'study of the home') and economy (the 'management of the home'). There are now professional societies of 'ecological economics', and many of the top-class economists now accept that economics relies on maintaining ecosystems and the services they provide us. Most recently a report, 'Growth isn't possible' (Simms et al, 2010), by the New Economics Foundation has summarized in detail why endless growth not only will not continue to bring us benefits, but just isn't possible if we are to maintain the ecosystem services on which humanity relies. Rather than a steady-state economy, they prefer to call it a 'dynamic equilibrium' economy. There are also 'degrowth' movements, most notably in France (Latouche, 2010).

Solving climate change will not necessarily cost the Earth either. In fact the McKinsey Report (2008) estimated that the carbon revolution would cost between 0.6 and 1.4 per cent of GDP by 2030, when the global spending on insurance is already 3.3 per cent of GDP. A report on making Australia fully powered by renewable energy in 10 years finds this would cost 3 per cent of GDP a year (Wright and Hearps, 2010). Is it economic to solve climate change? This has the question back to front. We should ask whether it is economic *not* to solve it. It may indeed cost a lot of money to take strong action to cut carbon emissions by 80 per cent by 2050, just as it cost a lot to finance the Space Race. It won't cost more than we already spend on the military, however (Pittock, 2009). On the more immediate (and easy level) one obvious change is to remove the huge subsidies, tax incentives and preferential tariffs governments give fossil fuel companies (Pittock, 2009). In a climate change world, why should we subsidize the biggest carbon polluters? Rather we urgently need to provide subsidies, tariffs, low interest loans and investment to renewable energy and energy efficiency technologies.

Getting the message across

So how do we get the message across? Every one of us must know someone (family or friend) who is in denial about climate change. The public seems largely unaware of the impending crisis. This 'obliviousness' of the public is not surprising, says James Hansen (2009), as global warming is as yet slight compared to day-to-day weather fluctuations. Hansen asks in frustration, 'How in the world can a situation like this be communicated credibly?'. He also points out his belief that if the public had a better understanding of the climate crisis, they would 'do what was needed to be done'. We have already pointed out failings with a media owned predominantly by conservative interests. So how do we get the message across? Well, first and foremost one must accept that you can only get it across to someone who will listen and meet you half way. They have to be interested in delving into the scientific facts. They have to be interested in weighing the probabilities and the risks. They have to understand there is always some uncertainty and judge the preponderance of scientific evidence. There are some who will never 'hear' what we have to say in this book. Their denial is so strong that they will discount everything, as they already 'know' the truth. For them the elephant in the room is enormous but remains invisible.

It's not going to be easy to get the message across, largely because there are many people who won't hear and don't want to know. So we can't get the message across to everyone. However, as Zerubavel (2006) notes, there is also a tendency within society to *break with denial*. It is these people that one needs to take the message to, people who are true 'skeptics' looking for the truth. People who are willing to stop deluding themselves. People who will seek to bridge the gap between concern and action (Cohen, 2001). To such as these one can communicate, and to such as these we write this book. Fear does not motivate people, in fact people freeze up and some go into denial. A climate catastrophe is of course something one should worry about, but we need to get the message across in measured and reasoned debate, not in an emotional tirade. People switch off to a tirade, but some will listen to reasoned debate. Getting the message across is going to need both reason and patience. The facts are there, it is just a matter of putting them to those who have an open mind. The facts will then speak for themselves to anyone who can make a rational assessment of risk. Other books have other ideas as to how to get the message across, and some will work for some people somewhere (Diesendorf, 2009; Hoggan, 2009; Hulme, 2009; McNeil, 2009; Pittock, 2009). It has also been noted that schools represent a huge missed opportunity to combat consumerism, and fail to teach a basic understanding of ecology (Assadourian, 2010).

Communication to the public is one thing, getting the message across to governments is quite another. When one of us started working on environmental issues, he used to think that governments would do things 'because they were right'. It took a while to understand that governments do things because they are politically expedient. Even scientists on the IPCC Working Group II acknowledged that politicians delude themselves with a curious optimism that humans can avoid the consequences of climate change (Parry et al, 2008). Cohen (2001) notes that at the political level, 'We simply cannot tolerate states of denial. There is no room for compromise.'

Getting the message across to politicians requires that you think about votes and lobbying. Politicians will undertake action when the public *forces them to* – it's that simple. There are exceptions of ethical politicians, but en masse they are political animals and will respond to political lobbying. Probably nowhere in the world is that lobbying yet strong enough to force effective climate change action. This is yet another aspect of denial, as people deny that their involvement in political action can *make a difference*. In fact possibly one of the oddest outcomes of the failure at Copenhagen in 2009 was that climate change has fallen off the political agenda somewhat. One would have thought that the failure by politicians to come up with a meaningful treaty (with binding targets) would have galvanized people to lobby politicians harder. Instead, the opposite seems to be happening, and some people seem now to deny the whole issue. We desperately need to remember the comment attributed to anthropologist Margaret Mead (InterculturalStudies, 2010):

> Never doubt that a small group of thoughtful, committed citizens can change the world. Indeed, it is the only thing that ever has.

Adapt or mitigate?

Another key debate is about whether to *mitigate* climate change (that is slow and then halt it) or to *adapt* to it. In recent years there has been a focus in places to speak about 'adapting to climate change'. In some ways this is one of the silliest debates around climate change. On the one hand we have already had 0.7 degrees Celsius of climate change which we will simply *have* to adapt to. There is no choice. Also there is another 0.6 degrees Celsius of warming on the way (Hansen, 2009). We will have to adapt to this too. Up to two degrees of warming, ecosystems will have reasonable adaptive capacity. However, ecosystems simply cannot readily adapt to six degrees or ten degrees of warming in 100 years: they will collapse and many species will go extinct. Hansen (2009) has pointed out that it is insane to speak of adapting to the collapse of the ice sheets and a sea-level rise of five metres that would flood many of the world's largest cities. It is thus not a case of either/or – we have to do *both* as they are necessary and complementary (Pittock, 2009). We have to adapt to the warming that is here or already in the pipeline and we have to mitigate climate change as quickly as possible to ensure that we do not warm the world further than this, and in fact cool it by dropping CO_2 levels to 350 ppm. This will mean we not only have to reduce emissions to zero, we need in fact to go *negative* and take carbon out of the atmosphere. Inevitably we will have to adapt to the changes we have already caused. Mitigation action now will have its most significant effects decades into the future. However, if we fail to mitigate, then we stand a very good chance of plunging the world into runaway climate change. Humans are one of the most adaptable species on Earth. Nonetheless, we have to realize that beyond a certain point other species *cannot adapt* – they go extinct. The fossil record is full of these. We do indeed have to adapt, but even more importantly we have to *mitigate*.

Sustainability

Climate change action is a subset of reaching *sustainability*. Sustainability and sustainable development are terms that arose from the *Our Common Future* report (WCED, 1987). The terms reflect the growing groundswell of concern about what is happening to the world (Soskolne, 2008). Sustainability is a word that can encompass many meanings. One description is that it is an attempt to provide the best outcomes for the human and natural worlds into the future. At the heart of the concept of sustainability is a vision of achieving human and ecosystem wellbeing together. Sustainability is generally considered to be made up of three strands – social, economic and ecological (sometimes called environmental). All three of these are necessary. Think of sustainability as being a three-legged stool, with each strand being a leg. For the stool to function, all three legs must be in place. Sustainability and its three strands are often not defined, but they should be. One of us (Washington, 2009) was involved in an attempt to define them, as shown below (WCC, 2008):

- *Social sustainability* is often confused with social justice or social responsibility, but while it is related to these, it has a different focus. Social sustainability aims for a society that can live in a long-term balance with the world and its ecosystems – in other words, a world at peace, both among people and between people and nature. A sustainable society will require fairness (equity) and justice, locally and globally, both within this generation and between our generation and future generations.
- *Economic sustainability* is about creating an economy that is sustainable over the long term, not just a short-term growth economy. This means not damaging the ecosystem services that underpin our society. Environmental economics has now become the cutting edge of economics, and in many ways is integrating ecology and economics through environmental accounting.
- *Ecological sustainability* is about taking action to solve the Earth's environmental crisis by monitoring, restoring and supporting the biodiversity and ecosystems (including ecosystem services) that support us. In terms of urgent challenges, it means greatly reducing our carbon footprint by controlling our greenhouse gas emissions. This means not exceeding the Earth's carrying capacity, which can result in ecosystem breakdown and massive species extinctions (Daily and Ehrlich, 1992).

People historically have tended to devote the majority of their time to their society and their economy. To return to the 'three-legged stool' analogy, it is the third leg – ecological sustainability – that has received less attention, and it is this one that may collapse. Certain interests worldwide seek to shift the focus of 'sustainability' primarily to an economic or social focus, so that they can continue business as usual, which may not be ecologically sustainable. Social and economic factors must remain a key part of the decision-making process, but in order to respond to the urgency of the environmental crisis, extra weight needs to be given to restoring the balance, by focusing on the long-overlooked side: ecological sustainability. The book *Climate Code Red* (Spratt and Sutton, 2008) notes that because of climate change, sustainability is now not so much a 'radical idea as simply an indispensable course of action if we are to return to a safe-climate planet'. Without a stable climate we cannot reach sustainability (Pittock, 2009). Erik Assadourian (2010) explains that institutions now will have to be fundamentally oriented to sustainability. Deniers of course hate both the term 'sustainability' itself and the philosophy behind it. They deny that there are any environmental problems and thus the need for a sustainability philosophy to solve them.

Market and civic environmentalism approaches

So assuming we want to reach sustainability and slow, then halt, then reverse climate change, how do we do it? We know we need to reduce carbon emissions by at least 80 per cent by 2050 (Pittock, 2009). What is the best way? Different approaches have been suggested, and as Hulme (2009) points out, our views on these will be affected by how we perceive governance and politics. As a market economy, the most obvious approach by economists has been to put a *price on carbon*, so that the price signal forces people to emit less CO_2. This can be done either by a carbon tax (sometimes called a 'fee and dividend', Hansen, 2009) or by an emissions trading scheme (ETS) or both, as has been done in some countries. At first glance these approaches may seem the same, as both put a price on carbon to reduce emissions. However, Hansen (2009) argues they are poles apart.

A fee and dividend carbon tax puts a price on carbon at source, either at mine or well-head or port of entry. The total money raised is revenue neutral. It can be divided by the country's population and paid as a dividend to legal adult residents or via tax reductions. In this way it is transparent and the public can have greater trust in the system than with an ETS. Those who are carbon-thrifty thus make money; those who are carbon-wasters pay extra. The State of British Columbia in Canada brought in a fee and dividend scheme in 2008 (and did so within six months). This was $10 a tonne of CO_2, ramping up to $30 a tonne by 2012 (Hansen, 2009). This is revenue neutral, with a direct Climate Action Dividend of $100 to residents, along with tax reductions. A carbon tax is often criticized on the basis of cost. A carbon fee of $115 a tonne in the US would increase the cost of electricity by eight cents per kilowatt hour. If returned to the public, this would result in a dividend of $3000 a year to legal adults. Hansen (2009) points out that in general governments don't like the dividend system as it means they have to give the money back to the people.

Most governments tend to favour an ETS, which was a suggested mechanism to reduce carbon emissions in Annex I of the Kyoto Protocol. An ETS sets a cap and then carbon permits are traded at a set price. Production of more CO_2 than one has permits for invokes a cost penalty. It has been argued by economists (for example by Garnaut, 2008) that an ETS is the *cheapest* way to send a price signal – provided you do not provide free credits to polluting industries (as the European Union did). However, the cap and trade system means the cap is also a *floor* beyond which CO_2 emissions will not drop. Using a cap and trade system means you are committed to a certain amount of carbon pollution for that year – no matter what the public does altruistically in terms of energy conservation or installation of renewable energy. Any savings made by the public would be reallocated to the big carbon polluters to use that year. It thus minimizes the effect of other actions (such as civic environmentalism) and actually slows down the rapid reduction of CO_2 emissions. Hansen (2009) argues that the fossil fuel lobby spends a lot of money to ensure that if governments do something about climate change, it is an ETS approach. The reason is that it will allow business-as-usual emissions to continue for as long as possible. Hansen describes an ETS as 'carbon indulgences'.

There are thus valid doubts about whether a cap and trade ETS is the right way. It has been called the 'commodification of carbon'. The eco-anarchists and some in the Left see a market approach (of any sort) as being the *cause* of the problem. For example, the climate campaign group Rising Tide challenges the institutions of the capitalist state, seeking a fundamental transformation of consumption patterns to pave the way for a more equitable and eco-centric world order (Hulme, 2009). There is in fact an ethical problem with the commodification of carbon (especially in an ETS). It is an ongoing part of the commodification of nature as a whole. These parts of nature were once in the public domain, but individual ownership is being applied to them so that they can be traded by the market economy.

Carbon trading is also a top–down hierarchical approach (Hansen, 2009). This is yet a further instance of the modernist and resourcist mentality seeking to commodify the natural world, take away ownership 'in common' and giving ownership to those with sufficient money. This approach is thus part of the modernist worldview that is in need of change. There are also those who say that the ETS won't work to actually reduce CO_2 levels, that it will create a huge bureaucracy to trade carbon but make little real impact on CO_2 levels. Science journalist Fred Pearce (2008) notes:

> Many fear that carbon capitalism is already out of control, delivering big profits while doing little to halt global warming. They are deeply sceptical of the notion that market forces can fix climate change.

On the other hand, parts of the world already have an ETS (such as Europe), or are moving towards one, so there is a practical argument for taking part in this. Hansen (2009) argues that it's not good enough to say that an ETS is a 'done deal' and thus we should make the best of it. He points out that starting with the *wrong* thing can be worse than having nothing, as it could lock us in to decades of pretend action, with little real effect. We agree with Hansen that a fee and dividend carbon tax would make far more sense. It would be faster to put in place and would not require a huge bureaucracy. The reality is that in a market-based society, we desperately need a price signal on carbon. The fee and dividend direct carbon tax would be a better price signal system. However, if a nation is stuck with an ETS, then one needs to make it work as well as possible. But is a market approach the *only* thing we should be doing? Indeed it is not.

Another approach has been called 'Civic Environmentalism'. This has been said to challenge the state-centred beliefs of governments and the market-centred beliefs of neo-liberal environmentalists (Hulme, 2009). This is a bottom–up, grassroots approach where you take many small meaningful steps to reduce carbon emissions. Civic environmentalism seeks to transcend political ideologies and build coalitions of policy actors *beyond* the State, such as business, local government, community groups and non-governmental organizations (Hulme, 2009). Civic environmentalism goes beyond green consumerism, which has been criticized for sometimes being a false solution (Hamilton, 2010). It can be false if it fails to take place along with political action and if it still promotes consumerism. On the other hand, the range of climate action projects that can be done through civic environmentalism is enormous. Some practical examples of what can be done are:

- *Sustainable building*, which can save up to half the energy (and water) a building requires (Hulme, 2009);
- *Energy efficiency*, for example turning off your 'power vampires' such as all the standby appliances in the house that use power even when they are supposedly 'off' (Stoyke, 2007); people in the US, Canada and Australia use about twice as much electricity per person as those in Japan or Europe (Hansen, 2009);
- *Home sustainability audits* to find out how you can save energy and water (ask your council or energy supplier);
- *Changing incandescent light bulbs* to compact fluorescent or LED;
- *Using solar or heat pump hot water systems* (saving around 30 per cent of a house's electricity use);
- *Sustainable transport* (use bus, rail, bike or hybrid vehicles);
- *Turning green waste into 'biochar'* (charcoal) that can sequester carbon into soils is an important *carbon-negative* technology;
- *Installing solar PV panels or wind turbines* to feed electricity into the grid;
- *Using GreenPower* so your electricity doesn't come from coal-fired power stations (and instead supports renewable energy);
- *Buying carbon offsets* if you fly overseas for a trip, so your trip is carbon neutral; though Hansen (2009) describes carbon offsets as 'carbon indulgences', if you are going to travel by plane anyway, it is better to buy offsets than do nothing;
- *Reducing waste and methane* produced by domestic waste (for example by composting your organic matter at home) is another way of reducing your carbon footprint;
- *Thinking about the 'food miles'* of what you buy and buying locally grown produce where possible can save a lot of energy in transporting food; and
- *Sustainable business* is another huge area where simple cost-effective changes can make a big reduction in energy use.

However, civic environmentalism also goes beyond the above. It involves promotion of ideas such as community carbon reduction action groups (CRAGS), use of courts to force reductions in greenhouse gases, citizens pledges, technology standards and voluntary carbon offsets (Hulme, 2009). The jury is out in terms of comparing the two, but it may well be that civic environmentalism will actually reduce society's carbon footprint *more* than an ETS. Similarly, strong Mandatory Renewable Energy Targets (MRETs) and the renewable energy revolution may make as big a difference as an ETS (and possibly more). We fully support the need for 'silver buckshot' solutions as suggested by Hulme (2009), so in regard to any question as to whether one should use a carbon price *or* civic environmentalism, the answer would have to be 'use both!'. The urgency is such that *any* realistic approach to reducing carbon emissions should be pursued that does not create other environmental problems (see the nuclear discussion in Chapter 7). The value of civic environmentalism is that you don't have to wait for unwieldy governments to act. The failure of the 2009 Copenhagen COP15 conference to deliver a binding treaty with targets shows the wisdom of actions that don't rely on governments. Individuals, groups, businesses and local government can act and make a real difference to carbon emissions. It has been argued that inelegant but attainable bottom–up approaches to climate governance are likely to be more effective than elegant but impractical top–down ones (Prins and Rayner, 2007).

When the proposed ETS came out in Australia (Commonwealth, 2008), and the extent of the free credits to carbon-polluting industries was revealed, there was a statement by some environmental groups that making personal reductions in carbon footprint was 'pointless', as the savings would just be given to the polluting industries. However, no reduction in carbon emissions is pointless. We should be massively encouraging civic environmentalism on climate. We should never say it is pointless, as no matter how unwieldy and slow to act an ETS may be, civic environmentalism can be done immediately and can reduce carbon emissions. It is easy, cost-effective and can be done by everyone. Let's not wait for governments to act, let's act ourselves!

The unsettling challenges of climate change call forth extreme voices. Some advocate a return to the authoritarian certainties of the nation state (eco-authoritarianism), while eco-anarchism seeks to finally overthrow the antiquated capitalist state (Hulme, 2009). Climate change (like sustainability) is often co-opted to support whatever argument somebody is promoting. We have argued for an ethical examination of our values and a new worldview and new approach to economics. However, it is somewhat foolish to scare people with ideas of radical social change and the immediate abandonment of the market economy. This just plays into the hands of the conspiracy theorists (and deniers), who see it as a Marxist plot. This is not an either/or situation. The reality is that market solutions and civic environmentalism will both play a part as components of the 'silver buckshot' that reduces, then halts climate change.

A farewell to coal

Humanity is hooked on fossil fuels, but coal releases the greatest percentage of CO_2 into the atmosphere through power stations. Coal is not just king, it is a dictator. Each year around the world 100 new large-scale coal-fired power plants are constructed (Hamilton, 2010). Hansen (2009) points out that 'clean coal' is a figment of the imagination, and if any government tries to tell you they will reach an 80 per cent cut in carbon emissions by 2050 without getting rid of coal, then they are 'lying through their teeth'. He points out that energy-efficiency is great, but it must be part of a strategic policy that leaves most of the fossil fuels in the ground. Hansen (2009) does not dismiss carbon capture and storage out of hand (see Chapter 7), but he does argue that coal use must be prohibited until it can be shown that CO_2 *can* be safely stored and it actually happens. He argues that coal emissions must cease in the next 10 years, a difficult (but honest) scenario. He believes the present situation is analogous to that faced by Abraham Lincoln with slavery and Winston Churchill with Nazism – the time for compromises and appeasement is over. Hansen (2009) says we are not ready to stop using oil and gas, so coal emissions have to stop immediately. Australia is the biggest coal-exporting country in the world, making a lot of money from its export. It will thus find it harder than most to kick the coal habit. However, Hansen (2009) is right: an ETS is probably not going to be able to deliver the emission cuts necessary in time. We have to kick the coal habit, and kick it quickly. This clearly infuriates the coal lobby, who seek to use 'jobs' as a key argument, even though mining in fact produces comparatively few jobs, certainly less than a renewable energy economy would (McNeil, 2009).

If coal needs to be abandoned, even more so do we need to avoid using tar sands and oil shale, which produce even more CO_2 than brown coal (for a given amount of energy produced). However, projects continue to be planned for a major increase in Alberta tar sands and a pipeline to carry the synthetic oil to the US (Hansen, 2009; Hoggan, 2009). Government claims of future carbon reductions are thus inconsistent with their actual actions in exploiting every last bit of fossil fuel available. This is probably one of the biggest cognitive dissonances concerning climate change. Our governments say one thing, but they do another. Hansen notes that in 2009 there were 2340 registered energy lobbyists in the US capital, a major problem. Hansen (2009) proposes a 'Declaration of Stewardship' with:

1   A moratorium on coal-fired power stations that do not capture and sequester carbon;
2   A fair and gradually rising price on carbon emissions; and
3   Measures to improve energy-efficiency.

Hansen (2009) believes that the forces for 'business-as-usual' and fossil fuel interests will seek to ensure that any climate change agreements reached will be minor steps. He concludes that 'the real battle by young people for their future is just beginning'.

References

ABC Lateline (2009) www.abc.net.au/lateline/content/2009/s2772906.htm
Asian Correspondent (2009) 23 December, see http://us.asiancorrespondent.com/rwdb-jfbeck/india-boasts-of-scuttling-climate-talks
Assadourian, E. (2010) 'The rise and fall of consumer cultures', in L. Starke and L. Mastny (eds) *State of the World 2010: Transforming Cultures from Consumerism to Sustainability*, Earthscan, London
Atkinson, D. (2008) *Renewing the Face of the Earth: A Theological and Pastoral Response to Climate Change*, Canterbury Press, London

Barry, P. (1995) *Beginning Theory: An Introduction to Literary and Cultural Theory*, Manchester University Press, Manchester, UK/New York

Baudrillard, J. (1993) 'The evil demon of images and the precession of simulacra', in T. Docherty (ed) *Postmodernism: A Reader*, Columbia University Press, New York

BBC (2006) 'Earth is too crowded for Utopia', BBC News online, 6 January, http://news.bbc.co.uk/2/hi/science/nature/4584572.stm

Berry, T. (1999) *The Great Work*, Belltower, New York

Butler, C. (2002) *Postmodernism: A Very Short Introduction*, Oxford University Press, Oxford, UK

CEC (2009) 'Carbon trading is Hitler-style genocide!', *Citizens Electoral Council Newsletter* (Australia), vol 6, no 12, August/September, http://cecaust.com.au/main.asp?sub=pubs&id=newcitizen.htm

Cohen, S. (2001) *States of Denial: Knowing about Atrocities and Suffering*, Polity Press, Cambridge, UK

Commonwealth (2008) 'Carbon Pollution Reduction Scheme: Australia's low pollution future', White Paper, Commonwealth Government, Canberra, Australia, December

Crotty, M. (1998) *Foundations of Social Research: Meaning and Perspective in Research Process*, Allen and Unwin, Sydney, Australia

Daily, G. and Ehrlich, P. (1992) 'Population, sustainability, and Earth's carrying capacity: A framework for estimating population sizes and lifestyles that could be sustained without undermining future generations', *Bioscience*, vol 42, pp761–771

Daly, H. (1973) 'The steady state economy', in *Toward a Steady State Economy*, Freeman and Co, New York

Daly, H. (1980) *Economics, Ecology, Ethics: Essays towards a Steady State Economy*, Freeman and Co, New York

Derrida, J. (1966) 'Structure, sign and play in the discourse of the human sciences', in H. Adams (ed) *Critical Theory Since Plato*, Harcourt Brace Jovanovich, New York, pp1117–1118

Diesendorf, M. (2007) *Greenhouse Solutions with Sustainable Energy*, UNSW Press, Sydney, Australia

Diesendorf, M. (2009) *Climate Action: A Campaign Manual for Greenhouse Solutions*, UNSW Press, Sydney, Australia

Dobson, A. (2008) 'Climate change and the public sphere', *Open Democracy*, 1 April, see www.opendemocracy.net

Docherty, T. (1992) *Postmodernism: A Reader*, Harvester Wheatsheaf, New York

Doran, P. and Zimmerman, M. (2009) 'Examining the scientific consensus on climate change', *Eos, Transactions American Geophysical Union*, vol 90, no 3, p22

Eckersley, R. (1992) *Environmentalism and Political Theory: Toward an Ecocentric Approach*, UCL Press, New York

Ehrlich, P. (1968) *The Population Bomb*, Buccaneer Books, New York

Ehrlich, P., Ehrlich, A. and Holdren, J. (1977) *Ecoscience: Population, Resources, Environment*, WH Freeman and Co, New York

Flavin, C. (2010) 'Preface' to L. Starke and L. Mastny (eds) *State of the World 2010: Transforming Cultures from Consumerism to Sustainability*, Earthscan, London

Foucault, M. (1979) *Power, Truth, Strategy*, Prometheus Books, Buffalo, NY

Fromm, E. (1976) *To Have or to Be*, Abacus Books, New York

Gare, A. (1995) *Postmodernism and the Environmental Crisis*, Routledge, London/New York

Garnaut, R. (2008) *The Garnaut Climate Change Review*, Garnaut Climate Change Review, see www.garnautreview.org.au

Georgescu-Roegen, N. (1971) *The Entropy Law and the Economic Process*, Harvard

University Press, Cambridge, MA

Graff, J. (2010) 'Reducing work time as a path to sustainability', in L. Starke and L. Mastny (eds) *State of the World 2010: Transforming Cultures from Consumerism to Sustainability*, Earthscan, London

Hamilton, C. (2010) *Requiem for a Species: Why We Resist the Truth about Climate Change*, Allen and Unwin, Sydney, Australia

Hansen, J. (2009) *Storms of My Grandchildren: The Truth about the Coming Climate Catastrophe and Our Last Chance to Save Humanity*, Bloomsbury, London

Hardin, G. (1968) 'The tragedy of the commons', *Science*, vol 162, pp1243–1248

Hartmann, B., Meyerson, F., Guillebaud, J., Chamie, J. and Desvaux, M. (2008) 'Population and climate change', *Bulletin of Atomic Scientists*, 16 April, www.thebulletin.org/web-edition/roundtables/population-and-climate-change

Hay, P. (2002) *Main Currents in Western Environmental Thought*, UNSW Press, Sydney, Australia

Higgins, P. (2009) 'The planetary rights', www.treeshaverightstoo.com/the-planetary-rights

Hoggan, J. (2009) *Climate Cover Up: The Crusade to Deny Global Warming*, Greystone Books, Vancouver, Canada

Houghton, J. (2008) *Global Warming: The Complete Briefing*, Cambridge University Press, Cambridge, UK

Hulme, M. (2009) *Why We Disagree about Climate Change: Understanding Controversy, Inaction and Opportunity*, Cambridge University Press, Cambridge, UK

InterculturalStudies (2010) Margaret Mead quote, see www.interculturalstudies.org/Mead/biography.html

Karoly, D. (2009) Statement by Prof. David Karoly of the University of Melbourne on ABC Four Corners, 9 November, see /www.abc.net.au/4corners/content/2009/s2737676.htm

Knudtson, P. and Suzuki, D. (1992) *Wisdom of the Elders*, Allen and Unwin, Sydney, Australia

Kristeva, K. (1992) 'The other of language', in K. Murray (ed) *The Judgement of Paris: Recent French Theory in a Local Context*, Allen and Unwin, Sydney, Australia, pp23–37

Latouche, S. (2010) 'Growing a degrowth movement', Box 22 (p181) in L. Starke and L. Mastny (eds) *State of the World 2010: Transforming Cultures from Consumerism to Sustainability*, Earthscan, London

Layard, R. (2005) 'The national income: As sorry tale', in R. Easterlin (ed) *Growth Triumphant: The 21st Century in Historical Perspective*, University of Michigan Press, Ann Arbor, MI

Levinas, E. (1989) 'Ethics as first philosophy', in S. Hand (ed) (1994) *The Levinas Reader*, Basil Blackwell, Oxford, UK, pp82–83

Lyotard, J. (1992) 'Answering the question: What is postmodernism?', in T. Docherty (ed) *Postmodernism: A Reader*, Harvester Wheatsheaf, New York

McCright, A. and Dunlap, R. (2000) 'Challenging global warming as a social problem: An analysis of the conservative movement's counter-claims', *Social Problems*, vol 47, no 4, pp499–522

McCright, A. and Dunlap, R. (2010) 'Anti-reflexivity: The American conservative movement's success in undermining climate science and policy', *Theory, Culture and Society*, vol 27, nos 2–3, pp100–133

McKinsey (2008) *The Carbon Productivity Challenge: Curbing Climate Change and Sustaining Economic Growth*, McKinsey Global Institute, Washington, DC, www.mckinsey.com/mgi/publications/Carbon_Productivity/index.asp

McNeil, B. (2009) *The Clean Industrial Revolution: Growing Australian Prosperity in the Greenhouse Age*, Allen and Unwin, Sydney, Australia

Monbiot, G. (2006) *Heat: How to Stop the Planet Burning*, Penguin Books, London

Monbiot, G. (2009a) 'Leaders bicker while the biosphere burns', *Sun-Herald* (Australia), 20 December

Monbiot, G. (2009b) 'The population myth', www.monbiot.com/archives/2009/09/29/the-population-myth/

Neumayer, E. (2007) 'A missed opportunity: The Stern Review on climate change fails to tackle the issue of non-substitutable loss of natural capital', *Global Environmental Change*, vol 17, nos 3–4, pp297–301

Norgaard, K. (2006a) '"People want to protect themselves a little bit": Emotions, denial and social movement nonparticipation', *Sociological Inquiry*, vol 76, no 3, pp372–396

Norgaard, K. (2006b) '"We don't really want to know"', *Organisation and Environment*, vol 19, no 3, pp347–370

Oelschlaeger, M. (1991) *The Idea of Wilderness: From Prehistory to the Age of Ecology*, Yale University Press, New Haven, CT/London

O'Neill, B., Mackellar, F. and Lutz, W. (2001) *Population and Climate Change*, Cambridge University Press, Cambridge, UK

Oreskes, N. and Conway, E. M. (2010) *Merchants of Doubt: How a Handful of Scientists Obscured the Truth on Issues from Tobacco Smoke to Global Warming*, Bloomsbury Press, New York

Parry, M., Palutikof, J., Hanson, C. and Lowe, J. (2008) 'Squaring up to reality', *Nature Reports, Climate Change*, vol 2, pp68–70

Pearce, F. (2008) 'Carbon trading: dirty, sexy money', *New Scientist*, no 2652, 19 April

Pittock, A. B. (2009) *Climate Change: The Science, Impacts and Solutions*, CSIRO Publishing, Melbourne, Australia

Plimer, I. (2009) *Heaven and Earth: Global Warming: The Missing Science*, Connorcourt Publishing, Ballan, Australia

Prins, G. and Rayner, S. (2007) 'Time to ditch Kyoto', *Nature*, vol 499, pp973–976

Simms, A., Johnson, V. and Chowla, P. (2010) *Growth Isn't Possible: Why We Need a New Economic Direction*, New Economics Foundation, London

Sneddon, C., Howarth, R. and Norgaard, R. (2006) 'Sustainable development in a post-Brundtland world', *Ecological Economics*, vol 57, no 2, pp253–268

Soskolne, C. (ed) (2008) *Sustaining Life on Earth: Environmental and Human Health through Global Governance*, Lexington Books, New York

Spash, C. (2007) 'The economics of climate change impacts a la Stern: Novel and nuanced or rhetorically restricted', *Ecological Economics*, vol 63, no 4, pp706–713

Spratt, D. and Sutton, P. (2008) *Climate Code Red: The Case for Emergency Action*, Scribe Publications, Carlton, Australia

Starke, L. and Mastny, L. (2010) *State of the World 2010: Transforming Cultures from Consumerism to Sustainability*, Earthscan, London

Stern, N. (2006) *The Economics of Climate Change* (Stern Review), Cambridge University Press, Cambridge, UK

Stoyke, G. (2007) *The Carbon Buster's Home Energy Handbook: Slowing Climate Change and Saving Money*, New Society Publishers, New York

UN (2009) 'World population to exceed 9 billion by 2050', press release by United Nations Population Division, 11 March, www.un.org/esa/population/publications/wpp2008/pressrelease.pdf

Walker, G. and King, D. (2008) *The Hot Topic: How to Tackle Global Warming and Still Keep the Lights On*, Bloomsbury Press, London

Washington, H. (1991) *Ecosolutions: Environmental Solutions for the World and Australia*, Boobook Publications, Tea Gardens, Australia

Washington, H. (2006) *The Wilderness Knot*, PhD thesis, University of Western Sydney, Sydney, Australia

Washington, H. (2009) 'Embedding sustainability in an Australian council', *Journal of Sustainability*, vol 2, no 2 (e-journal), 1 August, http://journalofsustainability.com/lifetype/index.php?op=ViewArticle&articleId=63&blogId=1

WCC (2008) *Sustainability Charter*, Willoughby City Council, Sydney, Australia, see www.willoughby.nsw.gov.au/Sustainability-Charter.html

WCED (1987) *Our Common Future*, World Commission on Environment and Development, Oxford University Press, Oxford

Wright, M. and Hearps, P. (2010) 'Australian sustainable energy stationary energy plan', University of Melbourne Energy Research Institute/Beyond Zero Emissions, http://beyondzeroemissions.org

Zerubavel, E. (2006) *The Elephant in the Room: Silence and Denial in Everyday Life*, Oxford University Press, New York

7

Rolling Back Denial: The Technological Solutions

Technologies – Appropriate and Inappropriate

One argument put forward by some environmentalists has been 'science got us into this mess'. This taps into a tendency in the community known as the 'revolt against science', or at least a suspicion of science (Passmore, 1975; Washington, 1991). One should indeed question the unbridled scientific 'can do' optimism which argues that humans are masters of nature and can do anything, as this is 'progress'. This belief is 'Cornucopianism' (Oreskes and Conway, 2010) and is one reason why some are suspicious of science: not because of the data discovered or even the process, rather it is a suspicion of the outdated modernist philosophy of domination of nature (Hulme, 2009). What is it that we are actually 'progressing' towards? Progress today should be measured as progress towards a sustainable future, not the ability to 'master' nature. This scientific hubris about 'progress' is still around today, and is even promoted by some who speak out against denial (Specter, 2009). It is thus not science as a whole that people should be suspicious of, just the 'domination of nature' and Cornucopian worldviews within our society (including some scientists).

There is a need for social responsibility in science, and there is a movement by that name (and also a Union of Concerned Scientists). Philosophically this is a far more responsible approach than unbridled Cornucopian optimism that science can do anything it wants. More scientists are now speaking out on climate change and other environmental issues than before, due to the severity of the problem and the sense of urgency they feel. This is long overdue, as scientists have abrogated their responsibility to society for too long. Being objective should not mean being mute and having no responsibility to the Earth, its ecosystems and peoples. The denial movement is now frantic in part because more climate scientists *are* speaking out, and we hope this speaking out accelerates. So the problem has not been science or even technology per se – it has been that they have not been *appropriate*.

Appropriate to what? Appropriate to the reality we face. Appropriate to the fact that humanity faces an environmental crisis, and chief among the problems is climate change. Appropriate to the rapidly reducing time-frame over which we need solutions. We would never say 'if it's not done in 10 years, it will be too late', because effective action using appropriate technology is *never too late*. However, accepting reality means acceptance of the risk of runaway climate change, and that this would have great impact on the Earth, its biodiversity and its peoples. This means there is an urgency, one that we share, a cause of deep concern that is never far from the surface. We understand why James Hansen (2009) says he is studying Gandhi's 'civil resistance' and why he has been present at attempts to block coal trucks. However, this urgency can lead people to set absolute timelines and targets that may not be achievable. There is a risk (and one of us has a friend who does this) that people may say 'Well it's too late anyway!' and go into denial that way. We need action and strong action now, and we need it in many different ways, the 'silver buckshot' we spoke of in Chapter 6.

So in terms of appropriate technology – are there solutions? Yes there certainly are. This is one of the most frustrating aspects of the whole debate – the denial of real and workable solutions. There is a wealth of solutions out there to roll back climate change, and good grounds for optimism that large emission cuts can be achieved at moderate cost (Pittock, 2009). Amory Lovins of the Rocky Mountain Institute details how we can transform industrial production so as to use less resources and energy. This is explained in his book *Natural Capitalism* (Hawken et al, 2010; see also www.natcap.org). Climate change is not an irrevocable decree of fate to which we must submit. It is a human-caused problem and has human-invented solutions, *provided we act*. Barrie Pittock (2009) notes that if people are panicking about climate change, it is because governments and business have not fully taken up the technological challenge to solve it through ingenuity and innovation. As research and demonstration continue, technologies are becoming cheaper by the year. We thus understand the frustration of scientists who know the solutions exist, but cannot get adequate funding to bring them into commercial production. The fossil fuel industry receives huge subsidies from government, while the renewable energy industry receives a trickle. Significant emission reductions can be achieved at a future cost of only a few per cent of GDP (Pittock, 2009). One of the most frustrating aspects is that appropriate technology, such as renewable energy, will create a large number of green jobs, far more jobs than the fossil fuel and mining industries combined (McNeil, 2009). Yet those who supposedly support job creation will in the same breathe oppose renewable energy. The problem, Pittock (2009) concludes, has always been *lack of political will*.

Renewable Energy

Key among these appropriate technologies is renewable energy. The Sun radiates to Earth each year something of the order of 7500 times (EPI, 2008), 10,000 times (Pittock, 2009) or 18,000 times (Shell, 2008) as much energy as humans consume. There is thus no problem with there being enough renewable energy available. The issue has always been harnessing this effectively and economically. The renewable energy sources available are solar energy through thermal and photovoltaic systems, wind power, wave power and tidal power, hydroelectricity, bioenergy, and geothermal (including hot rocks). These are all available essentially forever (in human history terms). Why then has there been a history of ignoring or even *repressing* renewable energy? Why have patents on renewable energy inventions been bought up and sat on? Why was there a concerted (and clandestine) campaign to stop and recall an efficient electric vehicle in America (see www.whokilledtheelectriccar.com)? Why is there a concerted campaign even today to dismiss renewable energy as a minor player or as 'off with the fairies'? The answer is simple – oil and coal. Society went down the coal path in the industrial revolution and became addicted to coal for stationary energy use and steam trains. Then oil was discovered, and provided a simple liquid fuel for transport. We became addicted to both, and they were originally plentiful and cheap. They make great wealth for corporations, who will fight to continue this until they are stopped in the public interest. Coal is still plentiful, though we have reached peak oil, so cost is rising. Due to climate change we need alternatives to both.

And the alternatives exist. We will not list them in great detail, as others such as Mark Diesendorf (2007), Barrie Pittock (2009), Ben McNeil (2009) and Matthew Wright and Patrick Hearps (2010) have already done this. One can summarize them as:

- *Wind power.* The cost of wind energy has come down hugely over the last 30 years. It is already cheaper than nuclear electricity and should soon rival coal-fired electricity in cost (Diesendorf, 2009a). Wind power has grown 28 per cent a year since 2000. At the end of 2006 there was 94 GW installed. Over 20 GW was installed in 2007. By 2012 it is expected there will be 240 GW. By 2050 it has been predicted that wind energy will provide up to 17 per cent of world power (Pittock, 2009). Already Denmark draws 21 per cent of its electricity from wind (Hamilton, 2010). The potential for wind power is huge, with one study showing that the US has the potential to produce over twice its current electricity consumption (Pittock, 2009). The wind doesn't always blow in any one spot, but it does blow *somewhere* all the time. A widely distributed wind power network will thus function in part as base-load power, though it will need other forms of peak-load backup (Diesendorf, 2007; Wright and Hearps, 2010). Noise and bird death are over-rated problems with wind power. For every 10,000 birds killed by human activities, less than one bird death is caused by a wind turbine (Pittock, 2009).

- *Solar.* Solar thermal is ideal for water heating. Electricity can be produced either by solar thermal or by photovoltaic (PV), the efficiency of which is increasing (and is more practical for domestic situations). There are currently 354 MW solar thermal electricity installed in the Mojave Desert in the US (EPI, 2008) and 545 MW installed worldwide (Greenpeace, 2009). Solar thermal capacity is growing rapidly and is expected to reach 6400 MW by 2012 (EPI, 2008). Some 14,500 MW are either under construction or proposed (Hamilton, 2010). A proposal is under consideration for a vast solar thermal installation in the Sahara that could provide a sixth of Europe's electricity needs (Kanter, 2009). Solar thermal storage systems (such as molten salts of sodium and potassium nitrate) can also store solar energy for almost eight hours for later use. In this way solar thermal can provide base-load power, that is power day or night (Diesendorf, 2007; Pittock, 2009). It has been claimed that solar thermal could supply seven per cent of the world's energy needs by 2020 and a quarter by 2050 (Greenpeace, 2009). A Californian company, Ausra, has developed efficient solar thermal systems which they claim could supply 90 per cent of the US electricity grid (Pittock, 2009). An Australian study shows solar thermal could provide 60 per cent of stationary power in just 10 years (Wright and Hearps, 2010).

  There were 620 MW of solar PV in 2003, 2821 MW in 2007 and in 2017 it is estimated there will be 23,000 MW (Pittock, 2009). New solar PV technologies continue to emerge, such as the Nanosolar panel that could produce solar electricity at a third of the cost of current panels, a price competitive with fossil fuel electricity. Together the prospects for rapid growth of solar (thermal and PV) are excellent and they can supply energy on demand. This is contrary to the views expressed by nuclear and denial advocates. The two main central problems of solar – remoteness from markets and the need for storage to counter its intermittent nature – have now been largely solved (Pittock, 2009).

- *Geothermal and hot rocks.* Geothermal traditionally harnesses the steam produced naturally by the Earth's heat. This produced 9 GW of electricity in 2005. The top 2km of the Earth's crust in the US could provide current power demands for 30,000 years (Pittock, 2009). Australia does not have major regions of geothermal steam, but does have areas of *hot rocks* (or hot fractured rocks). With these you need to pump water down to produce steam, which is then captured and returned to a turbine. One cubic kilometre of hot granite at 250 degrees Celsius has the stored energy equivalent of 40 million barrels of oil (Geodynamics, 2009). The company Geodynamics (2009) in Australia has demonstrated 'proof of concept' and has a 1 MW demonstration electricity station due to commence operation shortly in South Australia. They plan to develop a 500 MW power station by 2016, and eventually build up to 10,000 MW. Electricity derived from hot rocks will be base-load power, and estimates put its cost at AU$45/MWh, less than the cost of black coal electricity. Australia's total hot rock energy resources are likely to be comparable to its demonstrated reserves of coal and natural gas (Pittock, 2009).

- *Hydroelectricity*. This has major potential in many countries, though less potential in Australia. However, large hydroelectricity dams (such as the Three Gorges in China) generally have major environmental and social impacts. Small- and medium-scale hydro projects in widely distributed areas are thus better options.
- *Wave and tidal power (and ocean currents)*. The power of the tides has been harnessed in various places in the world (for example the 240 MW plant on the Rance Estuary in France, Pittock, 2009). One proposed tidal power station on the Severn could provide 4.4 per cent of the UK electricity supply. Wave power has been harder to harness, but there is an operating 2.2 MW wave power plant in Portugal and another being built in Scotland. An Australian company has successfully tested the CETO wave power system, where 500 buoys could produce 100 MW of electricity (Pittock, 2009). The potential of wave power is enormous and would be base-load power.
- *Bioenergy*. Plants store solar energy in wood, fibre and oils. These can be burned to produce energy for both stationary sources and transport. Wood and plant oils are the oldest form of renewable energy. Unless there is major transport involved (using fossil fuels), or inputs of fertilizers produced with fossil fuels, then such bioenergy comes close to being carbon neutral. Plants take up CO_2, which is then released when they are burned. Diesendorf (2007) notes that bioenergy offers both threats and opportunities. If poorly implemented, it could result in soil depletion, consumption of scarce water resources and loss of biodiversity. If implemented appropriately, on the other hand, it could have very low environmental impacts and could help restore degraded land. Biofuels are much discussed and confusion is rife. They can be useful in reducing carbon emissions (especially regionally), especially if sourced from plantations or agricultural residues. They can be harmful if you clear existing rainforest to grow oil palms, or if you clear old growth forest. Bioenergy must demonstrate a significant *net* carbon reduction over its whole life-cycle. It should not come from native forests but from plantations or agricultural wastes. Bioenergy electricity plants could be used to provide peak-load demand in an integrated renewable energy system. Genuine waste residues from plantation (not old growth) forestry activities and farm crops are one obvious source of bioenergy.

It is estimated that by 2040, Australia could produce 30 per cent of its electricity from bioenergy from agricultural and forestry wastes (Diesendorf, 2009a). It is therefore a significant but overlooked source of renewable energy. Biomass is also important in terms of replacing 'energy-dense' construction materials. Wood has an energy density of 1–3 MJ/kg, whereas steel has 34 and aluminium 170 (Pittock, 2009). Bioenergy can also be obtained from the production of *biochar* (charcoal), where this is then used as an agricultural product that sequesters carbon into soil and also improves water and nutrient retention. Biochar is thus not just carbon neutral, it is *carbon-negative*, removing carbon from the atmosphere and putting it in soils (Pittock, 2009). This is one of the most important carbon-negative technologies available, and could have great value in removing CO_2 from the atmosphere given we have overshot the likely safe level of CO_2. It has been estimated that by 2100 biochar could sequester as much carbon as is currently emitted annually by fossil fuels (Pittock, 2009). It is a tragedy that the carbon-negative technology of biochar – a significant solution – has been overlooked and received minimal support from governments.

The use of all these technologies (often suited to remote locations) has been improved by the ability to use high-voltage direct current transmission cables with emission losses of only three per cent over 1000km (Pittock, 2009). Australia is one of the sunniest countries in the world, yet has a woeful history of seizing this potential. Instead, China is now the biggest solar producer in the world, followed by Germany. Australia has good wind resources also, but it has a poor history of researching and supporting wind turbine technology (Diesendorf, 2009a). Australia also has a major 'hot rock' potential, but lack of vision means that time is being wasted.

There is some pessimism about society's speed of change to renewable energy, even in countries which have made a major effort. In Germany in 2008, winter wind provided 20 per cent of electricity, but as an annual average wind and solar provided only 7.3 per cent of electricity (Hansen, 2009). To solve climate change will thus require a rapid and major conversion to renewable energy, as we have delayed for so long. We are talking about the need for an urgent program similar to the scale of the Marshall Plan (which provided money to reconstruct Europe after the Second World War) or even the Space Race. Possibly we may be talking about something more of the order of the effort put into the Second World War. This effort would be a key part of the 'Great Work' – a rapid deployment of resources and technology to roll out renewable energy (in all its forms) to solve climate change. To put the economics of this in perspective, as mentioned earlier (see page 123), the money needed would be much less than what we already spend on the military (Pittock, 2009), and it has shown that Australia could become renewable-powered in just 10 years at a cost of three per cent of GDP a year (Wright and Hearps, 2010).

Renewable energy is thus entirely feasible. However, unless we reduce consumerism, the sheer scale of renewables required to supply an increasingly affluent world in the time required would be mind-boggling (Assadourian, 2010). We therefore need a renewable conversion that goes hand-in-hand with a reduction in consumerism. We need both together. For years we buried our heads in the sand and denied the potential of the wealth of renewable energy on our doorstep. Now it is time to wake up and 'seize the day'. The technologies exist, are feasible and economic – all we need is the political will.

One inappropriate technology to discuss here is 'geoengineering' (nuclear and carbon capture and storage are discussed in the following sections). Geoengineering is actually a category of technologies aimed at cooling the planet by engineering actions. This idea is very much part of the ideology of dominating nature. Geoengineering includes placing mirrors in space to deflect sunlight, adding aerosols (mainly sulphate) to the stratosphere to reflect light, fertilizing the oceans (mostly with iron, a limiting nutrient) to encourage algal growth to remove CO_2, or using 'artificial trees' that sequester CO_2. Space mirrors may be expensive, but sulphate aerosols and ocean iron addition would be cheaper (and may be able to lower global temperatures by two degrees). One cost estimate puts the cost of sulphate injection at U$25–50 billion a year (Crutzen, 2006). One newspaper survey reported that half of climate scientists believe that cutting emissions will not be enough and we will be forced to pursue geoengineering (Connor and Green, 2009). However, once you start relying on geoengineering, you can't stop, as then climate change will return with a vengeance (as CO_2 will have continued to increase). The James Hansen (2009) view on sulphate aerosols is that you don't solve one pollution problem with another serious problem. Sulphate additions in the stratosphere would reduce the efficiency of solar power stations, affect ozone levels and may affect the Indian Monsoon (Pittock, 2009) and thus markedly increase world hunger (Robock et al, 2008). There would also be a reduction of the blue skies we grew up with, as instead the sky will become increasingly 'whitened' (Crutzen, 2006). It would also do nothing to stop the acidification of the oceans due to increasing CO_2 levels. There would also likely be an increase in acid rain to the surface as the sulphate enters the troposphere. Geoengineering is yet another excuse to continue business-as-usual, rather than actually face up to reality and reduce emissions. The temptation to rely on geoengineering as a fall-back excuse (and thus not reduce emissions) is dangerous (Pittock, 2009). Geoengineering is part of the denial of the overall problem.

Climate change action – despite what the deniers claim – is not about going back to live in caves. It is about a rational assessment of reality, of our situation, and a transition to a carbon-free economy. It won't mean a drastic plunge in the standard of living, or the end of the car (though possibly less reliance on this), or the end of electricity use. The price of electricity will rise – as it should. In terms of its environmental and climate impact, coal-fired electricity has been too cheap for too long. We have not been paying the true cost of such electricity in terms of environmental impacts. However, a home energy-efficiency (sustainability) audit can generally save you the cost of this price increase, as most houses waste lots of energy. With energy conservation in your home, rising electricity prices need not end up being a *net* cost. Acting on climate change is thus not going to send us back into the caves. In fact it is more likely that climate change action will lead to an improvement in the quality of life in real terms. Less pollution, cleaner skies, less freak weather and heatwaves. Appropriate technology – harnessing the creative potential of humanity as part of the Great Work (Berry, 1999) of Earth repair – is a major part of the solution to the environmental crisis and climate change.

Is Nuclear Power the Way Out?

We conclude that nuclear power is not the solution to climate change, as you don't solve one serious problem with another. Even if it was the only option for non coal-fired electricity, the serious problems around nuclear power would make one question it. Energy expert Amory Lovins (quoted in WADE, 2006) notes:

> So the big question about nuclear 'revival' isn't just who'd pay for such a turkey, but also why bother? Why keep on distorting markets and biasing choices to divert scarce resources from the winners to the loser – a far slower, costlier, harder and riskier niche product – and paying a premium to incur its many problems?

However, nuclear isn't the only option – it is more expensive than renewable energy options such as wind (Diesendorf, 2009a), so why is society debating its merits? The reason is due to the powerful nuclear and mining lobbies, who (due to concern over climate change) see a chance to resurrect their nuclear fantasy. Nuclear power is one issue that tends to polarize even climate scientists. Hansen (2009) has come out in support of nuclear power, especially fast breeder reactors (FBRs). We understand the deep concern about climate catastrophe that has motivated Hansen to propose nuclear as an alternative. However, we repeat his own advice regarding geoengineering – it is not wise to solve one serious pollution problem with another. This argument applies here also. Nuclear power is not a viable solution for the following reasons:

- It's not carbon neutral anyway. Nuclear power requires the mining of ore, and its processing to yellowcake. This involves energy that comes from fossil fuels. Gavin Mudd and Mark Diesendorf (2008) have shown that just in terms of onsite energy consumption it takes 20–50 tonnes of CO_2 to produce one tonne of U_3O_8 (yellowcake). With current high grade ores (>0.1% U_3O_8) this might mean that the carbon footprint of a uranium power station was 10 per cent of that of a coal-fired one. That doesn't sound too bad. However, high grade ores are limited, and with low grade ores (<0.01% U_3O_8) the carbon footprint will be a greater percentage of a coal-fired power station – perhaps approaching that of a gas-fired power station (Mudd, 2009). It also takes energy to build and dismantle nuclear power plants, transport nuclear materials (Pittock, 2009) and quarantine nuclear wastes for millennia, so the above figure is an underestimate.
- Nuclear energy is too slow to deploy anyway. It takes many years to build and commission a nuclear power station. The International Energy Agency envisages a four-fold increase in nuclear electricity by 2050. This would require the construction of 32 nuclear power plants every year and would reduce CO_2 emissions from the energy sector by only six per cent. By contrast, Amory Lovins and Imran Sheikh (2008) show that wind farms could generate the same power for 60 per cent of the construction costs, and could be installed in a year or two.
- Nuclear power is not cheap. An MIT study estimated the cost of nuclear electricity at 6.7 cents per kWh. This was more expensive than fossil fuel

electricity and wind power in the US (around 4–5 cents per kWh) (Pittock, 2009). We should be spending each dollar in ways that displace the most carbon soonest, and this is not nuclear (Lovins and Sheikh, 2008).

- It is debatable if there are enough total uranium reserves (especially high grade reserves) to provide a low-carbon future if fossil fuel power stations are to be replaced (Diesendorf, 2009b; Mudd and Diesendorf, 2010), *unless* we move to FBRs. Such a system converts the common uranium 238 isotope into plutonium, which can then be recycled to fuel additional power plants. These FBRs require liquid sodium to cool them (which bursts into flame on contact with water or water vapour). There are major questions regarding safety around FBRs. There is potential for a large (non-nuclear) explosion that might rupture the reactor vessel and disperse radioactive material into the environment (Kumar and Ramana, 2009). A partial fuel meltdown occurred at the Enrico Fermi FBR in the US in 1966. A sodium leakage and fire occurred at Monju FBR in Japan in 1995, and the Russian BN-600 FBR has suffered repeated sodium leaks and fires (Kumar and Ramana, 2009). A pro-nuclear MIT study (Ansolabehere et al, 2003) did not expect that the breeder cycle would come into commercial operation during the next three decades. There is also the practical question as to whether reprocessing of fission reactor waste in FBRs is really the answer (Garwin, 2009). India has proposals to build hundreds of FBRs by mid-century. However, few FBRs are currently producing electricity, and none are doing so on a commercial basis (Diesendorf, 2007).

- The nuclear fuel cycle produces weapons grade uranium and plutonium. It thus increases the risk that fissionable material may fall into the hands of terrorists (even impure plutonium can still work as a dirty bomb).

- Nuclear power stations produce highly radioactive waste that must be separated from the environment for tens of thousands of years, longer than recorded human history. It is never really a case of 'disposal' where you can forget about such waste. It must be monitored for thousands of years. Do we really believe our society can guarantee this for future generations?

- Nuclear power stations cannot blow up like a bomb but they can melt down like Chernobyl and release large amounts of dangerous radioactivity, causing cancer and genetic defects over a wide area

- When nuclear power stations reach the end of their design life, they are so radioactive that dismantling them is a problem. For a standard-sized reactor there are at least 130 million pounds of radioactive waste produced that must be removed and stored at radioactive waste sites for thousands of years (Wald, 2009).

- The costs to insure a nuclear power station are huge (of the order of several billion dollars). Thus governments must insure them against accidents, as no insurance company would do so. Surely that demonstrates the risks involved? One thing that insurance companies excel at is the estimation of risk.

These considerations suggest that nuclear fission reactors are unlikely to play a major role in replacing fossil fuels and reducing total emissions by 2050 (Pittock, 2009). Apart from Asia (China, India, Korea) and Russia there are few new commitments to build new nuclear power plants (Deutch et al, 2009). President Obama, however, has recently announced an $8 billion programme to build a new generation of reactors in the US.

It is often said that nuclear *fusion* is the future, as this does not require uranium and is free of risks. However, this is a half-truth. Fusion has never worked economically to date and this is at least 30 years away. If the experimental ITER fusion reactor is successful (commencing 2016), a prototype nuclear fusion power station may be built starting in 2026, with a possible commercial power station commencing in 2045 at the earliest (Diesendorf, 2007). However, the most efficient fusion reactor requires both deuterium and tritium. Deuterium is present in the sea, but large-scale tritium production for fusion would initially have to come from fission reactors (though later it could come from the fusion reactors themselves). Nonetheless, the high-energy neutron output of fusion reactors may also be used to breed fissile material to run fission reactors. Indeed a fission/fusion reactor is seen as desirable for efficiency reasons (Gerstner, 2009). Fusion would thus probably not 'replace' fission but be added to it. Fusion power stations also become highly radioactive over their lifetime (Atkinson, 1989), and like fission reactors have to be dismantled with care. The radioactive waste must be stored safely for thousands of years. Fusion thus will take decades to arrive and may not in fact replace fission reactors. It therefore cannot be seen as the 'magic bullet' to solve our climate problems.

Given the above, why would we rush into a nuclear future? Nuclear power is a false solution. It offers little, it offers late and it doesn't mean a huge cut in the carbon footprint. It is expensive and provides its own high risk to future generations. Accepting reality means we need to accept *all* of reality. We can't reject denial about climate change but then deny the serious problems around nuclear power. Nuclear power is not the path to a sustainable low-carbon future. We should not fall prey to the spin and propaganda of the nuclear and mining industries. Nuclear energy is not the way to solve human-caused climate change.

Is Carbon Capture and Storage the Solution?

Again we believe not – carbon capture and storage (CCS) is a 'buzz' word. The reason it is supported by governments is that if it worked it would allow 'business-as-usual' to continue. It is in fact part of denial. We are deluding ourselves that we don't need to change, that we can just put the nasty CO_2 somewhere 'away', where it won't do bad things. Hansen (2009) notes that in regard to CCS, the phrase 'capture ready' is an illusion, a fake designed to get approval for proposed coal-fired power plants. CCS is not the answer because:

- It would come too late. It cannot be applied to existing power stations effectively. To work successfully, the coal would need to be gasified and the

CO_2 collected under high pressure to be liquefied and then pumped underground. It cannot be used to retrofit existing power stations, so there would be a huge cost involved in building replacement power stations. The International Energy Agency estimates that by 2030 the world will need 200 power plants fully equipped with CCS to limit warming to three degrees Celsius. A study by MIT (2007), *The Future of Coal*, suggests that the first commercial CCS plants would not be operating till 2030 at the earliest. The IPCC estimates that by 2050 only 30–60 per cent of power generation will be technically suitable for CCS (Hamilton, 2010).

- It requires huge amounts of energy to liquefy CO_2 and pump it underground. To use it on a coal-fired power plant would increase the amount of coal consumed by 25–40 per cent to compress, liquefy and pump the liquid CO_2 to underground storage sites (Metz et al, 2005). For every three coal-fired power stations you build you would thus need to build a fourth one just to provide the power for this.

- CCS (like nuclear waste) is never disposed of 'forever'. Rather, any CCS disposal site would need to be monitored for thousands of years. If the CO_2 escaped, it is potentially dangerous and causes death that was once called 'choke-damp' by coal miners. An example of mass CO_2 poisoning occurred during the Lake Nyos tragedy in Cameroon in 1988, where 1700 villagers and 3500 livestock died due to a CO_2 eruption from a volcanic lake (Holloway, 2001).

- If we were to use this for all our coal-fired power stations, the volume of liquefied CO_2 to be disposed of would be very large. It would thus be an oil industry in reverse. In order to capture just a quarter of emissions from the world's coal-fired power stations would require pumping in twice the volume of oil pumped out now by the oil industry (Goodell, 2008). This huge operation would create many problems, and inevitably there would be leaks.

- It probably won't work in terms of removing enough CO_2. By 2050 probably only 20–40 per cent of coal-fired CO_2 emissions would be technically suitable for capture. Of these, 5–15% of CO_2 is not captured by the process anyway. If there was 0.5 per cent leakage from these storages (quite likely), then by 2100 there could still be 10 Gt of CO_2 being released, more than the present rate of CO_2 emissions (Pittock, 2009). We would therefore have undertaken a hugely expensive process that did not reduce carbon emissions in a major way.

- It isn't cheap and probably would never be economic without a carbon price of U\$30 a tonne (Pittock 2009). Currently CCS research is overwhelmingly funded by governments and not industry (which should tell us something about its economic viability). In 2009 President Obama allocated U\$3.4 billion to CCS research while Australia allocated A\$2.4 billion (Hamilton, 2010). With a \$30/tonne carbon price, alternative technologies such as renewable energy would present a more attractive solution than CCS.

- Only some areas have the geology that is suitable for CCS. For example, in Australia the main coal areas of the Sydney basin and the Hunter do not have suitable geology, yet these are the sites of many of the coal-fired power stations in the State of New South Wales.

Thus, CCS is not the silver bullet. The IPCC view is that CCS could only be a small part of the solution to carbon emissions (Pittock, 2009). CCS is really part of implicatory denial. By ignoring the realities, we allow ourselves to continue with business-as-usual. CCS provides us with a way to salve our consciences. It may not be a complete fairytale, but 'hot rocks', geothermal or other forms of renewable energy provide a far more likely solution to climate change than CCS ever will.

References

Ansolabehere, S., Deutch, J., Driscoll, M., Gray, P., Holdren, J., Joscow, P., Lester, R., Monas, J. and Todreas, M. (2003) *The Future of Nuclear Power: An Interdisciplinary MIT Study*, Massachusetts Institute of Technology, Cambridge, MA, http://web.mit.edu/nuclearpower

Assadourian, E. (2010) 'The rise and fall of consumer cultures', in L. Starke and L. Mastny (eds) *2010 State of the World: Transforming Cultures from Consumerism to Sustainability*, Earthscan, London

Atkinson, A. (1989) 'The environmental impact of fusion power', *Energy Policy*, June, pp277–283

Berry, T. (1999) *The Great Work*, Belltower, New York

Connor, S. and Green, C. (2009) 'Climate scientists: It's time for plan B', *The Independent*, 2 January, www.independent.co.uk/environment/climate-change/climate-scientists-its-time-for-plan-b-1221092.html

Crutzen, P. (2006) 'Albedo enhancement by stratospheric sulfur injections: A contribution to resolve a policy dilemma', *Climatic Change*, vol 77, nos 3–4, pp211–220

Deutch, J., Forsberg, C., Kadak, A., Kazimi, M., Moniz, E. and Parsons, J. (2009) 'Update of the MIT 2003 future of nuclear power', http://web.mit.edu/nuclearpower/

Diesendorf, M. (2007) *Greenhouse Solutions with Sustainable Energy*, UNSW Press, Sydney, Australia

Diesendorf, M. (2009a) *Climate Action: A Campaign Manual for Greenhouse Solutions*, UNSW Press, Sydney, Australia

Diesendorf, M. (2009b) 'Is nuclear energy a viable option?', paper presented at Conference on Nuclear Energy, Petaling, Jaya, Malaysia, 10 October, by Dr Mark Diesendorf, Deputy Director of the Institute of Environmental Studies, NSW University, Sydney, Australia

EPI (2008) 'Solar thermal power coming to a boil', Earth Policy Institute, www.earth-policy.org/index.php?/plan_b_updates/2008/update73

Garwin, R. (2009) 'Reprocessing isn't the answer', *Bulletin of the Atomic Scientists*, 6 August

Geodynamics (2009) *Power from the Earth*, Annual Report, see www.geodynamics.com.au/IRM/content/report_annualreport.html

Gerstner, E. (2009) 'Nuclear energy: The hybrid returns', *Nature*, vol 460, no 7251, pp25–28

Goodell, J. (2008) 'Coal's new technology: Panacea or risky gamble', *Yale Environment*, vol 360, 14 July

Greenpeace (2009) *Concentrating Solar Power, Global Outlook 09: Why Renewable Energy is Hot*, Greenpeace International/SolarPACES/Estela (European Solar Thermal Electricity Association), Amsterdam, The Netherlands

Hamilton, C. (2010) *Requiem for a Species: Why We Resist the Truth about Climate Change*, Allen and Unwin, Sydney, Australia

Hansen, J. (2009) *Storms of My Grandchildren: The Truth about the Coming Climate Catastrophe and Our Last Chance to Save Humanity*, Bloomsbury, London

Hawken, P., Lovins, A. B. and Lovins, L. H. (2010) *Natural Capitalism: The Next Industrial Revolution*, 2nd edition, Earthscan, London

Holloway, M. (2001) 'Trying to tame the roar of deadly lakes', *New York Times*, 27 February

Hulme, M. (2009) *Why We Disagree about Climate Change: Understanding Controversy, Inaction and Opportunity*, Cambridge University Press, Cambridge, UK

Kanter, J. (2009) 'European solar power from African deserts?', *New York Times*, 18 June

Kumar, A. and Ramana, M. (2009) 'The safety inadequacies of India's fast breeder reactor', *Bulletin of the Atomic Scientists*, 21 July

Lovins, A. and Sheikh, I. (2008) *The Nuclear Illusion*, Rocky Mountain Institute, Boulder, CO, www.rmi.org/rmi/Library/E08-01_NuclearIllusion

McNeil, B. (2009) *The Clean Industrial Revolution: Growing Australian Prosperity in the Greenhouse Age*, Allen and Unwin, Sydney, Australia

Metz, B., Davidson,O., de Coninck, H. C., Loos, M. and Meyer, L. A. (eds) (2005) *IPCC Special Report on Carbon Dioxide Capture and Storage*, Working Group III of the Intergovernmental Panel on Climate Change, Cambridge University Press, Cambridge, UK and New York, available in full at www.ipcc.ch

MIT (2007) *The Future of Coal: Options for a Carbon Constrained World*, Massachusetts Institute of Technology, Cambridge, MA

Mudd, G. (2009) Personal communication from Dr Gavin Mudd, environmental engineer, Monash University, Victoria, Australia

Mudd, G. and Diesendorf, M. (2008) 'Sustainability of uranium mining and milling: Toward quantifying resources and eco-efficiency', *Environmental Science & Technology*, vol 42, no 7, pp2624–2630

Mudd, G. and Diesendorf, M. (2010) 'Uranium mining, nuclear power and sustainability – Rhetoric versus reality', paper presented at the Sustainable Mining Conference, Kalgoorlie, Western Australia, 17–19 August

Oreskes, N. and Conway, E. M. (2010) *Merchants of Doubt: How a Handful of Scientists Obscured the Truth on Issues from Tobacco Smoke to Global Warming*, Bloomsbury Press, New York

Passmore, J. (1975) 'The revolt against science', in P. Gardner (ed) *The Structure of Science Education*, Longman, Hawthorne, Australia

Pittock, A. B. (2009) *Climate Change: The Science, Impacts and Solutions*, CSIRO Publishing, Melbourne, Australia

Robock, A., Oman, L. and Stenchikov, G. (2008) 'Regional climate responses to geoengineering with tropical and Arctic SO_2 injections', *Journal of Geophysical Research Letters*, vol 13, doi:10.1029/2008JD010050

Shell (2008) 'Why has technology advanced so slowly in the energy sector?', Jotman Green blog, www.jotgreen.com/2009/07/why-has-technology-advanced-so-slowly.html

Specter, M. (2009) *Denialism: How Irrational Thinking Hinders Scientific Progress, Harms the Planet and Threatens Our Lives*, Penguin Press, New York

WADE (2006) *World Survey of Decentralised Energy 2006*, World Alliance for Decentralised Energy, Washington, DC, www.localpower.org/documents_pub/report_worldsurvey06.pdf

Wald, M. (2009) 'Dismantling nuclear reactors', *Scientific American*, 26 January

Washington, H. (1991) *Ecosolutions: Environmental Solutions for the World and Australia*, Boobook Publications, Tea Gardens, Australia

Wright, M. and Hearps, P. (2010) *Australian Sustainable Energy Stationary Energy Plan*, University of Melbourne Energy Research Institute/Beyond Zero Emissions, Melbourne, Australia, http://beyondzeroemissions.org

8

Summary and Conclusion

We shall wrap up by reviewing the chapters to see what we have learned about denial, both of environmental problems in general and specifically about denial of climate change. We shall then move to a conclusion.

Summary

In Chapter 1 we noted that denial is not the same as skepticism. In many ways they were shown to be opposites. Skeptics seek the truth; deniers deny it. We discovered just how common denial is within humanity. The nature of science was examined in terms of uncertainty and probability. There is always uncertainty, and hence scientists speak in terms of probability. Science doesn't 'prove' things: it shows what is most probable. Thus for any issue in science, we speak of the 'preponderance of evidence'. We discussed the peer review process, which deniers hate as their arguments fail under rational analysis. The way scholars have categorized denial arguments was related (for example cherry-picking of data). We also examined what deniers have argued motivates climate scientists, which ranged from greed to being 'anti-human'.

The basics of climate science were covered in Chapter 2. We distinguished between climate and weather, and found that human civilization developed during the stable climate of the last 8000 years. The 'forcings' that drive climate were discussed. The key to current warming is the human-produced greenhouse gases that cause an energy imbalance that warms the atmosphere and oceans. We examined the natural and human-caused greenhouse effect. The 0.7 degree Celsius global temperature increase observed over the last century can only be explained by incorporating *both* types of warming. The carbon cycle was explained, along with the way human carbon emissions from fossil fuels are throwing this out of balance. We examined the positive and negative feedbacks on climate, where positive feedbacks now dominate. The science behind 'runaway' climate change was investigated, along with its risks. We considered what a 'safe' level of CO_2 might be, which many scientists believe is 350ppm, lower than the current level. The 'greenhouse gamble' roulette wheel was discussed, which showed that taking policy action on climate change improved the odds that we would avoid runaway climate change. We also looked at the likely impacts of climate change, which will progressively become worse as temperature rises (and lead to massive species extinctions). We finished by discussing scientific and ethical 'disconnects', where government policy was disconnected from both the actual climate science and also from ethics.

The five main types of climate change denial arguments were explained in Chapter 3 – conspiracy theories, fake experts, impossible expectations, misrepresentation/logical fallacies, and cherry-picking. The nine most common denial arguments were examined under these types. The claims made in each of these denial arguments were listed, along with the actual science. 'Climategate' was one example, where emails between climate scientists from the University of East Anglia were hacked and published. The confusion over the terms used in the emails was explained, such as reference to 'decline' that referred to decline in tree-ring growth and *not* global temperatures. The increasing trend by deniers to put forward 'fake experts' was examined; where such people often deem themselves 'experts' through being spokespersons for denial groups such as think tanks. We examined claims that climate models don't work, when actually they have predicted both observed historical warming and temporary cooling due to a volcanic eruption. One logical fallacy examined was the claim that climate has changed in the past, so change today must be natural. The fact that climate has changed naturally over time does not mean humans cannot change it for the worse by releasing greenhouse gases. Finally we examined cherry-picking, a favourite type of denial argument. One argument was that temperature measurements are 'unreliable', when in fact global temperature increase has been observed from both multiple land-based stations and satellite measurements. Another argument is that global warming stopped in 1998, when in fact both land and oceans continue to warm. Global temperature continues to rise, and the Sun is not responsible, for we have been in a solar minimum period for the last few decades. Finally we looked at the claim that global warming was 'good' and saw that overall the rapid climate change now happening could not be seen as good. Rather it is potentially catastrophic.

The long history of denial of many environmental issues was related in Chapter 4. Indeed, most climate change deniers also deny the world has *any* environmental problems. This was brought to prominence with denial of the impact of the pesticide DDT (and indeed Naomi Oreskes and Erik Conway, 2010, note that deniers have recently returned to that theme). That was followed by denial of environmental problems such as biodiversity loss and population, denial of acid rain, denial of the impact of tobacco smoke, denial of the risk of nuclear winter, and denial of CFCs causing the ozone hole. The history of 'greenscamming' was examined, where front organizations that sound like environment groups are set up to sow confusion and doubt. We detailed the fossil fuel industry funding of denial groups, many of them conservative think tanks. The PR tactics used by denial groups to confuse the public were exposed. The trend to 'non-denial' denial was examined, where climate change is accepted, but then it is argued that regrettably it is just too difficult or costly to take action. The link between conservative think tanks and denial emerged, where regulation of the free market due to climate change was seen by conservatives as an attack on 'liberty'. Much of climate change denial is thus an *ideologically* driven attack on regulation, and one willing to abandon both reason and science. We closed the chapter by looking at one recent denial book, *Heaven and Earth* (Plimer, 2009), and examined its claims, which differed markedly from mainstream climate science.

The key question of whether we let denial prosper was addressed in Chapter 5. We considered humanity's fear of change, society's failure to discuss values, a fixation on economics and society, and our ignorance of ecology and exponential growth. The chapter looked at how some of us are gamblers willing to gamble on future climate, no matter what the risks. The role of the media in aiding denial was examined – how it loves controversy and how its coverage is biased in support of denial. Media coverage suggests that science is equally split regarding the cause of climate change, whereas the reality is that 97 per cent of climate scientists acknowledge humans are the cause. We related how a climate science hoax was set up by a journalist to show the media bias about climate change. The hoax was accepted by the media, and almost nobody checked on its accuracy. The problem of scientific 'reticence' was considered, where scientists have not explained climate science effectively. Government denial was examined, where they use 'spin' to *pretend* they are taking action. Finally, we looked at the psychological types of denial, where denial can be *literal* (for example the denial industry), *interpretive* (for example government spin) or *implicatory* (where one accepts the issue but chooses to ignore it). We showed that implicatory denial was the most common form of denial among 'we the people'. Thus the science has become more certain year by year, but due to implicatory denial more people let themselves ignore this – and fail to act.

Turning to the ways in which we might 'roll back denial', Chapter 6 examined the 'big picture' of doing this. One obvious answer was to 'accept reality'. Climate change denial was shown to be part of the denial of the environmental crisis as a whole. Such denial has been incredibly successful, and we discussed why. One key answer was *because we let it*. Society has let a denial prosper that has become a pathology that threatens the future. Implicatory denial within society has let many of us accept a more comfortable delusion by denying climate change. In our view it is not too late to roll back denial, accept reality, and solve climate change and other environmental problems. To this end we need a vision, a 'Great Work' of Earth repair (Berry, 1999). We examined what stopped society accepting reality. Chief among the reasons was society's consumer worldview. Ideologies also played a part, such as modernism and postmodernism. The latter of these has not proven to be more of a solution than the former, and they both play a part in denial. We examined key related issues, such as over-population (which society also denies). We looked at how we should go about solving climate change. Changing our worldview and ethics were shown to be a key place to start. Changing our economy from perpetual growth to steady-state was another. The need to both adapt and mitigate in regard to climate change was made clear. We looked at how to get the message on climate change across and the need for ongoing political pressure. Sustainability and its meanings were investigated. The market and civic environmentalism approaches to climate change were detailed. In regard to market solutions, we discussed an emissions trading scheme (ETS) and a carbon tax and the values of each. Civic environmentalism was considered, where the community can act even if governments are slow to do so. We concluded the chapter on why we needed to say farewell to coal.

In Chapter 7 we turned to the technological solutions to rolling back denial of climate change. Often denial of climate change goes hand-in-hand with denial of its solutions. The wealth of *appropriate* technologies that can reduce our carbon footprint was considered. Chief among these was renewable energy in its many forms. Many of these are already cost-effective, and some only need a price on carbon to become so. We argued that the inappropriate technology of geoengineering was part of denial. We also examined nuclear power and found it was not an appropriate solution, for one should not replace one pollution problem with another. Nuclear offered little, offered it late and didn't cut carbon pollution in a major way. Carbon capture and storage (CCS) similarly failed on many grounds. It too would come late, involve great cost, require huge amounts of energy to liquefy and pump CO_2, and probably not cut emissions markedly. It was concluded that CCS was part of a delusion that we can continue the business-as-usual approach which has led to the climate crisis. Overall, the chapter acknowledged that technological solutions exist and are economic. The problem remains *lack of political will* and the continuing government failure to support and encourage appropriate technology.

Conclusion

In conclusion, what have these chapters told us about denial? We have laid out the nature and dangers and incredible weaknesses of climate change denial. As far as we know, denial is a uniquely human trait, an amazing ability to reject reality and retreat into delusion. It may be a function of the complexity of our minds. It may be a function of our evolutionary heritage, the interaction between our reptilian brainstem and our rational cortex (Rees, 2008). Under the stress of a difficult reality, our brainstem may over-ride our rational cortex. Whatever the cause, denial is a siren song of delusion and represents a real risk to the human psyche. Today it is not just a personal risk, however, but a delusion that has become a pathology. It is a pathology that threatens the stable climate in which our civilization evolved. It is a pathology that threatens the web of life with which we evolved, our brother and sister species who share this Earth. It is a pathology that threatens our societies and those we love. We not only share this Earth, we *depend* on the ecosystems and ecosystem services it provides for our human survival. The majority of us may now live in cities (UN, 2007), but our roots are in the Earth. Anything that attacks the ecosystems we rely on is ultimately an attack on ourselves and our children. Climate change – which we are the cause of – is such an attack.

So the question is whether each of us can take stock and recognize the seeds of denial within ourselves. We cannot lay all the blame on others, whether industry, governments or other countries. We need to accept that we are part of the problem and thus need to be part of the solution. There is always an ember smouldering within society to confront denial (Zerubavel, 2006), and we need to fan that ember to burst into flame. We need to stop denying we are in denial. We need to accept reality – and do something about it. We need also to stop denying the workable *solutions* to the climate crisis, such as renewable energy. The climate crisis is not a fixed and immutable doom laid upon the world. It is a human-caused problem that has human-created solutions – if we use our intelligence and creativity. We have shown that the solutions exist. We can roll back denial and move to an ecologically sustainable future. The key first step is to stop the delusion, to stop denying we have problems that need to be faced – and solved.

The final chapters of this book were finished in draft the day after the 2009 Copenhagen COP15 conference finished in disarray. After two years of prevarication and procrastination, the conference itself got bogged down in parochial politics. It became a bargaining session where money and politics were the issue, not the science, not the action required by the science, not the ethics and not finding a sustainable future. Journalist George Monbiot concluded that this was the chaotic, disastrous denouement of a chaotic and disastrous summit. The process was sabotaged by particular states, supported by the energy industries (Monbiot, 2009). Thus immediate self-interest trumped the long-term welfare of humankind. So to some extent Copenhagen was an opportunity lost. Too many of those involved were denying things at some scale. Too many were and are set in their ways and cannot act in response to the climate crisis.

This is hardly surprising, as climate change in the end is showing us we need to change the way we view the world, that we need to move beyond consumerism and move to an eco-centric worldview (Assadourian, 2010). It is a major, inconvenient and unpalatable truth for a modernist and consumerist society. It is a major reality check. On the other hand, we agree with Mike Hulme (2009) and Barrie Pittock (2009) that climate change really is an *opportunity to get things right*. Something will come out of the Copenhagen experience, and there will be reductions in greenhouse gases because of it (provided we keep the pressure up on our politicians). Some action is always better than none. But the agreements that flow out of Copenhagen alone will almost certainly not be enough. The top–down approach will not be enough. It will need the simultaneous revolution in the expansion of appropriate technology and renewable energy. It will also need strong action through civic environmentalism. In Russia they used to talk of a 'kind Tsar' that would look after them. However, we can no longer expect a kind Tsar to solve these problems. We have to solve them ourselves – but that also means acting politically to *make* our governments solve them.

The reality of climate change is a wake-up call that forces us to acknowledge that all is not well with the world and our custodianship of it. It is the canary in the coal mine warning us of the toxic choke-damp (CO_2) and the danger involved. It is a wake-up call that denial is a dangerous element in the human psyche that can become a pathology. But climate change is truly an opportunity for us to get it right, to heal the damage our society, our numbers, our technology and our carbon fuels have done to the world. It is the chance to abandon denial and accept reality, ethics and responsibility. It is the chance to move to a dream of Earth Repair, the Great Work of our time (Berry, 1999). We can no longer say it's not economic to solve climate change. We have to, and thus we can *make it economic*. It certainly won't cost more than the U\$1531 billion a year we spend on the military (SIPRI, 2010). One Australian study suggests it would take only three per cent of GDP over 10 years to become 100 per cent renewable energy-powered (Wright and Hearps, 2010). It's what we value that counts, not just the dollars and cents (Pittock, 2009). Just as there are many paths to the truth, there are many paths to climate change solutions. These are the 'silver buckshot' solutions that must work together to halt climate change (Hulme, 2009). We see no need to choose between the approaches of the carbon marketeers and the eco-anarchists. They both have some validity and both can reduce carbon emissions. Silver buckshot means you *use what works*.

If we have the vision, the dream of Earth repair, the faith and hope that we can solve the climate crisis, then 'yes we can'. If we believe we can make a difference, then we will. If we despair, give up our hope of solving these issues, if we abdicate our choice to act, then we will fail. We either choose to act for a sustainable future or we contribute to a growing environmental disaster (Pittock, 2009). Climate change action is not about doom and gloom: it's about a new future, new technologies, new markets and a new worldview of how we live on Earth. It won't be simple or easy, but if we can face and conquer our denial, then our future is exciting as we make a better world. Can we roll back denial? *We can if we choose to.*

By way of concluding, we think each of us needs to pause and think. We need to return to the basics, and ask ourselves some deep, soul-searching questions:

- What do we value? If we value the diversity of life we share this world with, if we value those in poverty around the world (and believe we should help them), if we value the rights of future generations, then we need to stop denying the problems we face.
- What do we believe in? If we believe in the *reason* that underpins science,

then we need to accept what the peer-reviewed mainstream science tells us. We may not like it, but we must no longer deny it – in our own interests and in the interests of those we love.

- How much risk are we willing to run? Do we gamble on the future of the world or do we plan responsibly?
- What do we fear? Personally, our greatest fear is that humanity's lack of action will leave a vastly impoverished world to the future.
- Do we accept a responsibility to others and the future? If we do, then it's up to *us* to act, not others.

We think the last question is crucial. Denial is part of humanity; it has probably been with us since humans first evolved. There are those who operate from greed and deliberately create a denial industry to confuse people. This is immoral and destructive. Similarly, there are the denial spin-doctors in government who seek to use 'weasel words' and fool the public that they are taking meaningful action, when often they aren't. However, when it gets down to it, there is also denial in 'we the people'. We let ourselves be duped and conned, we let our consciences be massaged, we let our desire for the safe and easy life blot out the unpleasant realities. We delude ourselves. However, if a large part of the public abandons denial, they can fairly quickly turn around corporate denial, especially if it costs the corporations profits. If a large part of the community tells our politicians that they want real action, not weasel words, then politicians will actually act. We are not powerless drones who cannot change things. En masse, if we accept the dream of Earth Repair, we have the vision, the creativity and the power to solve climate change, and at the same time make the world a better place. That nobody should deny.

References

Assadourian, E. (2010) 'The rise and fall of consumer cultures', in L. Starke and L. Mastny (eds) *2010 State of the World: Transforming Cultures from Consumerism to Sustainability*, Earthscan, London

Berry, T. (1999) *The Great Work*, Belltower, New York

Hulme, M. (2009) *Why We Disagree about Climate Change: Understanding Controversy, Inaction and Opportunity*, Cambridge University Press, Cambridge, UK

Monbiot, G. (2009) 'Leaders bicker while the biosphere burns', *Sun-Herald* (Australia), 20 December

Oreskes, N. and Conway, E. M. (2010) *Merchants of Doubt: How a Handful of Scientists Obscured the Truth on Issues from Tobacco Smoke to Global Warming*, Bloomsbury Press, New York

Pittock, A. B. (2009) *Climate Change: The Science, Impacts and Solutions*, CSIRO Publishing, Melbourne, Australia

Plimer, I. (2009) *Heaven and Earth: Global Warming: The Missing Science*, Connorcourt Publishing, Ballan, Australia

Rees, W. (2008) 'Toward sustainability with justice: Are human nature and history on side?', Chapter 6 in C. Soskolne (ed) *Sustaining Life on Earth: Environmental and*

Human Health through Global Governance, Lexington Books, New York

SIPRI (2010) *Yearbook 2010*, Stockholm International Peace Research Institute, Stockholm, see www.sipri.org

UN (2007) *World Urbanization Prospects: The 2007 Revision*, United Nations, New York, see www.unpopulation.org

Wright, M. and Hearps, P. (2010) *Australian Sustainable Energy Stationary Energy Plan*, University of Melbourne Energy Research Institute/Beyond Zero Emissions, Melbourne, Australia, http://beyondzeroemissions.org

Zerubavel, E. (2006) *The Elephant in the Room: Silence and Denial in Everyday Life*, Oxford University Press, New York

Appendix

Greenscam and Denial Groups

Greenpeace's 'Exxon Secrets' List of Groups Funded by Exxon

See www.exxonsecrets.org/html/listorganizations.php for further details – the website lists the amounts of funding to these groups, sourced from public documents.

60/Sixty Plus Association
Accuracy in Academia
Accuracy in Media
Acton Institute for the Study of Religion and Liberty
The Advancement of Sound Science Center, Inc.
The Advancement of Sound Science Coalition
Africa Fighting Malaria
Air Quality Standards Coalition
ALEC (American Legislative Exchange Council)
Alexis de Tocqueville Institution
Alliance for Climate Strategies
American Coal Foundation
American Conservative Union Foundation
American Council for Capital Formation Center for Policy Research
American Council on Science and Health
American Enterprise Institute for Public Policy Research
American Enterprise Institute-Brookings Joint Center for Regulatory Studies
American Friends of the Institute for Economic Affairs
American Petroleum Institute
American Policy Center
American Recreation Coalition

American Spectator Foundation

Americans for Tax Reform

Annapolis Center for Science-Based Public Policy

Arizona State University Office of Climatology

Aspen Institute

Association of Concerned Taxpayers

Atlantic Legal Foundation

Atlas Economic Research Foundation

Blue Ribbon Coalition

Capital Legal Foundation

Capital Research Center and Greenwatch

Cato Institute

Center for American and International Law

Center for Environmental Education Research

Center for Security Policy

Center for Strategic and International Studies

Center for the Defense of Free Enterprise

Center for the New West

Center for the Study of Carbon Dioxide and Global Change

Centre for the New Europe

CFACT – Committee for a Constructive Tomorrow

Chemical Education Foundation

Citizens for a Sound Economy and CSE Educational Foundation

Citizens for the Environment and CFE Action Fund

Clean Water Industry Coalition

Climate Research Journal

Communications Institute

Competitive Enterprise Institute, listed by Hoggan (2009) and said to be a leader in the US denial industry

Congress of Racial Equality

Consumer Alert

Cooler Heads Coalition

Council for Solid Waste Solutions

DCI Group

Defenders of Property Rights

Earthwatch Institute

ECO or Environmental Conservation Organization

European Enterprise Institute

ExxonMobil Corporation

Federalist Society for Law and Public Policy Studies

Fraser Institute

FREE (Foundation for Research on Economics and the Environment)

Free Enterprise Action Institute

Free Enterprise Education Institute

Frontiers of Freedom Institute and Foundation

George C. Marshall Institute

George Mason University, Law and Economics Center

Global Climate Coalition

Great Plains Legal Foundation

Greening Earth Society

Harvard Center for Risk Analysis

Heartland Institute

Heritage Foundation

Hoover Institution on War, Revolution and Peace, Stanford University

Hudson Institute

Illinois Policy Institute

Independent Commission on Environmental Education

Independent Institute

Institute for Biospheric Research

Institute for Energy Research

Institute for Regulatory Science

Institute for Senior Studies

Institute for the Study of Earth and Man

Institute of Humane Studies, George Mason University

Interfaith Stewardship Alliance

International Climate Science Coalition

International Council for Capital Formation

International Policy Network (North America)

International Republican Institute

James Madison Institute

Junkscience.com

The Justice Foundation (formerly Texas Justice Foundation)

Landmark Legal Foundation

Lexington Institute

Lindenwood University

The Locke Institute

Mackinac Center

Manhattan Institute for Policy Research

Media Institute

Media Research Center

Mercatus Center, George Mason University
Mountain States Legal Foundation
National Association of Neighborhoods
National Black Chamber of Commerce
National Center for Policy Analysis
National Center for Public Policy Research
National Council for Environmental Balance
National Environmental Policy Institute
National Legal Center for the Public Interest
National Mining Association
National Policy Forum
National Wetlands Coalition
National Wilderness Institute
New England Legal Foundation
New Zealand Climate Science Coalition
Pacific Legal Foundation
Pacific Research Institute for Public Policy
Peabody Energy
PERC (Property and Environment Research Center), formerly Political Economy
Research Center
Public Interest Watch
Reason Foundation
Reason Public Policy Institute
Science and Environmental Policy Project
Seniors Coalition
Shook, Hardy and Bacon LLP
Small Business Survival Committee
Southeastern Legal Foundation
Stanford University GCEP
Statistical Assessment Service (STATS)
Tech Central Science Foundation or Tech Central Station
Texas Public Policy Foundation
United for Jobs
University of Oklahoma Foundation, Inc.
US Russia Business Council
Virginia Institute for Public Policy
Washington Legal Foundation
Weidenbaum Center on the Economy, Government, and Public Policy
Western Fuels
World Affairs Councils of America
World Climate Report

Other Greenscam/Denial Groups

American Coalition for Clean Coal Electricity (ACCCE), listed by Hoggan (2009)

Americans for Balanced Energy Choices (ABEC), listed by Hoggan (2009)

Australian Climate Science Coalition (ACSC), listed by Hoggan (2009)

Business Roundtable (New Zealand), listed by Greenpeace (2010)

Center for Energy and Economic Development (CEED), listed by Hoggan (2009) (group now defunct)

Climate Audit, listed by Oreskes and Conway (2010)

Climate Science Coalition, listed by Hoggan (2009)

Environmental Literacy Council, listed by Greenpeace (2010)

The European Science and Environment Forum (ESEF), listed by Enting (2007)

Global Warming Policy Foundation (UK), listed by Greenpeace (2010)

Information Council on the Environment (ICE)

Institute of Public Affairs (Australia), listed by Greenpeace (2010)

The Lavoisier Group in Australia, listed by Enting (2007)

Science and Public Policy Institute (SPPI), listed by Hoggan (2009)

Scientific Alliance (UK), listed by Hoggan (2009)

References

Enting, I. (2007) *Twisted: The Distorted Mathematics of Greenhouse Denial*, Australasian Mathematical Sciences Institute, Melbourne, Australia

Greenpeace (2010) *Dealing in Doubt: The Climate Denial Industry and Climate Science*, Greenpeace International, Amsterdam

Hoggan, J. (2009) *Climate Cover Up: The Crusade to Deny Global Warming*, Greystone Books, Vancouver, Canada

Oreskes, N. and Conway, M. (2010) *Merchants of Doubt: How a Handful of Scientists Obscured the Truth on Issues from Tobacco Smoke to Global Warming*, Bloomsbury Press, New York

Note also that the website www.desmogblog.com has a research database of key individual climate deniers.

Index